VOID

Library of
Davidson College

OXFORD THEOLOGICAL MONOGRAPHS

Editorial Committee

J. BARR   R. C. MORGAN

P. W. BIDE   K. T. WARE

J. MACQUARRIE   B. R. WHITE

M. F. WILES

Oxford Theological Monographs

THE ENGLISH SEPARATIST TRADITION

By B. R. White. 1971

THE PRINCIPLE OF RESERVE IN THE WRITINGS OF
JOHN HENRY NEWMAN

By R. C. Selby. 1975

GELASIAN SACRAMENTARIES OF THE 8TH CENTURY

By M. B. Moreton. 1975

THREE MONOPHYSITE CHRISTOLOGIES

By R. C. Chesnut. 1976

RITUALISM AND POLITICS IN VICTORIAN BRITAIN

By J. Bentley. 1978

THE ONTOLOGY OF PAUL TILLICH

By A. Thatcher. 1978

BECOMING AND BEING

By C. E. Gunton. 1978

CALVIN AND ENGLISH CALVINISM TO 1649

By R. T. Kendall. 1979

NEWMAN AND THE GOSPEL OF CHRIST

By Roderick Strange. 1981

HAMANN
ON
LANGUAGE
AND RELIGION

TERENCE J. GERMAN

OXFORD UNIVERSITY PRESS
1981

Oxford University Press, Walton Street, Oxford OX2 6DP
London Glasgow New York Toronto
Delhi Bombay Calcutta Madras Karachi
Kuala Lumpur Singapore Hong Kong Tokyo
Nairobi Dar Es Salaam Cape Town
Melbourne Auckland

and associate companies in
Beirut Berlin Ibadan Mexico City

Published in the United States by
Oxford University Press, New York

© Terence J. German 1981

All rights reserved. No part of this publication may be reproduced, stored in a retrieval system, or transmitted, in any form or by any means electronic, mechanical, photocopying, recording, or otherwise, without the prior permission of Oxford University Press

British Library Cataloguing in Publication Data
German, Terence J.
Hamann on language and religion.
– (Oxford theological monographs)
1. Philosophy and religion
2. Languages – Philosophy
I. Title
200'.92'4   B2992
ISBN 0-19-826717-7

Set by Hope Services, Abingdon, Oxon
and Printed in Great Britain
at the University Press, Oxford
by Eric Buckley
Printer to the University

In memory of
my mother
Irene Kaiser German

PREFACE

While puzzling over the section of the Second Preface to Kant's *Critique of Pure Reason* which includes allusions to the notion of transcendental illusions it was brought to my attention that a little-known German, Johann Georg Hamann, called the Wizard of the North, might be able to throw some light on the subject. Hamann had written a critique of the *Critique of Pure Reason* which was a revelation to me because it displayed a deep understanding of two major puzzles which run through Kant's work: language and religion. This book is thus entitled *On Language and Religion*.

Hamann was called a wizard because his works appear to be enigmatic and perhaps unclear. However, he could find a lack of clarity in the works of Kant whose use of language has been considered by some to be quite clear. Kant had thought about his *Critique of Pure Reason* for twelve years; he wrote it within five months in great haste, which made it difficult for many readers to grasp what he was attempting to say. Hamann understood perfectly some of the weaknesses in Kant's work. Some of them will be explained in this book.

My fascination and admiration for Hamann increased when I was led to read a work of Georg Wilhelm Hegel entitled *Hamann's Writings*. In this work Hegel seeks to refute many of Hamann's insights, but the intriguing point remains that some of Hegel's insights appear to be similar to those of Hamann. His interest in a comparison of the disciples of Jesus Christ with the pupils of Socrates was influenced by Hamann's writing *Socratic Memorabilia*. Hegel's monumental work *Phenomenology of Mind* attempts to deal with an operative individual unity which is central to Hamann's works. Goethe had understood this point about Hamann before it was clearly understood by Hegel.

Hamann's relationship to Hegel becomes even more intriguing when it is compared with his influence upon Søren Kierkegaard. Kierkegaard admired Hamann and called him his 'Emperor'. Like Hegel, he had read Hamann's writings on language and religion in depth. Kierkegaard then sought to use these Hamannian insights as part of his arsenal which he used to discredit Hegel concerning language and religion. As the present work *On Language and Religion* unfolds the reader will see that Hamann is a fascinating character who presents new insights concerning reality at the most surprising points in time. Hamann in a temporal sense did not wish to be understood too quickly, for he had the insight that the thoughts of a man which are caught too quickly are too quickly forgotten by other men.

Hamann was a man of the moment; his ideas flow from particular temporal experiences. It is hoped that people will be led by this book to read Hamann's writings themselves. The Nadler edition of them is not chronologically arranged. They are grouped by Nadler according to content, which tends to make them too organized from a logical point of view. The older Roth edition is chronological in form and therefore presents Hamann's views more faithfully in their temporal sequence of particular experiences. No one will ever be able to systematize totally the thought of Hamann, so one should not lament the difficulty of reading him in a chronological but unsystematic order.

I wish to thank Dr James Collins of St. Louis University for whetting my appetite concerning Hamann, Fr Avery Dulles, S.J., of the Catholic University of America consistently encouraged me to seek out philosophical religious insights in the writings of Hamann. Dr Jurgen Moltmann, of Tübingen University, helped me to see more clearly the relationship of Hamann to Martin Luther, while Dr Josef Simon of the same University helped me to grasp the linguistic complexities of Hamann's writings. I wish especially to thank Professor John Macquarrie of Christ Church, Oxford, for his patience and intelligent kindness as he helped me to discern more clearly the heart of the mystery of Hamann. I also wish to thank Sir Isaiah Berlin of All Souls, Oxford, for a series of conversations relating Hamann to Giambattista Vico. Mrs Gertrude Mellon kindly encouraged me to continue my work because of her interest in the relationship of Hamann to the Munster circle of mystics. Finally, I wish to thank Mr and Mrs J. P. McLaughlin for allowing me to spend some time in their home in Williamstown, Massachusetts, while writing this work.

Translations from the German are my own.

CONTENTS

I. Hamann's Methods or Styles of Human Living and Creating   1

II. Hamann's Views Concerning Human Creativity   46

III. Continuation of Hamann's Views Concerning Human Creativity   68

IV. Hamann's Fascination with Time in This World   94

V. Hamann's Communication with God and with His Fellow Human Beings   141

Select Bibliography   176

Index   185

I

HAMANN'S METHODS OR STYLES OF HUMAN LIVING AND CREATING

An old Latin phrase states *vestis virum facit*. There was a sense in both the Greek and the Latin worlds that the clothes made the man.[1] There is a sense also in which the style of living and writing of a man help to make up his character. Hamann had liked the writings of Buffon who said 'Le style est l'homme même'; style is the expression of the dynamic, energetic fashion in which a particular person lives. If that person, as part of his temporal living, should happen to write, his writing will be an expression of his living.

Johann Georg Hamann was a man who wrote on various levels because his life had many levels. A valid effort to begin to know him must consist in knowing something about his manner of living; within the process of Hamann's living one ought to know some of the particular experiences he was having at the time he was engaged in creating a particular piece of writing. It is also helpful to know what some other people thought of both his living style and the style of his writing.

Johann Georg Hamann intriguingly tells his friend, Lindner, 'you know that my manner of thinking is not connected . . .'[2] Hamann is honestly saying that in the eyes of the 'Public' his manner of thinking would not appear to be connected in the *Socratic Memoirs*. He later shows how his thoughts are connected by threads of communication that are invisible to 'the public' who think they are so smart. 'The public' could say 'the writer (Hamann) was witty, but he wrote in a strange fashion . . .'[3] Of course Hamann could play with the word 'wit' because it could be used in various ways in the latter part of the eighteenth century, as when, in translating Montesquieu's 'L'Esprit des lois', he calls it 'Witz der Gesetze'.[4] This statement serves also as a warning to any of Hamann's readers, but even more cryptic is his

---

[1] See Bruno Snell, *The Discovery of Mind*, translated by T. G. Rosenmeyer, Oxford, 1953.
[2] *Johann Georg Hamann, Briefwechsel*, ed. by Ziesemer and Henkel, Bd 1-7, Leipzig, 1949, I, p. 408.
[3] *Johann Georg Hamann, Sämtliche Werke, Historische–Kritische Ausgabe*, ed. by Josef Nadler, Wien, 1949-57, III, p. 253.
[4] *Hamanns Schriften*, ed. by F. Roth, Berlin, 1821-5, III, p. 158.

own previous warning that 'an outsider and an unbeliever can take my style for nothing but *nonsense* because I express myself in many tongues . . . chatter, criticism, mythology, riddles, and principles all mixed together . . . '[5] Hamann only wishes to communicate with those who can grasp exquisite communications.

Johann Georg Hamann was born in Königsberg in 1730 when it was a bustling, fast moving, trading city. During his university days in the early 1750s he was much influenced by the ideas of the Enlightenment, although he later felt that there never had been much order in his studies,[6] which would not have been too 'enlightened' in his day. But it is clear that at the time of his studies, although he may have claimed later that he was disorganized, he did, with his friend J. C. Berens, excel.[7] He apparently had a disciplined technique for reading books and at that time he wished to impress 'the public' with his enlightened knowledge.

When he was quite young, his friend J. C. Berens, who came from a wealthy merchant family, sent Hamann to London in order to do some business. He went through his business money quickly while living a dissolute life.[8] Then in great fear and trembling he read the Bible and experienced a conversion.

Some authors maintain that his one conversion experience in London was the major experience of his life. In fact, however, Hamann devoted his life to a series of communicating experiences with God which were all conversion experiences, for conversion was a sequential experience, a series of great moments.

Efforts to find strong Catholic tendencies in Hamann's relationships with the Gallitzin Münster circle of readers are untrustworthy,[9] for he remained devoted to Luther in his conversion process.

In 1759 Hamann refers to Luther as 'our Father Luther'[10] and in 1780 he tells a friend 'I read in Luther of the Knight of Tonaldo, on a narrow bridge, with a load on his back; beneath him was a

---

[5] Ziesemer-Henkel, I, p. 396. (Henceforth the J. Nadler edition is referred to as 'Nadler', the F. Roth edition as 'Roth', and the Ziesemer and Henkel edition as 'Ziesemer-Henkel'.)

[6] Nadler, II, p. 19.

[7] The professor of oriental languages at the University of Königsberg continued to *converse* with Hamann into his later life keeping him interested in the fascinations of oriental languages. Prof. G. Kypke died in 1779.

[8] Nadler, II, p. 211, and III, pp. 190 and 312.

[9] See Joseph Galland, *Die Färstin Amalia von Gallitzin und ihre Freunde*, Köln, 1880, pp. 105-25. See also Ziesemer-Henkel, I, p. 412 and Nadler, V, pp. 127-9 for Hamann's continual devotion to Luther in relationship to the London experience and the Enlightenment.

[10] Ziesemer-Henkel, I, p. 296.

sulphurous deep full of dragons and one was coming to meet him. At that point I certainly knew that I had found the key to myself.'[11] The key to the mystery[12] of himself opens the door to a self who is partially a man, a knight if you will, on the narrow bridge of life. It is a life in danger of falling prey to the special dragon among the dragons of evil who was coming to meet him in order to drag him into the sulphurous depths of hell. He is a man concerned about the state of his life in relation to God and to both the possible and the real evils of life in this world. His admiration for Luther over the course of at least thirty years of his life is grounded in admiration not only for Luther as a man of flesh and blood, but also for Luther the writer, and for Luther as he helps to represent the image of the knight, and of the Germans as a people who struggle creatively amidst the difficulties of this world. Hamann had no interest in being a Lutheran but he always insisted that 'I Lutherize . . . ',[13] partially because Luther in Hamann's eyes was interested in 'Paradoxa'[14] which interested him.

After the first conversion experience of 1759, in spite of the fact that he still read books voraciously, he read them alongside the many other activities of his busy life, for he had learned that one cannot learn easily from a book how to live.[15] And first and foremost, Hamann wanted to live.[16] During his conversion experience he was more interested in Luther than in the Lutheran Christianity of his contemporary age, for he was opposed to the hierarchical and metaphysical corruptions of Lutheranism.[17] Hamann's devotion to Luther and his effort to write in a Christian fashion hardly create the background for describing him as the 'first Christian man of letters',[18] but it is true to say that he became one of the great Christian men of letters, in some ways akin to Luther.

Hamann does not only worry about the state of his life in relation

---

[11] Ibid., IV, p. 209.
[12] Hamann's interest in mystery can still find him against the 'Schwärmerei', Nadler, II, p. 154 and Roth, VI, p. 227.
[13] Ziesemer-Henkel, I, p. 307.
[14] Nadler, I, p. 47, II, pp. 247 and 249. See also Nadler, I, p. 15, II, p. 211, III, pp. 190 and 312 for Hamann's views on Lutheranism.
[15] C. H. Gildemeister, *Johann Georg Hamann, des Magus im Norden, Leben und Schriften*, Bd. 1–6, Gotha, 1868, V, p. 445.
[16] Josef Nadler, *J. G. Hamann: Der Zeuge des Corpus Mysticum*, Salzburg, 1949, Ch. I.
[17] *Aus dem Briefwechsel des Magus im Norden*, ed. by Schmitz-Kallenberg, Münster, 1917, p. 92.
[18] E. Hirsch, *Geschichte der neuren evangelischen Theologie*, Gütersloh, 1952, IV, p. 177.

to God and the evils of this world, but he also worries about the state of life of his close friends, Immanuel Kant and J. Berens, for his creativity always takes the form of being ever perceptive towards the relations of people in their everyday lives. Part of the key to his writing of the *Socratic Memoirs* in 1759, which is one of his best public, creative works, is his desire to help his two friends through the daily difficulties of this worldly living.

It does not make much difference whether Hamann began writing in 1756 or 1759, although Volker Hoffmann thinks it does, because, although there is a developing progression in his style even in the early years, it is always rooted in a particular set of concrete circumstances concerning persons and places, and these take precedence over any progression of stylistic development.[19] This statement does not deny the fact that there is a certain temporal development in Hamann's style. Ultimately, his ability to help his friends is aided by the grace of God, but he can help that grace to be creatively effective in their lives, for he knows that in regard to his own life, he is dependent upon God in light of the fact that he is the knight of Tonaldo whom the dragon approaches with ferocity. He is a knight, in the true fashion of Luther's view of the world, who is dependent upon the power of God's sword to ward off the ferocious dragon and save him. He can say of himself, 'My soul, with all its moral deficiencies and basic crookedness, is in His hand. Its righteousness is the work of the Spirit, a Creator, a Redeemer; to make it sound rests neither in my power, nor in that of a friend.'[20] He knows that the glory of being human consists in his ability to be creative, but he still keeps in mind that man has a basic crookedness which can only be redeemed and changed creatively into a new way of living by God. Nothing in Hamann's own personality can effectively save him. Even his friends can bring him no complete salvation nor can he save his friends without the help of God. But God is the heart of man's ultimate salvation which can bring man integrated happiness. If man really begins to perceive life correctly, life will always give hints in the direction of a kind of faith, a kind of relation ultimately directed towards God.[21]

Hamann had trusted in his earlier years, in his years of happy enlightened relationships with J. Berens and Immanuel Kant, that in the true manner of the Enlightenment friendship among cultured persons

---

[19] Volker Hoffmann, *Johann Georg Hamanns Philologie, Hammans Philologie zwischen enzyklopädischer Mikrologie und Hermeneutik*, Stuttgart, 1972, p. 78.

[20] Ziesemer-Henkel, I, p. 302.

[21] See Chapter IV.

was the greatest gift in life.[22] He now sees that even cultured friends cannot save a person from the deep ravages of evil. His friends cannot totally save him through a humanistic type of redemption. One cannot search for a kind of existentially creative fidelity in friendship as one's total source of redemption in contradistinction to the invitation of redemption offered by God. The necessary help and grace for man's redemption must originate in God. Hamann realizes that he must finally say 'My soul, with all its moral deficiencies and basic crookedness, is in His hand. Its righteousness is the work of the Spirit, a Creator, a Redeemer; to make it sound rests neither in my power nor in that of a friend.[23] This passage of 1759 reflects Hamann's later held views about friendship, the Trinity as Spirit, Creator, Redeemer, God as special Creator, man as creative helper, and soul as an entity involving all of man's activity, a flesh/blood/spirit kind of reality in which these parts relate in a network of combined activities.

As Hamann's life progressed he could say of himself in relation to God 'without Thee, I am nothing; Thou art my entire being.'[24] He had at one time thought that marriage in itself could be the heart of his life, but when he was rejected by Catin, the sister of the Berens brothers,[25] one of whom he wished to save by writing *Socratic Memoirs*, he saw that marriage or love, even of a woman, was not the total answer to man's needs for ultimate love and redemptive happiness. He did later have a 'common-law' marriage in which he loved his wife and children very much, but he always linked their love with the love of God, just as, especially in the late 1750s, he could feel guilt towards both God and his fellow-man: 'I felt my heart thump, I heard a voice sigh in its depths and wail like the voice of blood . . . I felt my heart swell, and pour out in tears . . . '[26] because he had hurt both God and his fellow man.

This passage shows the early interest Hamann had in the power of the voice, of speech. There is a voice of blood which speaks out from the heart of any man; there is also the voice of God, and God could therefore be addressed in Hamann's favourite words 'Speak that I may see Thee!' Although he did experience a great deal of guilt and fear in the late 1750s, his relationship with God, which he wished his friends

---

[22] See Wolfdietrich Rasch, *Freundschaftskult und Freundschaftsdichtung im deutschen Schrifttum des 18. Jahrhunderts*, Halle, 1936.
[23] Ziesemer-Henkel, I, p. 302.
[24] Nadler, I. p. 83.
[25] Ziesemer-Henkel, I, p. 289.
[26] Roth, I. p. 212.

could also experience, became a loving relationship through the friendship of Jesus Christ, the Son of God. Hamann speaks of 'A friend [who is Jesus Christ in this context] who gave me the key to my heart, the way out of my Labyrinth . . . '[27] The notion of labyrinth was very popular in Hamann's time as a description of the human condition.[28] Jesus Christ helps him find his way out of the many confusions of the evil human condition so that he can live more happily and creatively in a new human condition informed by the love of God and the correct love of friends. The relationship Hamann always seeks to have with God and with his friends is one of basic equality rather than one of abjectly cringing before either God or other men. His relationships are based upon the virtue of liberty, the liberty to think and to act in relationship to God and to other men.[29] Hamann in his creative writing must have the freedom to think and act as the basis of his virtuous writing; he hopes that the intentions flowing from this liberty will bring forth creations useful to God and to other men.[30]

From the late 1750s and throughout the rest of his life, Hamann loved God without cringing before Him and His laws; he lived creatively and freely. It is not fair of Unger to infer that he interpreted his 'faith' or his relationship with God in such a way that it consistently met the conditions which were necessary to allow him to live in the way that he selfishly wished to live at a given point in time in contradiction to God's regular laws.[31] Some of Hamann's apparent floutings of God's laws beginning in his late life arose from the misconception caused by the fact that he sincerely advised his friend, E. F. Lindner, 'to turn the good inward while showing the evil outwardly—to seem worse than one actually is and to be better than one appears to be . . . '[32] At all costs, he wanted to avoid being a Pharisee.

Hamann contents himself with the fact that whatever a man truly believes in his heart is always a partial mystery to others. An onlooker can believe what he will from a man's outward appearance; the 'enlightened Public', onlookers disdained by Hamann, will be the most deceived.[33] When Hamann is thinking of this difficulty in relation to his *Socratic Memoirs* and to his two friends, Kant and Berens, he can write to another friend 'I do not preach in society, . . . it will always

---

[27] Nadler, II, p. 39.
[28] See Edna Purdie, *Studies in German Literature of the Eighteenth Century*, London, 1965, p. 142.
[29] Roth, I. p. 246.   [30] Ibid., I, p. 222.
[31] R. Unger, *Hamann und die Aufklärung: Studien zur Vorgeschichte des romantischen Geistes im 18. Jahrhundert*, Bd. 1–2, Jena 1911, I, p. 119.
[32] Ziesemer-Henkel, V, p. 17.   [33] Nadler, III, p. 67.

be my pride to be a lily in the valley whose fragrance ceases unnoticed, for one is to burn brightest in the foundation of the heart . . .'[34] That burning heart of his life he will communicate and reveal to those who know how to communicate creatively. In this manner goodness in a person becomes real goodness both in relation to God and in relation to other humans.

Hamann hated hypocrites and yet Unger implies that he is, in a sense, being hypocritical by forcing God to accept his way of living, his 'desired' way of being good. But Hamann is not just a pleasure-seeker who demands that God see his pleasure-seeking as good. He truly desires to communicate honestly and unhypocritically with God and other humans. He is always seeking to discover ways of creating through speaking and writing. He is intrigued by the 'dreams of an author'.[35] He is maddened in a metaphorical sense by the continuing thought that 'Nothing is left to be done except to discover and search out the implications of the fight over the bounds between *genius* and madness.'[36] Hamann is no simple pleasure-seeker who bends reality to meet his constant personal demands. He is brave enough to face the fact that creativity can cause events that are not pleasurable: the suffering of a genius, and the possibility of madness.

He has discovered one of the doors to creative reality which he knocks, bangs, and attempts to open wider as he proclaims to his close friend Herder 'Even if I were as eloquent as Demosthenes, I should not have more to do than repeat three times a single phrase: Reason is language, *logos*. This is the bone I gnaw at and shall gnaw myself to death over.'[37] Hamann is not saying that Reason is the written language or even just the spoken language. Language reaches down into the bones of man.

He hopes that his writings will be strong enough to reach into the bones of his friends, Kant and Berens. He had begun in 1758 to work on this door of reality which can help his friends to acquire the power of language but he is humble enough to know that the door hides fantastic depths of reality and, even in the 1780s, he is still exclaiming 'these depths are still obscure to me; I still await an apocalyptic angel with a key to this abyss.'[38] He spends his life feverishly searching for that key. He never searches for it just in the abstract levels of reasoning. He knows that 'the tapping of another human being's foot even serves to quicken our hearts.'[39] Our thinking is affected by and partially *is* our feet.

[34] Ziesemer-Henkel, I. p. 343.
[35] Ziesemer-Henkel, III, p. 207.
[36] Nadler, II, p. 104.
[37] Ziesemer-Henkel, V, p. 176.
[38] Ziesemer-Henkel, V, p. 188.
[39] Nadler, I, p. 200.

Hamann seeks to write with his whole self, a man of flesh, blood and spirit. He knows that he will be misunderstood, but he seeks creatively to discover new ways of communicating which causes him to mention to his friend Lindner that his thinking will not always appear to be connected.[40] He could playfully write to Lindner 'when you have the key to this mystery-filled letter, share it with me',[41] just as he could write to Herder 'You will be able to see the *chaos* of my feelings in all of my writing.'[42]

Whenever he writes, Hamann takes it for granted that speech and writing in his time are understood by the 'Public' in such a thick and stupid fashion that they are insulted when they begin to hear or read the truth[43] which is written by him. The 'Public' are fooled so easily, for 'the clarity of books is often deception and tangled thought.'[44] The 'Public', while believing that they are thinking clearly about reality, have actually deceived themselves concerning reality, in a series of tangled thoughts. What they perceive to be communication actually helps to destroy true communication by their act of compressing all reality into a *tangled* mass of reasonableness; for true communication demands more than mere reasonableness.

A writer who seeks to communicate well will find that his work will be read by one hundred persons, then possibly reissued and remembered by four. This indeed is 'the birth, the spot of life, and the death'[45] of a real communication in writing of which it will most likely be said by the 'enlightened Public' that 'the piece of writing could not communicate because it could not communicate with us.' Hamann knows that all great geniuses appear strange to average people,[46] even if these average people claim to be special as members of the 'enlightened Public', who are merely capable of playing games concerning their own supposed genius.

Hamann knows that 'the birthday of a genius will, as usual, be greeted by a martyr's feast of innocent children . . .'[47] He humbly feels he is a genius and ironically says 'do not look on me, for the reason that I am so black is because the "Genius" has burnt me.'[48] He knows he will be martyred by the 'Public' and partially understood by those who know how to communicate exquisitely. He can always say 'I write everything that my Muse says to me with red running eyes . . .'[49] Write he will, with personal passion.

[40] Ziesemer-Henkel, I, p. 408.
[41] Ibid., p. 62.
[42] Ibid, III, p. 393.
[43] Nadler, II, p. 183.
[44] Ibid, p. 183.
[45] Ibid, p. 243.
[46] Roth, IV, p. 364.
[47] Nadler, II, p. 214.
[48] Ibid, p. 107.
[49] Ibid, p. 107.

Before checking sections of Hamann's writings for their personally living style, it will be useful to see how some other persons connected with Hamann perceived him, either through having known him personally in everyday life or through his writings.[50] Søren Kierkegaard, who was deeply intrigued by Hamann's writings,[51] wrote of him that 'with everything in his life and soul, even to his last drop of blood, he is concentrated in a single word.'[52] It later becomes clear that Kierkegaard admired Hamann's intense devotion to the 'single word', *language*, which for Hamann included the fabric of living which had helped give Kierkegaard the powerful impetus to build his notions of what could be called an extentialist view of reality. Hamann was the 'Emperor' for Kierkegaard because Hamann awakened creative living as an individual in Kierkegaard, both in his writing and in other forms of activity. But Kierkegaard's living differed from Hamann's because Kierkegaard spent so much time running up and down the staircases of his mind.

Kierkegaard continues the statement on his 'Emperor', 'poor Hamann, you have been cut short to a paragraph by Michelet . . . I know that the paragraph-machine ploughs all your eloquence, all your inwardness, under a few scant words registered in the System as to your significance.'[53] It is in a sense true that man actually can only make 'postscripts' concerning life or a life in an unscientific fashion, as the title of Kierkegaard's book suggests, but these 'postscripts' or fragments of Hamann's, as in his work *Brocken*, which are ironically supposed to be at least partially scientific, do not deserve to be treated in a mere paragraph. Hamann was always writing snippets or postscripts about life, postscripts to his everyday experiences, snatches of experience which were not very systematic and therefore not very scientific in the then held understanding concerning the meaning of that word, from the viewpoint of the technical rationalists. Kierkegaard is lamenting the fact that Hamann's complex life-soul-blood view of language and other living realities has been cut short to a paragraph of explanation by a writer such as Michelet who tends to be categorical in his efforts to make sense out of history.

[50] See *Socratic Memoirs* and *Aesthetica in Nuce*.
[51] Kierkegaard had known of Hamann's writings since he was a child. See Torsten Bohlin, *Kierkegaards dogmatische Anschauung in ihrem geschichtlichen Zusammenhang*, Gütersloh, 1927, p. 60. He first speaks of Hamann in his Tagebücher in 1833. See Gerdes Hays *Sören Kierkegaard, Gesammelte Werke: Die Tagebüchen*, Düsseldorf, 1962-8, Bd. I, pp. 25, 127, 132, 135, 140, 198, and 309.
[52] Søren Kierkegaard, *Concluding Unscientific Postscript*, translated by David F. Swenson and Walter Lowrie, London, 1941, p. 224.
[53] Ibid., p. 225.

Kierkegaard disliked historians who sought to describe earlier creative thinkers within the confines of a paragraph of their uncreative thought, just as Hamann despised so-called historians who could encapsulate earlier ages in a systematically constructed, unliving fashion.[54] Both Kierkegaard and Hamann are deeply interested in the correct use of words, economy of style, and lack of ostentatious writing. Both Kierkegaard and Hamann construct the titles of their books or writings in such a fashion that the use of words can be a key to the entire work. But blithely to sum up all of Hamann in one little paragraph without actually having grasped his message in a nutshell . . . that one cannot do if he is really understanding Hamann. The eloquence in the writings and in the life of a person such as Hamann are ploughed under and disregarded by the paragraph-machine. In this passage, Kierkegaard evidently places great emphasis upon the word 'system', for in a real sense both he and Hamann hated the system and would have expected it to give them scant attention.

Kierkegaard continues his praise of Hamann in his private papers: 'At this time when it is a custom of habit for one author to ransack another, it is refreshing to come upon men whose individual personality stamps each word with its own physique so that it compels a person meeting the word in a strange situation to say to the writer, "Give to Caesar the things that belong to Caesar!"'[55] Lowrie states that this passage in Kierkegaard's papers is a reference to his 'Emperor', Hamann. Kierkegaard admires Hamann because he is a writer who does not ransack other writers in order to get ideas which he can quickly copy down and call his own. Hamann does imitate experiences from other writers, but he always makes them a living part of himself before he includes them in his writings. He never copies or superficially imitates another person, for he imitates the creative genius of another writer while deriding a person who imitates others in order to get ideas which he can quickly copy down and call his own.[56]

Hamann sought to have every word he wrote contain a quality that united it with his own physical personality. He thought as much with his belly as with his brain. He attempted to give his words the physique of his own physique. Most of his writings could not be imitated superficially; a man with an incisive eye could simply say to the superficial imitator 'Give to Hamann the things that belong to Hamann'.

It is interesting that Kierkegaard's master's thesis *On the Concept of Irony with Constant Reference to Socrates* appears to depend

---

[54] Roth, VI, p. 258, Nadler, II, p. 78 and *Golgotha and Scheblimini*.
[55] Walter Lowrie, *Johann Georg Hamann' An Existentialist*, Princeton, New Jersey, 1950, p. 174.   [56] See *Aesthetica in Nuce*.

considerably upon references to the interpretation of Socrates presented by Hamann in the *Socratic Memoirs*.[57] I am sure that Kierkegaard would have felt that he gave to Hamann the things that belonged to Hamann, that he had imitated the genius of Hamann's creativity correctly and had therefore made a part of his self what had originally been Hamann's creation. Hamann would most likely agree with this form of imitation although he would have lamented the fact that Kierkegaard usually thought too much.

Hamann influenced Kierkegaard not only in the development of his literary style but also in one of his most important attitudes to living, for when Hamann had decided that Catin Berens was meant to be his lawfully wedded wife according to the will of God, although she refused his proposal of marriage, he resolved to marry but only in a common-law sense. In a somewhat similar experience, Søren Kierkegaard's engagement to Regina Olsen was broken off. He evidently decided to follow Hamann's pattern of marriage to the extent that he would not have a lawfully married wife. But, for personal reasons, he followed a different course from Hamann and decided not to have a common-law marriage.[58] Hamann always entered dynamically into the lives of even those who only read his writings in spite of the fact that they may not have known him in the living flesh.

His writing, *Socratic Memoirs*, which will be investigated in this chapter in part, had this kind of effect upon the people who read it. Goethe analyses this effect in *Dichtung und Wahrheit*. 'His [Hamann's] *Socratic Memoirs* was especially liked by those persons who could not adapt themselves to the dazzling spirit of the time ... In the *Clouds*, an after-piece of the *Socratic Memoirs*, he had given some offence to the very same people.'[59] People never knew quite what to expect in Hamann's writings, but they knew each writing would present a new experience. We know that the *Socratic Memoirs* affected different persons according to their own perceptions; J. Berens and Immanuel Kant, the two people Hamann hoped to save in a somewhat Christian sense by their reading of the *Socratic Memoirs*, were not too moved by

---

[57] The thesis did not receive much acclaim in the beginning.
[58] Søren Kierkegaard, *Elterladte Papier, 1847*, Kopenhagen, 1877, p. 150. Kierkegaard did entertain the idea of keeping Regina as a mistress. See also George Price, *The Narrow Pass*, London, 1963, p. 72.
[59] Goethe, *Poetry and Truth: From My Life*, translated by R. O. Moon, London, 1932, p. 453. Hamann did this partially on purpose because some of these admirers were looking for an incorrect form of mysticism in *Socratic Memoirs*.

it. They were able to stand the dazzling light of their age because they had helped create it as members of the Enlightenment.

As Hamann himself writes in the *Clouds*, the first review of the *Socratic Memoirs* by an enlightened, dazzling source, the *Hamburgische Nachrichten* of December 1759 stated that 'No alchemist, no Jacob Boehme, no insane fanatic can write and speak more senseless, more unintelligible trash than what we are forced here to read . . .'[60] Alchemists at that time were still considered to be a little bit disconnected from the rest of reality. Jacob Boehme had indeed influenced Hamann although not as much as some suspect. The far-fetched sayings in the *Socratic Memoirs* could appear as nonsensical trash to the enlightened mind which is exactly what Hamann had hoped for in the first place. His words from various languages, however, ought to have impressed the enlightened ones since he could quote from the following languages which he had studied: Greek, Latin, English, Hebrew, Arabic, French, and smatterings of Egyptian hieroglyphics, plus Persian, Tibetan, and Latvian.

Hamann in his writings was seeking to unite the language experience, for the enlightened ones gave deference to language. They memorized languages, however, whereas Hamann sought to be creative with language which was at its heart poetical. All languages were based upon poetical experience and therefore flowed analogically from a similar poetical source of experience.[61] Although he did not consider himself to be either a theologian or a philosopher, he was seeking to attempt to accomplish one of the pleas of the noted theologian, Karl Rahner, who says' 'To the poet is entrusted the word. Alas that there is no theology of the word! Why has no one yet begun, like an Ezekiel, to collect the limbs strewn about upon the fields of philosophy and theology, and then to speak the word of the spirit over them so that they rise up a living body?'[62] Hamann spoke of the Horatian 'strewn limbs' in his *Aesthetica in Nuce* while he sought to have the living body of poetry present itself to those who could ask from it, 'Speak that I may see Thee'.

Hegel criticized Hamann's *Socratic Memoirs* in his typical fashion of admitting some merit but damning the bulk of the work. He claims that Hamann lacked 'objective content'[63] in most sections of it. Hegel does admit in his own confusing fashion that there is perhaps an

---

[60] Nadler, II, 86.   [61] See *Aesthetica in Nuce*.
[62] Karl Rahner, *The Word: Readings in Theology*, New York, 1964, p. 3.
[63] Hegel, *Hamanns Schriften* in *Berliner Schriften, 1818-1831* in *Sämtliche Werke*, Bd. XI, Hamburg, 1956, p. 254.

'appearance of an objective content'.[64] By stating that the *Socratic Memoirs* lacked objective content it was then quite easy for Hegel to reduce Hamann's other writings to an almost solipsistic[65] mass of material, for Hamann himself had sought to make the *Socratic Memoirs* one of his more public or objective works, whereas most of his other writings were indeed more heavily subjective than objective in style. Gildemeister could see that in actuality Hegel was often unclear in his own writings,[66] whereas he consistently criticized Hamann for being unclear.

Lettau thought that 'A line out of the writings of Hamann weighs as much as a book of Hegel.'[67] Gildemeister thought that Hegel's writings were 'watersoup'[68] in relation to those of Hamann which taste very good. Nadler does not think that Hegel understood Hamann in the first place,[69] but Gildemeister is more perceptive in stating that Hegel does not want to claim to understand Hamann.[70] By so doing, when Hegel does understand Hamann in his own subjective experience while denying that he can understand him in dealing with the 'Public', he can proceed more easily to use Hamann's views of reality as if they were his own original creations.

In the famous conversation between Goethe and Hegel concerning Hamann, Eckermann states 'A great deal was said about Hamann with respect to whom Hegel was chief spokesman displaying a deep insight into this extraordinary mind, such as could only have arisen from a most earnest and scrupulous study of the subject.'[71] Hegel knew the writings of Hamann quite well and could see that Hamann was not only dynamically creative in his writings but that his life and friendships had an 'energetic liveliness'.[72]

Hegel saw that Hamann's thoughts as expressed for instance in the *Socratic Memoirs* included many 'bombshells'.[73] He said that Hamann

---

[64] Ibid., p. 254.

[65] In so far as solipsism can be a sign of autism, it could be partially attributable to Hamann who often stammered because of a form of shyness, but Hamann was certainly no solipsist.

[66] Gildemeister, VI, pp. 325, 344, and 357.

[67] Lettau, *Johann Georg Hamann: ein Lehrer und Prophet unseres Volkes*, Gütersloh, 1882, p. 91.

[68] Gildemeister, VI, p. 398.

[69] Nadler, *J. G. Hamann: Der Zeuge des Corpus mysticum*, Salzburg, 1949, p. 484.

[70] Gildemeister, VI, p. 400.

[71] *Conversations of Goethe with Eckermann and Sorel*, translated by John Oxenford, London, 1892, p. 302.

[72] Hegel, *Hamanns Schriften*, in *Sämtliche Werke*, XI, p. 258.

[73] Ibid., p. 289.

indeed was an 'original'.⁷⁴ But Hamann's originality could not have fitted Hegel's system. Ultimately Hegel was afraid of Hamann's views concerning creativity which involved the question central in Hegel's thought concerning 'creation' and 'transformation'.⁷⁵

Some persons are of the opinion that Hegel stole ideas from Solomon Maimon, especially the idea of spirit in the world, so he could and most probably did steal from Hamann while seeking to destroy Hamann's own reputation. Hegel had been especially impressed with 'the Christian teaching of the Trinitarian God . . . '⁷⁶ He had read Hamann's writings on symbolic creativity, especially *Aesthetica in Nuce*, with special reference to language.

Perhaps Alexandre Kojeve's great commentary *Introduction à la lecture de Hegel* is correct in concentrating upon the complexity of word combinations in the *Phenomenology of Spirit*, which could have derived in part from Hamann's influence upon Hegel. It is puzzling why Hegel was so rough on Hamann and also treated his daughter with such contempt when she begged Hegel, after Hamann's death, to say and write kinder things about her father, but the puzzlement is partially banished by the fact that Hegel apparently profited from Hamann's demise. G. Gervinus also disliked Hamann very much and this influenced many people in the middle 1800s to ignore him.⁷⁷

Herder liked Hamann's style of writing both in the *Socratic Memoirs* and *Aesthetica in Nuce*; he used the *Aesthetica in Nuce* as a guide for his work on *The Spirit of Hebrew Poetry*. Werner Kohlschmidt states that without him [Hamann] Herder would not have been able to be a great leader in the 'Storm and Stress' period.⁷⁸ When he wanted to write an evaluation of Kant's first Critique, which he despised, he used the style of Hamann's *Metacritique*⁷⁹ as a guide. He was actually seeking to unite the insights of Kant with those of Hamann, Hume and Shaftesbury whenever that was possible and to destroy the rest of Kant's views on reality. When Herder, partially through the use of Hamann's *Metacritique*, had criticized Kant's *First*

---

⁷⁴ Ibid., p. 225.
⁷⁵ *Hegels Werks*, Berlin, 1835, 19 Bde., XVII, p. 73.
⁷⁶ Ibid., p. 72.
⁷⁷ G. Gervinus, *Zur Geschichte der deutschen Dichtung*, Leipzig, 1871.
⁷⁸ W. Kohlschmidt, *Geschichte der deutschen Literatur von Barock bis zur Klassik*, Stuttgart, 1965, Bd. II, p. 445.
⁷⁹ Hamann wrote this masterful work as a reaction against Kant's *Critique of Pure Reason*. It was not published until after Hamann's death because he did not wish to hurt Kant's feelings.

Critique, Kant was so angry that he wrote a scathing review of Herder's writings.[80]

Kant figures deeply in Hamann's writing of the *Socratic Memoirs* because Kant is one of the two friends Hamann hopes to save by his reading of the *Socratic Memoirs*. Kant had spent quite a bit of his earlier life in obscurity in Königsberg and in the early 1760s Hamann was actually better known than Kant.[81] They had met for the first time in 1756 long before Kant's great publicly accepted *Critique* of 1781. In the late 1750s, when the *Socratic Memoirs* were in gestation, Hamann could write of Kant 'We stand so near to each other . . .'[82] Hamann seeks to influence his friend, Kant, through the *Socratic Memoirs* although he ultimately fails in his task.

In history he came to influence Nietzsche, but in a negative sense, because Nietzsche decided he would present a different type of Socrates to the world.[83] However he admired Hamann's style. He also speaks gratefully of Hamann's soothing words of consolation.[84] He liked the fact that Hamann was unsystematic[85] and rejoices because Hamann writes in fragments.[86]

In fact, Hamann is the 'German Heraclitus'.[87] Life for him is a series of 'Fragmente'.[88] Cassirer may be pushing the point when he states, concerning Hamann, that 'what he gives are not fragments, but fragments of fragments. . .'[89] Nietzsche truly could write easily of Hamann that he was one of 'those overpowering artists who let a harmony sound forth from every conflict . . . bestow upon things their own power and self-redemption: they express their innermost experience in the

---

[80] *Herders Briefe an J. G. Hamann*, Berlin, 1889, p. 199. See also Friedrich Nicolovius, *Mancherley zur Geschichte der metacritischen Invasion*, Königsberg, 1800, pp. 9, 124, 128, 161, and 254 for parallels between Hamann and Herder over Kant's *Critique*.

[81] Wilhelm Koepp, *Der Magie unter Masken*, Göttingen, 1965, p. 168.

[82] Ziesemer-Henkel, I, p. 440. See also Heinrich Weber, *Hamann und Kant*, Nordlingen, 1903, pp. 4–23, which discusses the Hamann–Kant relationship from 1759 to 1779.

[83] Nietzsche, *Werke Die Philosophie im tragischen Zeitalter der Griechen*, in *Gesammelte*, Munich, 1920-9, IV, p. 161.

[84] Ibid., IV, p. 161.

[85] Gildemeister, VI, p. 228, Roth I, p. 413, and Gildemeister V, p. 285.

[86] G. S. Kirk, *Heraclitus: The Cosmic Fragments*, Cambridge, 1954, explains that Heraclitus wrote in fragments. Hamann had admired the fragments of Heraclitus very much.

[87] *Johann Georg Hamann: Lichtstrahlen aus seinen Schriften und Briefen*, Leipzig, 1874, p. 24.

[88] Roth, V, p. 278.

[89] Ernst Cassirer, *Freiheit und Form: Studien zur Deutschen Geistesgeschichte*, Darmstadt, 1961, p. 109.

symbolism of every work of art they produce—their creativity is gratitude for their existence.'[90] Understood paradoxically in a somewhat un-Nietzschean setting, the *Socratic Memoirs* describes Hamann well. He created humanly in time as he gratefully communicated with God.

It is now time to look at Hamann creating. When he was working on the *Socratic Memoirs* he was dynamically filled with many everyday experiences as well as being 'full of Hume.'[91] Rapin also had a great influence upon Hamann concerning his developing views of Socrates.[92] In conjunction with these various influences Hamann was aware of the fact that his own influence upon himself was decisive. He warned those who read him, in a letter to his friend, J. G. Lindner, that the *Socratic Memoirs* may appear to be unclear because he had to express a great deal and yet be 'brief'[93], which is part of his intended effort to put both his aesthetics and his religious views into a nutshell, as he did in writing *Aesthetica in Nuce*.

But his effort to be brief in discussing many things at once does not imply a condensed systematics. He states that the *Socratic Memoirs* are not systematic in a regular sense but are rather a series of flowing fragments.[94] He wanted a form of unity that still left room for diversity, a 'coincidence of opposites'.

He had first become interested in Socrates himself in 1753 by reading Plato's views on Socrates, so the fragments were gestating for quite some time. But this gestation of fragments was more than confused rubbish, for, as Eric Blackall knew well, 'For all his assertions of sensualism, Hamann writes a highly conscious and cerebral style—a style of intellect, of splendid intelligence, the expression of a mind that was exceptionally well-informed and incorrigibly nimble . . . '[95] Indeed Hamann was both sensual and incorrigibly nimble of mind, an apparent 'coincidence of opposites'. Blackall appears to admire Hamann's incorrigibly nimble mind but is suspicious of his sensualism, as if the mind helped to control sensualism. Hamann himself felt that emotion and

---

[90] Friedrich Nietzsche, *The Will to Power*, II, translated by Anthony M. Ludovici, New York, 1924, p. 852.

[91] Gildemeister, V, p. 27. See also pp. 492–6. Hume had a profound effect upon Hamann because he forced man to see that that which he may have termed to be certain knowledge was open to doubt. Perhaps man even needed a form of 'faith'.

[92] See Bernard Gajeck, 'Sprache beim jungen Hamann', Phil. Diss. München, 1959, p. 99.

[93] Ziesemer-Henkel, I, 324.

[94] Ibid., I, p. 431.

[95] Eric Blackall, 'Hamann's "fünf Hirten Briefe"' in *German Life and Letters*, Oxford, vol. XVIII, 1964–5, p. 117.

sensualism helped to control the more absurd reaches of the mind as a concept-making apparatus.

Hamann himself consistently insists 'In my mimetic style there rules a stricter logic and a closer connection than in the ideas of more lively minds.'[96] He is aware of the fact that 'without rules it is not possible to write . . .'[97] But he knows that the rules cannot be allowed to stifle the stirrings of spirit. At all costs he will create and be active, for he knows that 'Action, as Demosthenes said, is the soul of persuasion and also the style . . .'[98] In *Socratic Memoirs* he hopes to persuade his two friends, Kant and Berens, to become less enlightened and more Christian. His active creations are always related to surrounding circumstances[99] because 'My authorship is in very exact connection with my exterior circumstances . . .'[100] He often has too many reports at once to set forth from both heart and mind.[101] As circumstances change his active creativity changes and he can exclaim 'I express myself with many tongues . . .'[102] He does not pursue his observation that whenever he thinks he must be aware of the fact that he is experiencing sensations or vice versa because a too intense effort to be aware of this fact of reality would impede him from creating within temporality. He thus avoids one of the major pitfalls of the Linguistic Analysts who became tied up in the very process of seeking to discover relations between various levels of sensations,[103] turning their creative powers into 'word games' which are more stultifying than Kierkegaard's habit of running up and down the staircases of his mind.

His style is first and foremost *alive*, for 'what others call style is for me spirit . . .'[104] Style is the representation of the living flesh–blood–spirit human being. This experience on Hamann's part is very similar to Schiller's feeling that he was a kind of 'hybrid, hovering uncertainly between concept and image . . .'.[105] although Hamann's devotion to the feelings of the heart which create images was more intense than his devotion to the grasping of concepts. Schiller's interest in more abstract thinking arose from the rigours of his medical training whereas his image-making was apparent in his dramatic masterpieces. Schiller's friendship with Goethe, who was deeply influenced by

---

[96] Ziesemer-Henkel, I, p. 378.
[97] Roth, III, p. 172.
[98] Nadler, II, p. 116.
[99] Ibid, III, p. 138.
[100] Gildmeister, V, p. 444.
[101] Schmitz-Kallenberg, p. 20.
[102] Nadler, I, p. 396.
[103] See Bertrand Russell, *Our Knowledge of the External World*, Chicago, 1914, and 'The Relations of Sense-data to Physics' in *Scientia*, No. 4, 1914.
[104] Roth, V, p. 257.
[105] Elizabeth M. Wilkinson, *Schiller: Poet or Philosopher?* Oxford, 1961, p. 4.

Hamann, and his wrestling with Kantian metaphysics which was distrusted by Hamann, helped make him akin to Hamann, especially in regard to Kant's view that aesthetics was essentially subjective in a pejorative sense. Like Hamann, Schiller is not a systematic thinker. His aesthetic theories were more rationalistic than Hamann's but his relationship to Hamann was enhanced when he abandoned aesthetic philosophizing in favour of writing poetry. His view that aesthetics had to be a life-impulse was quite akin to Hamann's views expressed in *Aesthetica in Nuce*. He searches for a kind of 'coincidence of opposites' among apparently contradictory views of philosophy. His *Nervengeist* or nervous spirit is one of his most apt efforts to find a way of uniting body and spirit as contradictory aspects of reality. In his great work *Über naive und sentimentalische Dichtung*, we see him thinking that Goethe is a naïve poet in the sense that he is open to nature in a spontaneous fashion, whereas he himself is a sentimental poet who must react in various ways to his spontaneous experience of nature. He does not seem to think that the two kinds of poets could coexist in one man, whereas in fact Hamann could see this as a possible fact in a 'coincidence of opposites'. Perhaps Schiller's effort to deal with the mystery of nature in his late work *On the Sublime* is a movement in the direction of Hamann at this point.

We have presented many of the historical circumstances concerning the *Socratic Memoirs*. There is also a set of historical circumstances surrounding *Aesthetica in Nuce*, because Hamann writes only when he is actively concerned about a particular contemporary personal problem. The *Aesthetica in Nuce* was occasioned by the aesthetic writings of Lessing which Hamann thought were too humanistic because they denied God's position in helping man in the process of creating.[106] Lessing was deeply influenced by the writings of Christian Wolff whom Hamann despised, and by his friends, Friedrich Nicolai, whom Hamann disliked, and Moses Mendelssohn, whom Hamann liked as a person but with whom he quarrelled over some of his views. He was not a great original thinker but he did know how to transmit the ideas of others. He was in agreement with Hamann in desiring the German language to be free from the control of the French language and in his efforts to warn those following Winckelmann's slavish Classicism that poets must be free to create. He was, in a sense, neutral towards Christianity, a position which was unacceptable to Hamann. He was also devoted to Hermann Samuel Reimarus who attacked Hamann's beloved revelation.

---

[106] Ziesemer-Henkel, II, p. 17.

Lessing's study 'New Hypothesis Concerning the Evangelists Regarded as Merely Human Historians' in 1784 did not endear him to Hamann. His great expostulation that accidental truths of history can never become the proof of necessary truths of reason in the 1777 edition of *Über den Beiveis des Geistes und der Kraft*, is countered by Hamann's views on time his notion of the 'coincidence of opposites'. Jacobi, Hamann's old friend, was in complete agreement with Hamann on this point concerning Lessing's lack of interest in free will, which caused Jacobi to write his 'Letters to Moses Mendelssohn on Spinoza's Doctrine'.[107] Hamann felt that man's creative abilities flowed partially from animal passions[108] which was similar to Lessing's 'Fabeltheorie'—but God must also be given his acknowledged position in the creative process. There is an 'aesthetic Moses'[109] precisely because he co-operates with God's creativity in conjunction with his own creativity. In 1762 Hamann is very excited about his new writings, *Aesthetica in Nuce* and *Kleeblatt Hellenistischer Briefe*, which he affectionately calls his 'two new sausages'.[110]

Lessing had also written in a fashion repellent to Hamann about aesthetics, although, to a certain extent, he had been influenced by Leibnitz[111] whose views on aesthetics Hamann quite liked. He also had been influenced by A. G. Baumgarten. New aesthetical creations could make the world progressively better, just as Leibnitz held that the created world improves with the passage of time. Like Hamann, he claimed to have an unstable memory conjoined with great powers of aesthetical creative thinking.[112] He could exclaim 'when I have done something, I forget it almost completely in a few months, and rather than hunt for it in a chaos of sheets . . . I have to do the work all over again.'[113] Baumgarten saw aesthetics as 'the theory of beauty regarding the fine arts, an inferior sort of knowledge, the art of elegant thinking, the art which is knowledge through similitude or knowledge through sensitive perception.'[114] This is a difficult descriptive definition which

---

[107] See Ernst Cassirer, *Die Philosophie der Aufklärung*, Tübingen, 1932.
[108] Nadler, III, p. 38.   [109] Nadler, II, p. 163.
[110] Ziesemer-Henkel, II, p. 128.
[111] Ursula Franke, *Kunst als Erkenntnis: Die Rolle der Sinnlichkeit in der äesthetik des Alexander Gottlieb Baumgarten*, Wiesbaden, 1972, pp. 6–8.
[112] See G. E. Guhrauer, *Gottfried Wilhelm, Freiherr von Leibniz*, Breslau, 1842, vol. II, appendix p. 60.
[113] G. I. Gerhardt, *Die Philosophischen Schriften von G. W. Leibnitz*, Hildesheim, 1970, vol. II, p. 228. See also M. Gueroult, *Dynamique et métaphysique leibniziennes*, Paris, 1934, and Emilienne Naert, *Mémoire et conscience de soi selon Leibniz*, Paris, 1961.
[114] A. G. Baumgarten, *Aesthetica*, Leipzig 1907, p. 1.

has been twisted and interpreted since Baumgarten's time. For instance Kant in his early views on aesthetics is very akin to Baumgarten, whereas his later views differed.[115] Baumgarten himself worried whether his interest in poetics was unphilosophical.[116] His work on aesthetics was one of his only deviations from Wolffian philosophy. His pupil, G. F. Meier, followed his views on aesthetics closely. Meier's *Anfangsgründe aller schönen Künste und Wissenschaften*, published during Hamann's lifetime from 1748 to 1750, is much like Baumgarten's *Aestetica*. Baumgarten saw aesthetics as dealing with an inferior faculty which had a grasp of sense knowledge, but at least he gave this form of knowledge some merit. Hamann did not like his gnoseology which is a combination of aesthetics and logic. Hamann approved of his view that poetical beauty must be confused in the sense that it is not exceptionally clear and distinct.[117] Baumgarten had begun an apparently new interest in aesthetics which in time was taken up by the 'Public' with some enthusiasm in an intellectualist sense.

Hamann could say of this 'newest aesthetic' that 'the leading stem of his newest aesthetic, which is also the oldest, is: Fear God and give Him the glory, because the time of His judgement has come . . . the power that made heaven and earth and the sea and the springs of water.'[118] Man truly creates but in union wih God's creative power. Ultimately God is the best judge of aesthetics because He is the best Creator among creators. One must be able to have the experience of creating before one can claim to be capable of judging creations in depth, Bernard Berensen notwithstanding. This is what Hamann wishes to tell Lessing in a nutshell, and the followers of men such as Baumgarten. 'God is an author . . .'[119] and has the 'highest authorship.'[120] When God speaks, His speaking is like poetry.[121] Christ, who is also God, is synonymous with being a poet.[122] In Bonaventure's work, *De Reductione Artium ad Theologiam*, he shows beautifully how Christ is an author and a poet although not for exactly the same reasons as advanced by Hamann. Like Hamann, he reacted against claims at the University of Paris in his day that the philosopher was the noblest of men who can discuss any topic under the sun because he adheres to wisdom

---

[115] Compare Kant, *Kritik der reinen Vernunft*, 1781, with *Kritik der Unteilskraft*, 1790.
[116] *Aesthetica*, p. 478.
[117] See B. Poppe, *A. G. Baumgartens, seine Bedeutung und seine Stellung in der Leibniz-Wolffischen Philosophie und seine Beziehung zu Kant*, Münster, 1907.
[118] Nadler, II, p. 308.   [119] Ibid, I, p. 5.
[120] Roth, V. p. 82.   [121] Ziesemer-Henkel, I, p. 369.
[122] Ibid, I, p. 367.

rather than to fables. Unlike Hamann, who merely ridiculed metaphysics, he also made Christ the greatest metaphysician in contradiction to Aristotle.[123] God is a good judge of man's creations in this world.[124] God is the 'Poet at the beginning of the day'.[125] When man creates may he see that he does not create alone, but that God also creates with him. Man and God can communicate through their creative activities.

This is Hamann's message in a nutshell: if a man lives a life united with God and part of his living is aesthetic creation, then this is done in co-operation with God. Shaftesbury, who influenced the *Aesthetica in Nuce*, wanted the creative man's artistic objects to be like his act of living itself[126] so as to be valid human works. Hamann could agree with this view insofar as man experienced his everyday life and his artistic life in particular as impregnated by God.

Hamann wrote his little[127] work on aesthetics just as Christoph Otto von Schoenach had written his *Die ganze Ästhetik in einer Nuss, oder neologisches Wörterbuch* in 1754, but he entitled his work *Aesthetica in Nuce: eine Rhapsodie in Kabbalistischer Prose*. This little work influenced the following works historically: Herder's *Kalligone*, Schiller's *Die Künstler*, Jean Paul's *Vorschule der Aesthetik* (he considered Hamann to be one of the stars of the firmament), and Croce's[128] work also entitled *Aesthetica in Nuce*.[129]

[123] Much of Bonaventures writing is repetitious, but this particular writing is very thought-provoking because of its unique insights.
[124] Nadler, III, p. 132. [125] Ibid, II, p. 206.
[126] Shaftesbury, *Characteristics*, ed. by J. M. Robertson, London, 1900, Vol. I, p. 217. See also Christian F. Weiser, *Shaftesbury und das deutsche Geistesleben*, Second edition, Darmstadt, 1969. Like Hamann, Shaftesbury wrote for an exquisite person rather than for the 'Public' who desired intellectual clarity. He had no system of thinking. When his various thoughts were drawn together in *Characteristics of Men, Manners, Opinions and Times*, he wrote an introduction entitled 'Miscellaneous Reflections on the Preceding *Treatises*' in order to have people keep in mind the fact that he did not consider the book to be systematical. Although he was not exceptionally interested in religion he did plead for freedom of creativity. See also, Thomas Fowler, *Shaftesbury and Hutcheson*, London, 1882.
[127] Hamann thinks of his work as being a 'little' work because he is trying to put all of his experiences into a nutshell with the use of 'few' words. Economy of style is central throughout his life. See Ziesemer-Henkel, V, p. 88, and Nadler, III, p. 399.
[128] His more acclaimed book on aesthetics is entitled *Estetica come scienza dell espressione e linguistica generale*. Vico, whom Hamann knew hardly at all, but who is similar to Hamann in many respects, influenced Croce deeply. Croce is more intellectual than Hamann since he was partially influenced by Kant. See G. N. G. Orsini, *Benedetto Croce, Philosopher of Art and Literary Critic*, Carbondale, Ill., 1961.
[129] See Hermann Lotze, *Geschichte der Äesthetik in Deutschland*, Leipzig, 1913.

Hamann was intrigued by titles of works which had some influence upon him, like those of Jacob Boehme who gave titles to his works which were keys and summaries of the work in question. For example, Boehme had as a title for one of his works:

>Signatura Rerum;
>the Signature of All Things.
>Showing the Sign and Signification of
>The Several Forms of and Shapes in Creation;
>and what the
>Beginning, Ruin and Cure of
>Everything Is.
>It proceeds out of
>Eternity into Time and again out
>of Time into Eternity
>And Comprizes all Mysteries.'[130]

In this work, the *Signature of All Things*, Jacob Boehme states: 'Whatever is spoken, written, or taught of God, without the knowledge of the signature is dumb and void of understanding . . . but if his sound [that of another person such as God] and spirit out of his signature and similitude enter into my own similitude, and imprint his similitude into mine then I may understand him really and fundamentally, be it either spoken or written, if he has the hammer that can strike my bell.'[130]

Hamann never admitted to being deeply influenced by the mystical feelings of Boehme however, because he saw that Boehme's mystical feelings were 'insane fantasies' and 'mystical writings',[131] and he was

---

[130] Jacob Boehme, *The Signature of all Things*, London, 1969, introduction. Hamann did not live like the cobbler who, in 1600, looked at a pewter dish and because of the sunlight playing on it saw 'the Being of Beings, the Abyss of the Abyss, the eternal generation of the Trinity.' Both he and Boehme were influenced by the alchemical writings of Paracelsus. See also H. L. Martensen, *Jacob Boehme: His Life and Teaching*, translated by T. Rys, London, 1885.

[131] Nadler, II, p. 68. F. W. J. von Schelling, who was influenced by Hamann and Goethe, was much more deeply influenced by Boehme in his later writings, and was a romantic with an idealist twist. His later works are said to be somewhat existential. His view of art was similar to Hamann's because he felt a creation of art could never be fully known because it was a communication of the infinite in the finite. His *Über das Verhältniss der Bildenden Künste zu der Natur* insists that art is not abstract thinking which is quite Hamannian. Aesthetics helps create the real world. He felt that the Brunoian pantheistic view of God's activity in the world made sense in a vein somewhat similar to Hamann but more akin to Goethe. His God of 'eternal contrariety' does differ from Hamann's God who is more Christian. His view that man is the glory of creation and free creative activity is very Hamannian. His *Philosophie der Mythologie* copied with recognition by Cassirer in his *The Philosophy of Symbolic Forms* is anti-Hamannian in so far as it sees symbols as part of a Kantian *a priori* system. His existentialism is more negative

not much interested in mysticism *per se* in a positive sense, but criticized it often.[132]

Hamann in like fashion tells his readers that a title is 'a microcosmic seed, an Orphic Egg'.[133] He was following a long tradition in using the symbol of the egg. As Thomas Burnet had been able to say earlier in Hamann's century, 'the Mundane Egg . . . the world was Oviform, this hath been the sense and Language of all Antiquity, Latins, Greeks, Persians, . . . '[134] Often if Hamann wished to speak of the heart of his interest he would make use of the egg symbol, as when he wrote to his friend, Herder, 'Your theme of language, experience and tradition is my favourite idea, the egg I brood upon—my one and all—. . . '[135]

In speaking of a man's written works Hamann insists that 'the title of his works is simultaneously the signature of his name',[136] which is reminiscent of Jacob Boehme. The title of a work expresses the power and substance of the person who has a name, a signature, as the writer of the work. In the Title of *Aesthetica in Nuce* Hamann deals with the word *Aesthetica* in relation to the word *Nuce*. Both Goethe and Kierkegaard were correct in seeing that Hamann was always trying to express a great deal in a few words. His use of the notion of 'nutshell' in a title fits his desire for the creative qualitative unity of expression. The writing of Schoenach's, *Die ganze Ästhetik in einer Nuss*, of 1754, was the type of occasional contemporary writing which triggered in Hamann the desire to use words paradoxically from the title of another man's writings in an unsuperficial but valid mimetic fashion.

Hamann always desired some form of living creative unity. One of his favourite poets had been Horace who was concerned about the 'disjecta membra poetae', which Hamann quotes in the *Aesthetica in Nuce*. Horace loved a poetry of wit that had to be a little different because of the influence of the Greek writer, Archilochus. He is excellent at reproducing lively conversations from everyday life while

---

than the existentialism of Hamann because he constantly frets over 'Why is there anything at all' whereas Hamann accepts that fact as a given and goes on from there in the order of creativity. They could agree somewhat that the world as experienced by man is a kind of poetical language expression of creating spirit, but Hamann would insist that part of the creating spirit is man himself in a positive sense. See also Eric D. Hirsch, *Wordsworth and Schelling*, New York, 1962.

[132] Ziesemer-Henkel, I, p. 307, and II, p. 355, Gildemeister, V, p. 7, Nadler, II, p. 171, III, pp. 105, 107, 227, and 223.

[133] Nadler, III, p. 373.

[134] Thomas Burnet, *Telluris, Theoria Sacra: The Scacred Theory of the Earth*, London, 1726, vol. I, p. 86.

[135] Roth, VII, p. 292.   [136] Nadler, III, p. 372.

making many allusions, which is a feature of Hamann's style. He had a way also of using strange word orders. Many of his poems spring from particular occasions just as Hamann often wrote something because of a particular happening. He was no philosopher, just like Hamann. He was very interested in other people and enjoyed friendships in everyday life, as Hamann strove continually to do.

As a person Hamann's friend Herder was similar to him in relation to both the *Sturm und Drang* movement and the age of Romanticism. The Hebrew language also influenced Herder, who wrote 'they [the Hebrews] express by a single word, what we can express often only by five or more words.'[137] Hebrew is quite poetical and akin to the Ugaritic poetical texts, of the early fourteenth century BC. Herder's analysis of Hebrew poetry was affected by Michaelis's analysis described in *Beurteilung der Mittel, welche man anwendet, die ausgestorbene hebraeische Sprache zu verstehen*, published in Göttingen, 1757, which Hamann challenged in the *Aesthetica in Nuce*.[138] Michaelis had been influenced deeply on this subject by a former Bishop of Oxford, Bishop Lowth, who lectured '*De sacra poesia*' at Oxford in the early 1750s. After visiting Oxford in 1740, Michaelis published his German translation of the Old Testament in thirteen volumes which Hamann did not like. He did not translate the New Testament completely until 1792, four years after Hamann's death, but it is safe to say that Hamann would not have liked that translation either.

Herder had stated in his book on Hebrew poetry concerning Bishop Lowth that 'The beautiful and justly celebrated work of Bishop Lowth, *De sacra poesia Hebraeorum*, is universally known, and might seem to preclude the necessity of the present undertaking. A nearer comparison of its contents, however, will show that the present work is neither a translation, nor an imitation of it.'[139] With all due respect towards Herder, a comparison of the two works does quite clearly establish the fact that Herder's is at least a partial translation which at times is imitative. It is a fine work nonetheless. Lowth, of course, had studied in Germany at Göttingen where he may have encountered some views on Hebrew poetry especially related to the study of Hebrew poetry in Italy in the late Rennaissance. Bishop Lowth insisted upon putting

---

[137] J. G. Herder, *The Spirit of Hebrew Poetry*, translated by J. Marsch and Edward Smith, Burlington, 1833, p. 37. Hamann was quite influenced by Albert Schulten's *Origines hebraes*, concerning the Hebrew language.
[138] See R. Unger, *Hamann und die Aufklärung*, Jena, 1911, pp. 241-7; see also K. Gründer, *Figur und Geschichte*, Freiburg, 1958, pp. 173-7.
[139] Herder, *The Spirit of Hebrew Poetry*, Intr.

thoughts into a nutshell like Hamann, in the sense that 'brevity'[140] of words is good, while an accumulation of 'more words'[141] is detracting.

Herder's ability to read English was excellent, since Hamann, who was an expert translator of English, had taught him the language (cf. Hamann's partial translation of Hume's *Dialogues of Natural Religion* praised by Kant). Hamann especially liked having Herder read *Hamlet* in which the idea of 'nutshell' can be found. Like Shakespeare's *Hamlet*, Hamann wants to discover the heart or interior contents of the nutshell which gives us creative life. He is creatively also seeking like Novalis to put ideas into 'einem Punkte'.[142]

Novalis was influenced by Goethe, who put him in touch with Hamann's views of reality in Jena. He became a kind of romantic mystic after the death of Sophie von Kuhn. His *Hymnen an die Nacht*, which is like Edward Young's *Night Thoughts*, had an influence upon Hamann, but it is antithetical to Hamann's view that one should live in this world with joy because one can communicate creatively, although it does use the notion of a 'coincidence of opposites', because it is in the night that all polarities coalesce.[143] His *Heinrich von Ofterdingen* is more Hamannian as it seeks to explain how the poet is a muse who shows man where his true home is located. However, it is too mystical in its effort to release man from the finitude of this world as it seeks to place man in the poetic infinitude of true reality where he grasps his true self. Novalis also saw the world as a series of fragments in *Blutenstaub*, in regard to man's ability to think about the world, which is somewhat like Hamann's *Brocken*. He also detested the Enlightenment and the 'Public' who made up the Enlightenment. He exults in the freedom of the creative artist who becomes like the creative God. Hamann seeks to deal with his 'critical nuts' actively,[144] and in doing so helped to create the 'kernel-thought of the Romantic'.[145] Hamann's desire to write 'the most thoughts in the fewest words'[146] assisted others to become qualitatively creative. His study of the Torah had also helped

---

[140] Bishop Lowth, *Lectures on the Sacred Poetry of the Hebrews*, translated by Joseph Johnson, London, 1787, Lecture II, p. 168.
[141] Lowth, *Lectures on the Sacred Poetry of the Hebrews*, Lecture I, p. 350.
[142] Novalis, *Schriften*, ed. by Richard Samuel and Paul Kluchhohn, Leipzig, 4 Bd., 1928, II, p. 330.
[143] See B. Küpper, *Die Zeit als Erlebnis des Novalis*, Cologne, 1959. See also W. Dilthey, *Das Erlebnis und die Dichtung: Lessing, Goethe, Novalis, Hölderlin*, third edition, Leipzig, 1910.
[144] Nadler, II, p. 272.
[145] Ernst Zinn, *Wahrheit in Philologie und Dichtung in den Wissenschaften und die Wahrheit*, Tübingen, 1966, p. 135.
[146] Nadler, I, p. 165.

him to see that each word would have deep meanings in the order of creative wisdom.[147]

The section of the title investigated so far is *Aesthetica in Nuce*. The full title is *Aesthetica in Nuce: eine Rhapsodie in Kabbalistische Prose*. The word 'Rhapsodie' in Hamann's age popularly referrred to persons who were interpreters of reality both lived in a general sense and more specifically, reality as it comes into existence through human creativity The rhapsodist was originally known as a collector of literary pieces. Plinius Secundus was reputed to be the greatest rhapsodist among the Latins. But a rhapsodist was also a reciter of poems such as the Homeric poems, which fits Hamann's use of the word in the full title of *Aesthetica in Nuce* more exactly because he is primarily interested in the powers of poetic creation. Rhapsodists were also accused of arguing illogically and at times were referred to as ranters, which pleased Hamann, as he attempted to relate things in an apparently disconnected fashion giving an impression of a confused rambling nonsense except to those exquisite humans who could grasp the communication. A good rhapsodist would even be a good interpreter of interpreters. Shaftesbury, whom Hamann admired and some of whose works he translated into German,[148] was known in Germany as the writer of 'the rhapsody'[149] Hamann admired and some of whose works he translated into German,[148] was known in Germany as the writer of 'the rhapsody'[149] Hamann's 'Rhapsodie' is related both to Shaftesbury's 'Rhapsodie' and to his artistic views which are recognized as being 'Ästhetik', by Baumgarten.[150] Moses Mendelssohn, with whom Hamann had remonstrated, had also written a *Rhapsodie*. He is referred to as the greatest Jewish philosopher of his age since he was acknowledged by non-Jews. He was even called the Jewish Socrates. He was a close Wolff's views of metaphysics. Hamann had to dispute with him because he was directly interested in aesthetics and religion, while he wrote in a rather intriguing style. He followed Baumgarten's views on aesthetics, holding that aesthetics was an inferior form of knowing, residing in a special faculty which says to the mind 'I approve of this perceived object.' In this, he had a profound influence upon Kant. Hamann

---

[147] G. Scholem, *On the Kabbalah and its Symbolism*, translated by Ralph Mannheim, London, 1965, p. 63.
[148] Nadler, IV, p. 135.
[149] A. Altmann, *Moses Mendelssohn: Frühschriften*, Tübingen, 1969, p. 86.
[150] See Christian F. Weiser, *Shaftesbury und das Deutsche Geistesleben*, Darmstadt, 1969, Ch. V, Ästhetischen Geniessen, and Ch. XII, Religion. See also Otto Mann, *Hamann: Magus des Nordens, Hauptschriften*, Leipzig, 1937, pp. 66 and 99.

could agree with him that a genius, disregarding rules, produces beauty, except for the fact that Mendelssohn's genius was an idealizing factor in human creativity.[151]

Hamann is therefore following the example of well-known contemporary Germans by including the notion of 'Rhapsodie' in his title. He is always alive to his contemporary surroundings. His use of the word 'Rhapsodie' also demonstrates analogically the fight he was having with another interpreter: J. D. Michaelis who, as we have previously seen, had benefited from the 1754-5 lectures of Bishop Lowth of Oxford, concerning the creative aspects of Hebrew poetry. Hamann thought Michaelis was too rationalistic in his interpretation of Hebrew poetry. In 1758 Michaelis had translated into German some of Lowth's lectures concerning the Old Testament, which Hamann read and found disturbing. By 1762 he had his interpretative answer, his 'Rhapsodie', ready for publication. In the very same year, Bishop Lowth's work was discussed in the *Hamburgischen Nachrichten* which Hamann read[152] as it was related to Michaelis. Although he disliked Michaelis, he was not as rationalistic in his interpretation of the Bible as George Benson, in his *Einleitung Paraphrastische Erklärung und Anmerkungen über einige Bücher des Neuen Testaments*,[153] who held that each sentence of holy Scripture had just one meaning; but Michaelis is still attacked implicitly both in Hamann's *Rhapsodie* and in his *Hellenistische Briefe*. Hamann complains later to his friend, Lindner, that Michaelis has not benefited from his (Hamann's) efforts to help him change his rhapsodic view,[154] and therefore has not done much to correct his *Einleitung in die göttlichen Schriften des neuen Bundes*, which had been published again in Göttingen.

The Alexandrian school of Platonism flourished from the fourth to the seventh centuries. It was much occupied with the exegesis of various texts, as was Michaelis. It was quite non-Plotinian, and therefore truer to Platonism itself. It was liked by some Christians because of its Christian tinges, apparent especially in the writings of Bishop Synesius.[155] Although rhapsodic writings in the Enlightenment could

---

[151] See L. Goldstein, *Moses Mendelssohn und die deutsche Äesthetik*, Königsberg, 1904.

[152] Sven-Aage Jorgensen, 'Hamann, Bacon, and Tradition' in *Orbis Litterarum*, 16, 1961.

[153] George Benson, *Einleitung Paraphrastische Erklärung und Ammerkungen über einige Bücher des Neuen Testaments*, Leipzig, 1761.

[154] Ziesemer-Henkel, II, p. 183.

[155] See E. Eurad, 'Les Convictions réligieuses de Jean Philopon' in *Bulletin de l'Académie royale belgique*, Brussels, 1953, pp. 299-357.

refer to a kind of Alexandrian Platonism which is essentially inclined in the direction of Michaelis's translation and interpretation of the Bible, Hamann is more alive in his interpretation and therefore more faithful in grasping the experience of the Old Testament. Poets ought to be interpreters of the creative living God who is also a poet. Hamann can creatively proclaim 'I see myself . . . the rhapsodist has read, obeyed, thought, sought and found pleasing words . . .'[156]

Hamann writes that his Rhapsodie is in 'Cabbalistic Prose', but after many readings of the whole *Aesthetica in Nuce* one is convinced that it is not a cabbalistic tract; the word 'cabbalistic', for Hamann, is metaphorical in seeking to show that the work has complex intentions. The cabbala refers to the medieval period of Jewish mysticism found in the Bible and rabbinic tradition which takes on an occult form. The cabbala's view of creation runs contrary to Hamann's view because the mysticism of the cabbala demands more transcendence on God's part. Genesis shows God too immersed in the world; this is precisely what Hamann likes about the Book of Genesis. Hamann could agree with the cabbala's efforts to find hidden meanings in Scripture in general. He was not deeply influenced however by its efforts to develop layers of numerical symbolisms in Scripture. Its efforts to find the heights of human experience in this world were similar to his own lack of interest in an afterlife and his great desire to live creatively in this world. German cabbalism tended to be more practical whereas the Spanish variety was more speculative. The German form would have appealed more to Hamann.[157] Similarly, although Hamann was aware of the Masons[158] and had noticed the book *L'Art Royal du Chevalier de Rosecroix*,[159] he was not deeply devoted to the Masonic views of reality. Michaelis's *Beurtheilung der Mittel, welche man anwendet, die ausgestorbene Hebräische Sprache zu verstehen*[160] shows an anticabbalistic bias, but although Hamann disliked the views of Michaelis he did not write a strictly cabbalistic tract to counter Michaelis' cabbalistic stance. It is typical of his style to include the word 'cabbalistic' in his title with the partial purpose of teasing Michaelis. However, he certainly was no cabbalist and only speaks of the cabbala in his more private writings to his friend Lindner, and then only once.[161]

---

[156] Nadler, II, p. 217.
[157] See Christian D. Ginsburg, *The Kabbalah: Its Doctrine, Development and Literature*, London, 1920.
[158] Nadler II, p. 206, and III, p. 32.   [159] Nadler, III, p. 33.
[160] J. D. Michaelis, *Beurtheilung der Mittel, welche man anwendet, die ausgestorbene Hebräische Sprache zu verstehen*, Göttingen, 1757, pp. 88-92.
[161] Ziesemer-Henkel, II, p. 115.

Peter Kraft, in his *Zur Deutung von J. G. Hamanns kabbalistischen Prose*, in Wiener-Goethe-Verein, 1967, is unsure just how cabbalistic Hamann was either in his private life or in his writings, but if Hamann was deeply affected by cabbalistic practices it is a well-kept secret, quite impossible to settle definitively, because we do not have recordings of his daily talk which could give a deeper insight into his views on cabbalism than his writings, for everyday creative speaking was part of the heart of his life.

It is just as difficult to prove very much concerning Hamann's relationship to cabbalism as it is to prove how deeply Bosch[162] either was or was not a member of a heretical brotherhood which advocated sexual pleasure as the heart of reality (which some people say was the driving force for Hamann in his everyday life, since he felt that intercourse with his common-law wife placed him in union with God); or whether Jacob Boehme was really steeped in cabbalism at the heart of his life.[163] The most sensible view concerning Hamann's interest in cabbalism is that he relates its love of words to his own desire to be a 'Philologe', or lover of words,[164] and he also wishes to tease Michaelis.

In a letter Hamann states that the 'publisher' helped him decide to put Rhapsodisten and Kabbalisten together, which is not a very secret cabbalistic decision if Hamann were secretly cabbalistic and wanted to keep his cabbalistic practices outside the 'Public's' view. Perhaps the publisher was an ardent cabbalist, but this fact would not represent Hamann's deepest interior view of reality. On another level, his work, *per se*, is a secret to many persons who do not know how to communicate with it, and his writings could then be described in a sense as being 'cabalistico', just as his friend, Jacobi, metaphorically says of his other friend, Herder, that Herder's philosophical writings are 'cabalistico' without implying that Herder is a converted cabbalist when he is writing to Goethe.[165]

Aesthetica in Nuce: Eine Rhapsodie in Kabbalistischer Prose, in

---

[162] Bosch does not appear to have been optimistic about man's salvation in his enigmatic paintings. His landscapes are ominous and his monsters bizarre in shape. He is intrigued by the symbol of the egg, as in his great painting, The Garden of Delights, a symbol which also intrigued Hamann. See C. A. Wertheeim Aymes, *Hieronymus Bosch: Eine Einführung in seine geheime Symbolis*, Amsterdam, 1957.

[163] See *Der Spinozismus in Judenthums, oder die von dem heutigen Judenthum und dessen geheimen Kabbala vergötterte Welt*, Amsterdam, 1699.

[164] Nadler, II, p. 263.

[165] *Briefwechsel zwischen Goethe und F. H. Jacobi*, Leipzig, 1846, p. 73.

which the word *Prose* is a more rational playword in relation to *Poesie*, is Hamann's 'rock crystal'.[166] Hamann is the lover of God's creative word. He is the 'Philologe'.[167] Philology denotes a love of learning, which Hamann can see as a love of the Word who is God. A philologist loves speech, the process of communicating through talk which is at the heart of Hamann's view of reality, for he insists 'Speak that I may see Thee'. Philologists investigate the mysteries of both dead and living tongues. Homer was held to be the greatest philologian. Philosophers who considered themselves to be lovers of wisdom often considered philologians to be lovers of babbling. Vico based his new science on the facts residing in the domain of philology in opposition to Descartes who philosophized in too theoretical a fashion. Man must see the creation as a poetical painting, speaking in a creatively-alive fashion. Man, creatively alive, then seeks to establish communication with God in a loving awe that 'gives him the glory'. The glory of God is man fully, creatively alive.

This particular title of one of Hamann's works serves the purpose of showing how alive he is to the creative processes operating in his contemporary age which were exhibiting an added interest in the notion of aesthetics. Hamann wanted to grasp the pulsing heart of aesthetics, the kernel of aesthetics hidden within the aesthetical nutshell. He speaks as a rhapsodical interpreter like Michaelis and Mendelssohn while playing with the words 'cabbalistic' and 'prose'. Fritz Blanke sees *Aesthetica in Nuce* as presenting a 'body/spirit'[168] reality consisting in a 'creating together'[169] between God and man which was intended by Hamann as he sought to communicate creatively with God and other humans in time.

The title for *Socratic Memoirs* is as complex as the title for *Aesthetica in Nuce*. In its entirety, it is a complexly constructed and useful key to the entire work. The title says the work concerns the Greek, Socrates. It is a series of memoirs rather than a history, biography, or explication of Socratic texts. Hamann had played with the word 'opportunities' in relation to the word 'memoirs'.[170] Both words have a sense of temporality. The term 'opportunities' could also imply that worthwhile memoirs are composed of propitious opportunities which present

---

[166] Naddler, II, p. 268.
[167] Ibid., p. 266. See also Hans-Martin Lumpp, *Philologia Crucis*, Tübingen, 1970.
[168] Fritz Blanke, *Hamann-Studien*, Zürich, 1956, pp. 5-8.
[169] Ibid., pp. 9-14.
[170] Nadler, III, p. 100.

themselves to persons who know how to receive them. Hamann's use of the word 'memoirs' could testify to the influence of reading Winckelmann's[171] *Gedanken über die Nachahmung der Griechischen Werke* in the 1750s rather than to the masses of French 'historical' materials in *der Malerei und Bildhauerkunst* with which he was also acquainted.

When Hamann then states that the work is 'für die lange Weile des Publikums' (for the boredom of the 'public'), he is chastising the public who are too immersed in masses of superficially written material which is read on the ground that it is considered to be 'enlightened' reading. Hamann does consider himself to be 'the voice of a Preacher, who is like a desert to the Public' . . .[172] Both he and Herder wished constantly to escape from the insensibility of the 'Public'.[173] When Hamann thinks of great Berlin admired so by the 'Public' as the centre of intellectuality he exclaims 'Here is nothing, nothing, nothing . . .'[174] Hamann at this stage in his life most certainly is not concerned with being lauded by the 'Public' because 'A writer who is in haste to be understood today and perhaps tomorrow is in danger of being forgotten the day after tomorrow.'[175]

When Hamann writes for the 'boredom of the Public' there is the possibility that the majority of the 'Public' will read the *Socratic Memoirs* in the same manner in which they read so much other material, most of which is worthless junk. There is a twist in the Hamannian statement however, because Hamann begins the writing of the *Socratic Memoirs* with the foreknowledge that the majority of the 'Public' will not and could not grasp its true significance, for they will be bored in a special way from the reading of this work. Could the work paradoxically get bored by experiencing some of those who read it?

This work is 'zusammengetragen' (compiled or drawn together in a collective sense from various fragments of experience). This word appearing on the title page is the declaration by Hamann of his desire for unity in diversity which is the central principle of his life, as Goethe had seen so well, and as he sought to express later in *Aesthetica in*

---

[171] This first great work of Winckelmann's involved the various problems related to imitation which was one of the major interests of Hamann. His ideas were constantly shifting in a fragmentary fashion although some of his contemporaries sought to systematize his views. He held that beauty was indefinable; one simply had to experience it. The height of beauty was a divine communication which is similar to Hamann's view that the artistic creator is seeking not only to communicate with other humans but also with God. Winckelmann insisted that man spoke in images before he spoke in rational conceptual language which is part of the key insight of Hamann's *Aesthetica in Nuce*.

[172] Nadler, II, p. 108.   [173] Ibid., IV, p. 272.
[174] Nadler, IV, p. 274.   [175] Gildemeister, V. p. 616.

Nuce. This compiling or collecting has been done 'von einem Liebhaber der langen Weile' (by a Lover of Boredom).

This phrase, 'von einem Liebhaber der langen Weile', has at least three levels hidden in it. First, Hamann had been a lover of the enlightenment at one time and therefore, without them being aware of the fact, he spent much time in the boring pursuit of the enlightened search for knowledge through the reading of vast amounts of material which in itself was trite, but which he thought very perceptive. He laments in several letters to friends that he had wasted so much serious time on this pursuit compared with the reading of the Bible, which has the heart of the human condition on every page. Hamann did not give up the reading of books other than the Bible after his conversion, but he put them in their proper place: below the Bible in importance.

Secondly, Hamann, like Vico, never had a job which was very demanding. Vico never got a prestigious professorship and spent much time meditating on his writings. In his youth Vico had attended a Jesuit college which encouraged the interest in books already implanted in him by the fact that his father was a bookseller. His style of writing is quite obscure. He insisted that man can know only what he has helped to create, which is a central notion in Hamann's works. Most scholars agree that Hamann did not receive this notion from Vico. Just as Hamann insisted in his *Metacritique* that Kant attempted to say that there was only one method of inquiry in his *Critique of Pure Reason* whereas there are many methods, so Vico claimed that there were many methods of inquiry in contrast to Cartesianism. Vico insisted that language, even abstract language, was rooted in history and the earth.[176] There was a sense in which Hamann was a 'Lover of Leisure' in comparison with many good Prussians who worked hard in Königsberg and were proud of their menial tasks.

Thirdly, Hamann is being ironical, for he is re-interjecting the fact that he most assuredly could not be a lover of the type of activity which produces the boredom which consistently oppresses the 'Public'. But what then is he a lover of, in fact? Perhaps the opposite of the boredom of the 'Public'. He is a lover of creation, of a consistent effort through energy and dynamic activity to represent the mysteries of this world symbolically so that men can grasp the hidden meanings in creation. Hamann does not wish to seek to uncover some of the ambiguities and hidden meanings for those who know how to

---

[176] See *The Autobiography of Giambattista Vico*, translated by T. G. Bergin and M. H. Fisch, Ithaca, New York, 1944. See also A. R. Caponigri, *Time and Idea: The Theory of History in Giambattista Vico*, London, 1953.

communicate with his writings. This is why the title *Sokratische Denkwürdigkeiten* is related to another title-page, *Entkleidung und Verklärung*.[177]

This title page, read as an expression of the work, raises the following points of interest concerning Hamann's style of writing. He uses irony, paradox, and straightforward statements mixed together. His notion of energy or dynamism is intimated in Love. His views concerning the 'Public' who represent the enlightened ones is disparaging. He holds Socrates in great respect. He attempts through creative processes to bring forth memories from the past in such a way that they may live in the present and serve as a link between past and present. He attempts always to unite, collect, compile, and position a reality or experience so that it is a living, organic whole. He tries to communicate with people, if they can grasp the communication.

Hamann then states that this work is 'Mit einter doppelten Zuschrift an Niemand und an Zween' (With a Double Dedication to Nobody and to Two). The two special people are of course his two friends, Berens and Kant. Kant and Berens represent friends of Socrates, who represents Hamann.[178] 'Nobody' stands for the god who really is a nobody because he (it) is composed of the ignorance of the public masses. It (he) is the spirit of the age which worships something which really cannot be found in the nothing which it really is. Everybody knows this Nobody and yet Nobody cannot be identified. Hamann believed in the power of the devil or of Satan and in a sense he is challenging this Nobody, this idol, this false god who is a product of Satan, the devil. Part of the purpose of the *Socratic Memoirs* is the hope that it can free Berens and Kant from Nobody. This dedication is therefore a paradoxical dedication. In so far as Nobody is a creation of the ignorant activites of the Public there is also a sense in which Hamann could be hoping for a coincidence of opposites, a 'coincidence of opposites' which is one of his favourite views of reality received from Giordano Bruno.[179] Hamann would like to see the 'Public' saved from

---

[177] Nadler, III, p. 348.   [178] Ziesemer-Henkel, I, p. 373.

[179] Bruno was accused of heresy, as a Dominican, within the Catholic Church, partially as a result of his views concerning the reality of 'coincidence of opposites'. He was considered to be a Renaissance 'magus' just as Hamann was considered to be a 'magus' of the North. Bruno was influenced both by Ficino whom Hamann did not like and H. C. Agrippa. One of his most obscure and bizarre books was entitled *Thirty Seals*. He could be said to be a confused thinker just like Hamann, but the confusion does belie various levels of logicality. His magical hermetic religion saw itself as nature working in union with its own creative powers which is similar in certain respects to Hamann's view of reality. See Alexander Koyré, *From the Closed World to the Infinite Universe*, Baltimore, 1957.

their infatuation with Nobody whom they have created through their own unknowing ignorance. If Kant and Berens grasp the *Socratic Memoirs* correctly in so far as they are still related to Nobody, their reversal of interests concerning Nobody could bring about a change in the constitution or make-up of Nobody which would in turn change the views of the 'Public' who have helped paradoxically to create Nobody in the first place. Life is filled with ambiguities, so Hamann inserts these ambiguous facts into his writings.

Other points about Hamann's style arise from a reading of the *Socratic Memoirs* and *Aesthetica in Nuce*: they can be ambiguous in both intent and content; there are many instances of passages which can be interpreted correctly only by those who have some form of belief in what Hamann believes; persons must be treated as embodied; persons must be taken as organic or integral units; words are embodiments; clusters of words are organic or integral units; paradoxes are operative in the world of words; ugly metaphors can express hidden beauty; one must first be interested in material objects rather than abstract forms; analogous statements are the bonds of good language; irony brings out special forms of reality; imitation is good only if that which is imitated is the power of another person, of God, or of Scripture; originality is essential in writing; style is an expression of life; title-pages can be keys to a Hamannian work; reason and understanding both mean something different to him than to the members of the enlightenment; body and soul as realities are always intertwined; sentences and images are in groups which readers must perceive and grasp; sexuality is a strong symbol; so is time and space. Style gives a view of the 'human' Hamann. His whole life can be summed up in the effort to discover and interpret, and create 'language'. Every sentence can be interpreted in an 'unending'[180] number of ways. Every person gives his own interpretation. The sophists[181] hated Socrates because of his often repeated sentence 'I know nothing'.[182] What Socrates meant was that he was always searching to know more, to discover new meanings in old meanings, new things and levels in reality. Modern sophists (of Hamann's day) intellectualized *ad infinitum*, convincing people that they grasped Socratic ignorance. But Socratic ignorance cannot be grasped. Reality is always somewhat elusive. Reality is an

---

[180] Nadler, II, p. 72.

[181] The original sophists had been prophets and seers which would not have offended Hamann, but later sophists were noted for being rationalistic tricksters although this notoriety is perhaps undeserved.

[182] Nadler, II, p. 73.

Aesthetica in Nuce, but the contents of the nutshell are alive and changing sentences are always somewhat elusive. The basis of knowledge rests in grasping that we know nothing with certitude. We must believe.[183] Hamann takes the notion of Humean belief and interprets it to suit his purposes as he seeks to show that rationalistic science does not have the answer to all human questions. Propositional knowledge is partially illusory. One must believe, intuit, and imitate.[184] Both philosophers and poets, if they are true to reality, base their life on belief, intuition, and imitation, which is a combination of Socratic ignorance and aesthetic creativity.

Through belief, intuition, and imitation, one experiences that loving is greater than knowing. The height of human experience is loving God and other human beings.[185] Here Hamann has achieved his purpose of pointing out that human knowledge is not the ultimate answer to human life. The ultimate answer is love. Love of God makes man fully alive. This insight is hardly one of the presuppositions which undergirded the Enlightenment. The genius which came to Socrates and Shakespeare, giving them the power to create without aesthetical rules, was a genius rooted in their flesh and blood lives. Socrates loved his genius as a 'God'.[186] Many moderns seek to be like Socrates, but they are simply hypocrites because they love no genius as a god which they can admit as coming from outside themselves. They love their own intrinsic genius which they perceive to be their rationality, which in itself is actually weak.[187]

Three passages from *Aesthetica in Nuce* show Hamann's creativity alive. The first passage may speak for itself:

Poesie ist die Muttersprache des Menschlichen Geschlechts; wie der Gartenbau, älter als der Acker: Malerey, – als Schrift: Gesang, – als Schlüsse: Tausch, – als Handel. Ein tieferer Schlaf war die Ruhe unserer Urahnen; und ihre Bewegung, ein taumelnder Tanz. Sieben Tage im Stillschweigen des Nachsinns oder Erstaunens sagen sie; – – und thaten ihren Mund auf – zu geflügelten Sprüchen.

Poetry is the mother tongue of the human race just as the garden is older than the field, painting than writing, singing than declaiming, parables than inferences, bartering than commence. . . . their motion [that of our ancestors] was a boisterous dance. For seven days they sat in the silence of either reflection or astonishment, they then opened their mouth to speak forth winged words.

---

[183] Ibid., p. 73.　　[184] Ibid., p. 74.　　[185] Ibid., p. 74.
[186] Nadler, II, p. 75.　　[187] Ibid., p. 76.

This is a vibrant passage. Although Vico also held that language originated in poetry,[188] Hamann was not influenced in 1761-2 by this idea of Vico's since he did not begin to browse through a small section of Vico's writings until the 1770s.

Cassirer[189] states that 'the modern science of language, in its efforts to elucidate the "origin" of language, has indeed gone back frequently to Hamann's dictum that poetry is "the mother-tongue of humanity..."'[190]

The second text is intriguing:

Reden ist übersetzen — aus einer Engelssprache in eine Menschensprache, das heisst, Gedanken in Worte, — Sachen in Namen, — Bilder in Zeichen; die poetisch oder kyriologisch seyn können. Diese Art der übersetzung (verstehe Reden) kommt mehr, als irgend eine andere, mit der verkehrten Seite von Tapeten überein.

Zur Erläuterung kann nachgesehen werden Wachters *Naturae et Scripturae Concordia*.

Speech is translation — from angel-language into human language, that is, thoughts into words, — things into names; — images into signs [as living symbols]; which can be poetical or kyriological. [Here he refers to Egyptian demotic cursive writing which is the underside key to the meaning of a beautiful carpet and resembles Hamann's writings]. This type of translation (that is, speech) is more like the underside of a carpet than any other.

At this point Hamann refers to J. G. Wachter's *Naturae et Scripturae Concordia...*,

This is a very complex passage. The most intriguing section concerns the creative act of translating angel-language into human language. E. Metzke thinks Engelssprache is derived form Hamann's devotion to Luther's view that Holy Scripture is a translation from angel-language to human language.[191] There was also the influence of Judaic views concerning angels. As Scholem points out 'when even the angels come down into the world they don the garment of this world...'[192] Angel-language would have to become human language in order for humans to grasp it. Hamann links the language of angels to sight, as in his passage

---

[188] Giambattista Vico, *La Scienzia Nuova*, Rome, 1954, vol. I, p. 147.

[189] Cassirer's semi-Kantian views concerning language would not have pleased Hamann although he at least went in the direction of seeing the world as quite dynamic. His view that man is a symbolizing animal is very Hamannian. See *The Philosophy of Ernst Cassirer*, ed. by P. A. Schilpp, New York, 1949.

[190] Ernst Cassirer, *Language and Myth*, translated by Susanne K. Langer, New York, 1946, p. 34.

[191] E. Metzke, *J. G. Hamanns Stellung in der Philosophie des 18 Jahrhunderts*, Halle, 1934, p. 132.

[192] G. Scholem, *On the Kabbalah and its Symbolism*, London, 1964, p. 64.

'Speak that I may see Thee', when he says that man, by having the sharp eyes of an 'eagle',[193] can see the light of angels. The Sadducees,[194] as one Judaic strand, had denied the existence of angels,[195] but this was exceptional in later Judaic thought.

R. Joshua C. Levi said in the rabbinic tradition that 'An angelic escort goes before a man and the criers cry out before him. And what do they say 'Make way for the image of the Holy One . . . '[196] In some sects, Logos is seen as an angel of God.[197] Certain Jewish theories maintain that 'after Adam's creation, the angels are ordered to worship the image of God . . . '[198] Angels have the glorious work of communicating to man. Maimonides held that 'the angel is a prophetic image that appears only to those who are properly prepared to receive prophecy . . . '[199] Hamann is always patiently prepared to receive his prophetic angel. Maimonides was admired by Hamann because he was one of the most renowned Jewish wise men of all ages. His great work, *Guide to the Perplexed*, tries to help people who are torn between two opposing beliefs, although he does not present a 'coincidence of opposites' to help them in a fashion similar to that of Hamann. He purposely sought to be enigmatic towards the 'Public' of his age. He definitely wanted religious belief to have precedence over various intellectual systems, although in many respects he is quite Aristotelian.[200]

Egyptians and Persians, whose ancient mythology held Hamann's attention, also spoke of the translation of angelic speech into human speech.[201] Egyptian angel experience was often related to the Egyptian belief in the *Ka* which was the double or genius of a human Egyptian. This *Ka* completed man's reality of body and soul.[202] The *Ka* guarded

[193] Nadler, I, p. 71 and III, p. 144.

[194] The Sadducees were exceptionally reactionary. They simply refused to accept beliefs arising from oral tradition, one of which involved belief in the existence of angels. [195] Acts 23:8.

[196] Morton Smith, 'The Image of God: Notes on the Hellenization of Judaism with especial reference to Goodenough's work on Jewish Symbols', from *Bulletin of the John Rylands Library*, Manchester, vol. 40, No. 2, March 1958, p. 481.

[197] E. R. Goodenough, *By Light, Light: The Mystic Gospel of Hellenistic Judaism*, New Haven, Connecticut, 1935, p. 351.

[198] Morton Smith, 'The Image of God', p. 479. See also A. Marmorstein, *The Old Rabbinic Doctrine of God*, Oxford, 1937, p. 14.

[199] A. Reines, *Maimonides and Abrabanel, On Prophecy*, Cincinnati, 1970, p. 49 and 152.

[200] See A. Rohner, *Das Schöpfungsproblem bei Moses Maimonides, Albertus Magnus, und Thomas von Aquin*, Münster, 1913.

[201] Sven-Aage Jorgensen, 'Hamann, Bacon, and Tradition' in *Orbis Litterarum*, XVI, 1961, pp. 182 and 466.

[202] Adolf Erman, *Life in Ancient Egypt*, translated by H. M. Tirad, New York, 1971, p. 307.

the man, spoke to him and could speak also to his surrounding realities. This belief is quite similar to the guardian angel belief in Christianity. One could say 'as long as a man is with his *Ka* and goes with his *Ka*, so long is he also alive.'[203]

The Pythagoreans saw angels as unity multiplied in this way consisting in a kind of mathematical symbolization. Pythagoras himself had seen connection between religion and science, but many of his followers failed to retain this link, and so created the famous division between the *acusmatici* and the *mathematici*. Although they were interested in non-mathematical symbols their fascination with mathematics was a cause of Hamann's disliking them.[204] In other historical views, angels brought knowledge from God to man. They thought of their knowledge in angelic terms and then translated it into human knowledge. Hamann definitely felt some kind of force, call it angelic force if one likes, which proceeded from the transcendent and communicated with mankind. The Italian Renaissance had weakened this doctrine when Ficino became convinced that 'the soul is the greatest miracle of nature; it has replaced the Angel as the cosmic messenger winging its way up and down the ladder of the world.'[205] Ficino made the soul the centre of the universe to the disadvantage of body, which is anti-Hamannian. Since Hamann was not very interested in proving the immortality of the soul he was not too favourable to Ficino's main work, *Theologia Platonica de Immortalitate Animarum*.[206] Thus, whereas Hamann could still see angels speaking through us in an 'analogical' manner so related to our language[207] that their language could be mistaken as a kind of human language coming as if from human beings, the Italian Renaissance was beginning to say that this language did come from man himself, from his winged soul.

Hamann continues to trust the angel which speaks in him, whereas for Ficino the soul, in effect, takes the place of angels and in doing so becomes more spiritualized, a little less like flesh;[208] this is contrary to Hamann's perception that body and soul are very closely united. Ficino

---

[203] A. Erman, *Die Religion der Aegypter: Ihr Werden und Vergehen in vier Jahrtausenden*, Berlin, 1934, p. 209.

[204] See B. L. Van der Waerden, 'Die Arithmetik der Pythagoreer', in *Mathematische Annalin*, vol. 120, 1948, pp. 127–53.

[205] Michael J. B. Allen, 'The Absent Angel in Ficino's Philosophy', in *Journal of the History of Ideas*, vol. XXXVI, April–June 1975, New York, p. 233.

[206] See A. Robb Nesca, *Neoplatonism of the Italian Renaissance*, London, 1935.

[207] Nadler, III, p. 27.

[208] Allen, p. 234.

does not doubt that God can give ideas directly to man,[209] but angels lost their place in his communicating processes. He was probably influenced by the *De Rerum Principio*.

Duns Scotus insists that love of God is more important than knowledge of God, which would please Hamann. He allied the soul with the body more than some writers in the Scholastic tradition.[210] Jacob Boehme held that 'there is a real, intelligible, distinct sound and speech used by the angels . . . '[211] Oetinger, who also influenced Hamann, felt that men and angels were quite like each other in their ability to communicate.[212] Hamann, especially, would have accepted Oetinger's view that 'there is no creature without an inner spiritual essence that helps form the body. . .'[213] The eccentric Lichtenberg,[214] who wrote somewhat like Hamann, was interested in angels too, but felt that they would have a different form of metaphysical mathematical symbolical experience. These Lichtenbergian angels would probably think 2×2 was 3 but not in honour of the Trinity. E. Young held that angel language was 'the true language of the Gods . . . '[215] Since he spent most of his time writing and rewriting his poetry while a rector in Hertfordshire, it was to be expected that he should spend some time dealing with the question of angels and their relationship to various levels of language, in connection with the question of inspiration or genius which he dealt with at length in *Conjectures on Original Composition*.

Leibnitz had also thought of angel-language as being metaphysical in

---

[209] M. Ficino, *Théologie Platonicienne de l'Immortalité des Âmes*, ed. by Raymond Marcel, 3 vol., Paris 1964–70, vol. II, pp. 85, 156, 157, and 247.

[210] See Sebastian Day, *Intuitive Cognition*, New York, 1947.

[211] Jacob Boehme, *The Confessions*, translated by S. Palmer, London, second edition, 1954.

[212] Oetinger, *Biblisches und Emblematisches Wörterbuch*, Hildesheim, 1969, p. 128.   [213] Ibid., p. 92.

[214] He constantly satirized the members of the *Sturm und Drang* movement. He did have an aphoristic style of his own that intrigued Hamann. Perhaps because of his own aphoristic style he did not like the aphorisms of Hamann's friend, Lavater. He admired the philosophy of both Kant and Spinoza although he did criticize Descartes' rationalist view 'Cogito ergo sum' through a kind of linguistic analysis. In fact, Ludwig Wittgenstein imitated much of Lichtenberg on this point. He rejected the notion of soul because it was only a word unrelated to an actually existing something when he claims that 'everything is feeling'. One might think it to be quite similar to Hamann's views, but actually it arises from the influence of Spinoza. See F. H. Mautner and F. Miller, 'Remarks on G. C. Lichtenberg, Humanist-Scientist in *Isis*, vol. 43, 1952. See also A. Schneider, *Georg Christoph Lichtenberg, Précursor du romantisme*, Nancy, 1954.

[215] Edward Young, *Original Composition*, in *The Complete Works, Poetry and Prose*, London, 1854, p. 60.

a special sense; Hamann was in character with himself when he spoke negatively of 'the flattering light of the garments of an angel of reasoning.'[216] He truly believed that angels influenced the world and men in the world.[217] Unlike Jean Paul, who claimed that 'every poet gives forth his own angel . . .',[218] Hamann felt that angels exterior to man helped man to be creatively poetic. Hamann could at least agree with the general view of Leibnitz that if angels existed, in a sense they would have to have bodies.[219] He can explain 'I am always waiting for an apocalyptic angel with a key . . .'[220]

Not only does Hamann believe that man communicates with angels whose language is also a communication with God, but man can also communicate with God Himself, and this is the heart of his ability to communicate creatively also with angels and with other humans. He can say, exquisitely, 'this analogy of man to the Creator [through creative communication] gives all creatures their content and their character . . . the more capable we are of seeing and tasting, looking at things and grasping with our hands the loving kindness of God which is in creatures.'[221] Creatures can communicate the love and kindness of God. Hamann saw experience as rational, communicative, analogically alive in a series of comparisons. He knew that 'God, Nature, and Reason have an inner relationship to each other as light, eye, and all . . . or as author, book, and reader . . .'[222] Nature itself is 'an equation, an unknown size, an Hebraic word . . .'[223] When angels speak to man, they must speak analogically.

Hamann's life is a series of communications based on analogies.[224] He saw God as communicating with mankind analogically, just as Herder could see that the Hebrews knew that 'without a God, whose being is analogous to that of man, who thinks and feels as we do, no friendship or filial affection towards Him is possible . . .'[225] He enjoyed a friendship with a God who communicated with him analogically as a friend. The mysterious notion of analogy had run through Hebrew, Egyptian and, Oriental thought, and it much intrigued Hamann.[226]

---

[216] Nadler, II, p. 144. [217] Ibid., II, p. 277.
[218] Jean Paul Richter, *Vorschule der Aesthetik* in *Jean Pauls Sämtliche Werke: historisch-kritische Ausgabe*, Weima, XI, p. 57.
[219] *Die Philosophischen Schriften von G. W. Leibnitz*, II, p. 324.
[220] Roth, VII, pp. 151 and 152. [221] *Aesthetica in Nuce*.
[222] Gildemeister, VI, p. 22. [223] Nadler, III, p. 27.
[224] Ibid., II, p. 61.
[225] J. G. Herder, *The Spirit of Hebrew Poetry*, II, p. 12.
[226] H. Steinthal, *Geschichte der Sprachwissenschaft bei den Griechen und Römern mit besonderer Rucksicht auf die Logik*, Berlin, 1863, pp. 152 and 436.

Styles Of Human Living And Creating   41

Finally in *Aesthetica in Nuce*, Hamann has his unique insight ' "Speak that I may see Thee!" This wish was fulfilled in the creation, which is a speaking to the creature through the creature . . . '

Hamann's influence upon Herder from this passage is quite clear because Herder insists that the learning of language should not begin with the reading of a written word; it should begin 'through the ear'.[227] Erasmus had once said, 'loquere igitur, adolescens, ut te videam.'[228] Within the Erasmian context this could have merely meant that Erasmus, in a sense, not only had trouble seeing but felt also that the speech of a person helped others identify levels of his physicality. Harold Stahmer saw the phrase 'Speak that I may see Thee!' as critically important in the world-view of Hamann.[229] The interest Erasmus had in Scripture helped endear him in certain respects to Hamann. It is possible that Hamann also read his *Adagia*, a collection of three thousand proverbs garnered from classical authors. Erasmus disliked theological systems, just as Hamann did. He helped give rise to the Enlightenment because of his art of critical thinking.[230] Hamann wished reality at its heart to be a 'Speak that I may see Thee' between God and creatures and among creatures themselves.

In this passage and other passages of the *Aesthetica in Nuce*, Hamann is still deeply impressed with the creative process of 'seeing' as he was throughout the *Biblische Betrachtung*, but as his aesthetic creativity develops towards his *Magi und Morgenlande* he moves in the direction of linking seeing with showing. Life is a subjective/objective commingling experience.

The written language should never become so distinct from its utterance that it loses the power to represent the writer. French, in Hamann's eyes, was in grave danger of becoming such a language.[231] The body is always seeking to speak and a man should speak so as to express his body.[232] 'The true meanings of words are bodily meanings . . . What is always speaking silently is the body . . . '[233]

---

[227] See Herder's *Journal meiner Reise im Jahre 1769*, quoted in Bd. 6 of *Irrationalismus in Deutsche Literature*, Leipzig, 1935, p. 14.

[228] W. Boehlich, 'Die historisch-kritische Hamann Ausgabe' in *Euphorion*, 50, 1956, p. 350.

[229] Harold Stahmer, *Speak that I may see Thee: The Religious Significance of Language*, New York, 1968.

[230] See J. Walter Kaiser, *Praisers of Folly: Erasmus, Rabelais, Shakespeare*, Cambridge, Mass., 1963.

[231] Nadler, II, p. 134.

[232] E. Sharpe, 'Psycho-physical Problems Revealed in Language: An Examination of Metaphor' in *International Journal of Psychoanalysis* (21), 1940, p. 202.

[233] Ibid., p. 202.

Hamann's friend, Lavater, had remarked that he 'who writes as he speaks, speaks as he writes, looks as he speaks and writes—is honest.'[234] Lavater's fascination with facial expression as a reflection of the inner man is reminiscent of Hamann's dictum, 'Speak that I may see Thee'. He liked both Shaftesbury and Klopstock who also influenced Hamann. He even attempted to write in Klopstock's style of poetry in his *Joseph von Arimathia*. He was deeply interested in the notion of creative genius in his great work, *Physiognomic Fragments for Furthering Knowledge and Love of Man*.[235] Hamann wanted that type of honesty to exist between God and man and among human beings.

Hamann is in love with the act of communication. Poetry seeks to communicate Nature to man, God to man, and man to man.[236] This is a constant creative act. Hamann rejoices that 'Nature and writing are also the materials of the beautiful, creating, imitating spirits . . .'[237] Life itself is a communicative, creating experience of flesh and spirit. Once again one is reminded of Oetinger's remark that 'Each creature was first created chaotic,[238] then it was regulated and fashioned, and finally . . . into a pleasing, organic representation . . .'[239]

Just as Giordano Bruno had declared that the only rule for a poet was his manner of speaking,[240] so Hamann speaks according to his Genius,[241] and his Genius is so communicatively creative that he is not sure whether he 'has a genius or is a genius',[242]

Aesthetica in Nuce is a unique creative effort on Hamann's part. Unger is not grasping the truth when he says it is a religious pamphlet and not a work on fresh views concerning creativity,[243] for it is both. Hans-Martin Lumpp is closer to the truth on p. 162 of his book, and Balthasar perceives well that Hamann's view expressed throughout the writings is 'ambivalent'.[244] Nadler tries too hard to hellenize the *Aesthetica in Nuce*. Since the Hellenistic period is heavily scientific

---

[234] J. C. Lavater, *Aphorisms of Man*, London, 1788, p. 45.
[235] See J. Forssman, *Lavater und die religiösen Strömungen des 18 Jahrhunderts*, Riga, 1935. See also Ernst von Bracken, 'Die Selbstbeobachtung bei Lavater, Beitrag zur Geschichte der Idee der Subjektivitat im 18 Jahrhunderts' Münster, 1932, Diss. [236] Roth, II, p. 240.
[237] Nadler, II, p. 210. [238] Isa. 43.7.
[239] Oetinger, *Biblisches und Emblematisches Wörterbuch*, p. 92.
[240] Bruno ultimately was burned at the stake because of his dislike of rules.
[241] Ziesemer-Henkel, II, p. 80.
[242] Ibid., I, p. 371. See also Herman Wolf, *Versuch einer Geschichte des Geniebegriffs in der deutschen Äesthetik*, Heidelberg, 1923, and E. Zilsel, *Die Entstehung des Genie-begriffes*, Tübingen, 1926.
[243] R. Unger, *Hamanns Sprachtheorie*, pp. 233 ff.
[244] H. Balthazar, 'Hamanns Theologische Äesthetik' in *Philosophisches Jahrbuch der Görresgesellschaft*, Freiburg, Bd. 68, 1960, pp. 44-8.

and mathematical it is quite contradictory in spirit to the poetical views expressed in *Aesthetica in Nuce*. Nietzsche asked 'Is art a consequence of dissatisfaction with reality? Or an expression of gratitude for happiness enjoyed?'[245] Hamann is grateful for life; he would wish to remake reality only out of a sweet dissatisfaction with it as it is if reality as it is becomes controlled by 'enlightened' persons who make it static, unliving, uncommunicating.

The passages quoted from *Aesthetica in Nuce* have presented many aspects of Hamann's creative style. Two passages from the *Socratic Memoirs* will now be quoted in order to demonstrate a few more aspects of that style.

Hamann states: 'Wenn uns unser Gebein verholen is, weil wir im Verborgenen gemacht, weil wir gebildet werden unten in der Erde; wie viel mehr werden unsere Begriff im Verborgenen gemacht, und können als Gliedmassen unsers Verstandes betrachtet werden. Dass ich sie Gliedmaassen des Verstandes nenne, hindert nicht, jeden Begriff als eine besondere und ganze Geburt selbst anzusehen. Sokrates war also beschieden genug seine Schulweisheit mit der Kunst eines alten Weibes zu vergleichen, welches bloss der Arbeit der Mutter und ihrer zeitigen Frucht zu Hülfe kommt, und beyden Handreichung thut.' 'If our frame is hidden from us, because we were made in secret, because we are formed in the depths of the earth, how much more are our concepts made in secret, and can be regarded as members of our understanding. That I call them members of our understanding does not hinder our regarding each concept as a special and complete birth in itself. Socrates was thus unassuming (or modest) enough to compare his school-wisdom with the skill of an old midwife, who merely comes to the aid of the labouring mother and her timely offspring and gives them both assistance.'[246] Our bodies are made in the secret depths of the earth. Our concepts are made in even more secret depths of reality. Our concepts are members of our understanding. Hamann here does not mean understanding in the enlightened sense and that is why he is able to remind the reader that his view of understanding (which is sustained by the imagination) does not preclude the fact of it being somewhat secret. In fact every concept, even though it can be understood as being part of the understanding, is so special that it can be regarded as a birth in itself when it comes into creative being. A man like Socrates can help with the birth of a concept but he is not totally responsible for the concepts' existence. The full power of the birth remains a secret. One can ask the

[245] Nietzsche, *The Will to Power*, p. 843.
[246] Nadler, II, p. 66.

intriguing question: if a person creates a work of art (painting, poetry, music) does he, as a person, have the right to destroy that piece of art? Has he really only helped bring into existence something bigger than himself? Perhaps man serves only as a midwife in the birth of new concepts. The section on midwifery refers back also to the section in which Hamann tells us not only that the mother of Socrates is said by Plato to have claimed that she was a midwife, but that Socrates is said to have claimed 'I am the son of a midwife and myself have a midwife's gifts.'[247] Socrates aids the mother who is Nature, Scripture (sacred writings of the Greeks), God. Socrates also knew how to make good images like his father who was a sculptor. He was not only a good midwife helping to give birth to concepts; he was also a good maker of images which would be clusters of concepts.[248] As a sensitive, emotional man, Socrates was 'sincere'.[249] Apollo knew of the true worth which gave value to the human life of Socrates. Apollo is a god.[250] Modern intelligent people like Bayle would never grasp this reality of intelligence because they are too intelligent! 'God in fact descends to our weakness for our intellect does not grasp God.'[251]

The second passage from the *Socratic Memoirs* could speak directly to Hamann's friend, Kant.

A person must be willing to recognize that he does not know everything. He must be willing to take reality and puzzle with it, rearrange it in his experience to see what new discoveries can be made about its contents. All investigations of reality are interpretations of reality. Hamann explains that 'Ein sorgfältiger Augleger muss die Naturforscher nachahmen. Wie diese einen Körper in allerhand willkührliche Verbindungen mit andern Körpern versetzen und kunstliche Erfahrungen erfinden, seine Eigenschaften auszuholen; so macht es jener mit seinem Texte. Ich habe des Sokrates Sprüchwort mit der Delphischen Ueberschrift zusammen gehalten; jetzt will ich einige andere Versuch thun, die Energie desselben sinnlicher zu machen.

Die Worter haben ihren Werth, wie die Zahlen von der Stelle, wo sie stehen und ihre Begriffe sind in ihren Bestimmungen und Verhaltnissen, gleich den Münzen nach Ort und Zeit wandelber.' 'A precise interpreter must imitate the natural scientists. Just as they place a body in all kinds of arbitrary combinations with other bodies and devise artificial experiences to determine its properties, so he does with his text. I have

---

[247] Nadler, II, p. 66.   [248] Ibid., p. 67.   [249] Ibid., p. 68.
[250] Ibid., p. 68.   [251] Ibid., p. 69.

placed the aphorisms of Socrates beside the Delphic inscription; now I shall do other tests to make its energy more perceptible.'

And 'Words derive their value, like numbers, from the position where they stand, and their concepts are in their definitions and relations like coins changeable according to place and time.'[252]

Words do have value or worth. They derive their value from their position among other words just like numbers. Hamann was not antimathematical, for he uses mathematical analogies quite often. If mathematics is given its correct value it is an excellent science, but philosophers give it too much value in relation to its position in reality. Concepts can receive different meanings according to a particular time and place. Concepts are thus affected deeply by changes of place and changes in time.

The interpreters would do well to follow the example of the natural scientists in their interpretations. Hamann is not anti-scientific. He was anti-rationalistic and thought that many persons of the enlightenment who claimed to be scientific were, in effect, rationalistic. Concepts and sayings must be compared with other concepts and sayings to determine their force and power. Just as electricity was one of the great new discoveries of the natural sciences, so Hamann wanted people to grasp the existence of the energy, of the power which was held in language. Language was alive. Various interpretations are linked in their power and force, but the links are usually not seen unless the various concepts and sayings are placed in different positions in relation to each other. In this way Hamann sought to compare the aphorisms of Socrates with the Delphic inscription. He also made other tests and comparisons. And in fact his entire life became devoted to the task of interpretation.[253]

---

[252] Nadler, II, p. 71.

[253] It is quite possible that Hamann read some books of scientific interest previous to the writing of the *Socratic Memoirs* such as William Derham, *Physicotheologie, oder Natur-Leitung zu Gott*, translated by J. A. Fabricius, Hamburg, 1732 [Hamann would not necessarily have read the translation since he read English well], John Ray, *Drey physico-Theologische Betrachtungen von der Welt, Anfang, Veranderung und Untergang*, translated by Arnold, Leipzig, 1732, and J. J. Schmidt, *Biblischer Physics*, Leipzig, 1731.

II

HAMANN'S VIEWS CONCERNING HUMAN CREATIVITY

Hamann desired to be creatively human as the heart of his experience. What was the heart of a human being to Hamann—a soul, a spirit, a body? In discussing his style of living and style of writing creatively, insights have been given into his unsceptical views concerning human creativity. It is impossible to systematize those views of humanity or creativity, for systematization, which helps to explain his understanding of what makes up the heart of man, destroys Hamann. But one can begin. He had been influenced by Egyptian views concerning what it meant to be human.[1] A. P. Erman, in his fascinating book, *Die Literatur der Aegypter*, Leipzig, 1923, pp. 123 and 124, explains that for the ancient Egyptians the organ of speech constituted the soul in its very centre of power. Hamann gave great precedence to the power of speaking. He always thought that body and soul were intermingled. He never could define body or soul precisely because he thought they could not be precisely separated. He had special difficulty with the definition of soul, because he saw soul as linked to and possibly consisting of the elements which made up the experience of conscious mind as it is related to body. The organ of speech for him, as for the Egyptians, was very special because it consisted of a combination of body and mind or soul interacting creatively in an energetic way.[2]

An expert on the Egyptians, Wallis Budge, explains that 'A man (in Egypt) may think that he is directing the course of the boat of his life by his tongue, which he uses as a steering pole';[3] one can almost see Hamann shouting 'bravo' to this view, since it gives great power to speech in human living. Hamann did not keep his interest in the Egyptians to himself; he also transmitted it to his follower, Herder, who writes in his work on Middle Eastern poetry:

---

[1] Nadler, II, p. 211. See also Otto Mann, *Hamann: Magus des Nordens*, Hauptschriften, Leipzig, 1937, p. 112.
[2] Ibid., p. 122.
[3] See Sir E. A. T. Wallis Budge, *The Teaching of Amen-Em-Apt: Son of Kenekht*, London, 1924, p. 105.

> Whence art thou, hallowed voice
>   of ancient ages?
> And whither bound?
> And how, amid the storm of times
>   and nature's changes,
> Has breathed thy gentle breath?[4]
> 'God breathes upon his well-shaped work'.[5]

Hamann tells others analogically 'think about what the breath is which goes out of your mouth.'[6] He could write to his friend Jacobi, 'in your speech is your being . . .'[7] He had consistently disagreed with people like Winckelmann on the point that in the typical fashion of the Enlightenment they gave too much credit to the Greek mind rather than to the Egyptian and other creative influences which affected the Greek mind.[8]

The Egyptians gave great prominence to the act of speaking. So did Hamann, who was always in love with the phrase 'Speak that I may see Thee',[9] because speech helped to reveal the power of the interior man through a creative representation of this power which was usually more hidden. When man looks at other persons or at nature he must not look superficially; he must not place all of his belief in what he sees on the surface.[10] Hamann recognizes that even within his own mind there is a 'mental-translation.'[11] All levels of living are a kind of translation. Hamann could have been influenced by Martin Benson, the Bishop of Gloucester, who wrote *Essai sur les hiéroglyphes des Égyptiens*, Paris, 1744. He was also influenced by the effects of Arabic[12] in general upon European languages.[13] He was ahead of his contemporaries in studying the various aspects of speaking. Leonard Bloomfield states that most persons in the eighteenth century studying languages 'had not observed

---

[4] Part of *The Voice of Antiquity* in Herder's translation of *Hebrew Poetry*, p. 266. The Hebrews were influenced by the Egyptians concerning the power of the voice. See also Sir E. A. T. Wallis Budge, *Egyptian Magic*, London, 1911, vol. II, pp. 157-9.

[5] Roth, I. p. 15.

[6] Nadler, I, p. 76. See also Nadler, I, p. 16.   [7] Gildemeister, V. p. 516.

[8] *Aesthetica in Nuce*, Nadler, II, pp. 195-219 and *Konxompax*, Nadler, III, pp. 215-88.

[9] Nadler, III, p. 357.

[10] Ibid., II, p. 173.   [11] Ibid., p. 174.

[12] There are many Arabicisms included in the European language. Previous to 950 AD, Arabic had relatively few technical philosophical words. Hebrew and Arabic dovetail together linguistically. Although Arabic is a semitic language, it is more archaic than most semitic languages, giving it more mystery. Written Arabic has a great calligraphic elegance.

[13] Nadler, III, p. 309.

the sounds of speech, and confused them with the written symbols . . .'[14] Man must wait for another person to speak before he can truly begin to believe in what he is seeing. Man must hope that other men will respond to his appeal 'Speak that I may see Thee'.

Nadezhda Mandelstam's book concerning the creative activity of her husband Osip, *Hope Against Hope: A Memoir*, is a loving memoir similar to Hamann's *Socratic Memoirs*. It catches the experience of speech as the active expression of the heart of man in a fashion similar to the experience of Hamann as he sought to create under the direction of his Muse.[15] 'The whole process of composition' she says, 'is one of straining to catch and record something compounded of harmony and sense as it is relayed from an unknown source and gradually forms itself into words.'[16]

Hamann held that the source he listened to was his Muse, angel, Mother Earth, Christ, Nature, God. Osip Mandelstam loved his speech so much that he wrote a poem entitled 'Save my speech'.[17] Hamann also loved his speech and his words passionately. His speech flows from the Egyptians as does Mandelstam's in his poem 'The Egyptian Stamp'. Hamann exhausts himself in his search to awaken to the speech of Nature 'through journeys after the Arabians, through crusades of a philologian to the lands of the far East, and through the retranslating of their magic'.[18] He thought life itself was a form of translation; somehow he could live like the wizards of the East if he could translate their magical words and speech into his personal experience.

Hamann always enjoyed speaking with people directly because this activity revealed his inner powers. He also enjoyed writing letters as a revelation of self. He was just like Osip Mandelstam who, whenever his ' "inner voice" ceased, [after he had composed a poem] . . . was always eager to read the new poem to someone.'[19] Hamann always felt that the reader of a particular work actively participated in the work. He had written the *Socratic Memoirs* with the hope that his friends, Kant and Berens, would read it actively and be creatively changed in a direction away from subservience to the Enlightenment.

Hamann's hope against hope in relation to his two friends is similar to Mandelstam's habit of believing that 'the first reading [of a poem] rounds off, as it were, the process of working on a poem, and the first

---

[14] Leonard Bloomfield, *Language*, New York, 1933, p. 13.

[15] Nadler, II, p. 213.

[16] Nadezhda Mandelstam, *Hope Against Hope: A Memoir*, translated by Max Hayward, London, 1970, p. 82.   [17] Ibid., p. 83.

[18] Nadler, II, p. 211.   [19] *Hope Against Hope*, p. 83.

listener is felt to be a contributor to it.'[20] Hamann did not write the *Socratic Memoirs* for his own pleasure; the active power of that work would not be operative until his two friends, Kant and Berens, had contributed to its power and been transformed themselves. Their lives would become a new translation.

Hamann did not wish these persons to be transformed in an artificial sense; life was not a superficial translation for him, because he had grasped, like Mandelstam, that 'an ordinary translation is a cold and calculating act of versification ... The [average] translators sets himself in motion like an engine and then grinds out the required melody by a laborious mechanical process. He is deficient in what Khodasevich so aptly called "secret hearing".'[21] Hamann's 'secret hearing' is his 'Speak that I may see Thee'.[22]

Hamann desired his life to be a creative aesthetics. He liked *Aesthetica in Nuce* because the metaphor 'nutshell' represented for him the heart of his life. Kierkegaard saw him to be a creative person seeking to put his life-blood into a single word—the Logos, the Creator. Mandelstam's wife saw that 'A poem is like a word'.[23] A poem is an expression of life. Hamann studied the lives of different persons and had seen that they had different speech patterns. In the *Socratic Memoirs* he had seen that speech varied in the streets, shops, schools, stadiums, and fields; people talked differently on different occasions. He had noticed, like Mandelstam, 'at what point people switch from bureaucratic and ideological jargon to ordinary everyday speech.'[24] His life was a listening to the Muses and a speaking to the human beings around him with the necessity of writing to those with whom he could not speak in the flesh. His common-law wife could have written of his ' "sweet-voiced labour" '[25] as did Mandelstam's wife, Nadezhda.

Hamann was always fascinated by his tongue and mouth and lips because they all helped form his speech by which he could speak 'into the ear of God.'[26] Mandelstam in one poem says that 'his lips can never be taken away from him and they will still move when he is dead and buried.'[27] Hamann spends his life speaking; this is related to his paradoxical views concerning human death. Hamann was not a chatterbox, however. He had long periods of patient waiting in order to hear his Muse speak to him. Patience was one of his principal virtues because

---

[20] Ibid., p. 84.   [21] *Hope Against Hope*, p. 86.
[22] In checking the translation of *Hope Against Hope* with a Russian expert it appears that Max Hayward is no 'average translator'.
[23] *Hope Against Hope*, p. 86.   [24] Ibid., p. 105.
[25] *Hope Against Hope*, p. 216.   [26] Ziesemer-Henkel, V. p. 111.
[27] *Hope Against Hope*, p. 223.

it was through patient waiting that he heard what he would creatively speak.[28]

Hamann treasured creative patience. His poetical prose flowed from his flesh and blood and soul. The brain was so intimately linked with the rest of the body that in Hamann's experience thoughts in the brain could be 'felt', although one would not know in which 'cellula' a particular thought resided.[29] His written works were paradoxically composite creations as were his 'speakings' to friends. He could feel like Mandelstam that 'form and content [in written work] are absolutely indivisible [because] the process of working on his poetry, . . . was always born from a single impulse—the initial "ringing in the ears".'[30] Hamann listened to his Muse and then wrote and spoke with his whole being. His speech revealed his inner soul and he always asked of people 'Speak that I may see Thee'.

Mandelstam was so interested in speech that he could say of his poetic friend, Akhamatova, in reference to her lips, that 'looking at these lips you could hear her voice; her poetry was made of it and was inseparable from it . . . '[31] Hamann loved his tongue and its inflections because it helped to reveal his inner self. Speech was an intermingling of his body and mind. Speech was the heart of his creative active communication with God, with other human beings, and with nature. Thus Mandelstam with his 'The Egyptian Stamp' and Hamann with his love for the magic of the Eastern lands saw the organ of speech and the act of speech and writing as the heart of their lives: their soul, if you wish.

Hamann decided that there are special powers in the action of speech. In a true realist fashion he decides to study all possible areas from which man could learn to use the powers of speech more effectively. He listens to and watches animals closely because he believes that there is a sense in which animals help man to learn to speak.[32] Hamann also learns about spirituality through animals by analogy.[33] Man is the greatest animal for creative imitation.[34] Although he has great love for human beings as such, and thinks that speech is part of the heart of being human, he does not seek to restrict the power of speech in all its aspects strictly to the human character *per se*; he introduces the valid perception that in asking what it means to be human one must study animals as well as humans, because they can help teach man how to speak. Descartes had thought that animals were quite mechanistic, but by the time of Hamann

---

[28] Ziesemer-Henkel, II, 234 and Roth, VII, p. 234.
[29] Roth, III, p. 392.
[30] *Hope Against Hope*, pp. 224–5.
[31] Ibid., p. 226.
[32] Ziesemer-Henkel, III, p. 187.
[33] Nadler, III, p. 39.
[34] Ibid., p. 38.

and Herder many people thought that animals had a dynamic life.[35] It is also possible that Hamann had read P. Mocati, *Von dem körperlichen und wesentlichen Unterschiede zwischen der Struktur der Tiere und Menschen*, Göttingen, 1771, which was popular in his time.

Hamann does not, however, appear to be an evolutionist in the Darwinian or Bergsonian sense, because he does not say that non-rational or non-human speech preceded human speech in a progressive temporal series of events. He merely sees that at his point in time animals speak in their own way with their tongues, lips, and teeth, and that humans speak in their own way with their tongues, lips, and teeth. Human beings could learn more elements of the process of speaking by simply observing aniimals. Hamann becomes enthused with the idea of grasping the meaning of various animal voices.[36] He knows that human beings are also very animalistic. He knew Aristotle's definition of man as a rational animal, but he did not like the meaning of 'rational' in the period of the Enlightenment. He prefers to class man with the other animals in respect of many of his qualities, but he wishes to see man as special at least in degree, if not in kind, concerning his creative abilities, of which speech is the greatest, in so far as it reveals his inner mysteries in so special a manner.

Hamann also felt that nature spoke to him. The sounds of nature ring in his ears just as poems rang in Mandelstam's ears. Like Giambattista Vico, he would have felt that thunder is in a sense a form of sign language.[37] One must also study other languages as written and as spoken. Hamann always deplored the way in which written languages which were losing their spoken aspect. Although his analysis of the German language revealed to him that it had been deeply influenced by both English and French, he was proud that it was an exceptionally vital language.[38] He saw a definite degeneration in the French language because the sign or revelation of the writer in French was more dependent upon the eye than the ear.[39] Later in life he says that he has lost most of his interest in French,[40] because it is a dying language.

The written word is always deficient in relation to the spoken word. The great writer must seek to make the written word re-express the sign of his speech. One ought to be able to say to a poem by Klopstock, 'Klopstock, speak that I may see thee'. Klopstock had been mesmerized

---

[35] Robert Sommer, *Grundzüge einer Geschichte der deutschen Psychologie und Äesthetik*, Würzburg, 1892, pp. 103-6.   [36] Nadler, II, p. 123.
[37] Giambattista Vico, *La Scienza Nuova*, vol. 1, p. 147 (Rome 1954).
[38] Nadler, II, p. 125.   [39] Ibid., p. 134.
[40] Zchmitz-Kallenberg, pp. 2 and 3.

by Horace and Edward Young in a way similar to Hamann. He became the leader of the 'Bremen poets'. Hamann despised Frederick II because the latter disliked German. He leagued himself with Klopstock in fighting Frederick's slavish devotion to the French language. Unfortunately, Klopstock did not get on with Goethe, not because of Goethe's poetry, but because of his 'immoral' life. Hamann insists that language ought not to be analysed in the fashion of Diderot[41] so as to make it lifeless.[42] Since Diderot was editor-in-chief of the *Encyclopédie* it was to be expected that Hamann would dislike him. It is not clear if Hamann was ever aware of his famous aesthetical work, *Paradox sur le comédien*. However, Diderot's distrust of abstractions made him somewhat Hamannian in character. Actually, he disliked abstractions not because they robbed experience of its fleshly parts which was Hamann's argument against them, but because they decreased the clarity of the thinking process, since Diderot considered them to be merely reference signs to the real idea. Although his views on abstractions were not very similar to Hamann's, his more general interest in problems of communication was Hamannian. In his views on communication he did connect poetry and science, which was somewhat anti-rationalistic. His style of writing was also discursive, and could even appear confused at times. This style could have been due to his acceptance of Heraclitus's views concerning the flux of the universe which also intrigued Hamann.[43] Analysis of language that merely dissects it grammatically obscures the message of the power of the spoken word. Hamann knows that the 'concept from which one understands various aspects of speech is multi-meaningful.'[44] One can begin to analyse speech and the written word, but the full living reality of speech and the written word defy complete analysis.

Hamann could never understand why Moses Mendelssohn placed so much importance on the written word without reference to the spoken word. Both must always be intermingled and the spoken word must always be allowed to have its rightful power for those who can hear and see well.[45] Language is always rooted in a place, within a people, who are pulsing flesh and blood. One cannot totally translate one language into another, just as one cannot totally translate one people into another. In exasperation Hamann declares that if the rules evinced by

---

[41] Nadler, II, p. 125.
[42] Roth, I, p. 431. He claims that Diderot's views on aesthetics are 'idle talk'.
[43] See Arthur M. Wilson, *Diderot: The Testing Years (1713-1759)*, New York, 1957.
[44] Nadler, II, p. 125.   [45] Ibid., III, p. 309.

Mendelssohn were followed to the letter the ruler of China could rewrite German literature with great dexterity without ever speaking a word of German.[46] Sheer insanity! The heart of a language is its spokenness. Mendelssohn was too strictly reasonable.

Hamann exclaims to Herder that 'All chatter about reason is pure wind: language is its organ and criterion just as Young says . . .'[47] One of Young's first great anti-rationalist works, *Critical Forests*, reminds one of the forests in Hamann's *Socratic Memoirs*. Young consistently attacked enlightened views concerning the mind because mind was always related to body, as Hamann held.[48] Reason is based on language as its organ, as its source. The organ of language is first and foremost the mouth speaking. The hand may write but the mouth has first spoken. Before the mouth has spoken it has listened as part of the composite flesh and blood called man. Man's own heart speaks to him, animals speak to him, other persons speak to him, and material nature speaks to him.[49] Man ought to spend time patiently listening in order to speak in such a way that his spoken word will truly express the power latent in his person.

Hamann could lament with Peter Schneider in his book *Lenz*, about people who speak mere chatter because they have not first really listened. They are 'like deaf-mutes whose lip movements are a reflex accompaniment . . .'[50] To see a man merely babbling would be one of the saddest events Hamann could have experienced. Hamann insists that 'the trek from the thing to writing and from writing to the thing is always of necessity through and by means of language . . .'[51] Language for Hamann in this instance means the spoken language. Cannot someone like Mendelssohn see that the written language receives its life from the spoken language, which in turn receives its life from the 'thing' as living? One must mix the reading of words with the passions of the heart, but most men are too lazy.[52] One way or another, for better or worse, our reading and personal thoughts become 'mixed thoughts'.[53] It is simply impossible, of necessity to construct a view of reality which only sees the written language and the thing and yet hopes to arrive at a true grasp of reality. Hamann knows that Mendelssohn 'asserts with just about unbelievable and inexcusable conviction that writing is "the

---

[46] Ibid., 309.   [47] Ziesemer-Henkel, V, p. 108.
[48] See F. M. Barnard, *Between Enlightenment and Political Romanticism*, Oxford, 1964.
[49] Ibid., p. 109.
[50] Peter Schneider, *Lenz: Eine Erzählung*, Berlin, 1973, p. 74.
[51] *Golgotha and Scheblimini*, Nadler, III, pp. 309 and 310.
[52] Nadler, II, p. 335.   [53] Ibid., I, p. 299.

direct description of the thing". What a shame that mere philosophers who are born deaf can taken upon themselves this privilege . . . '[54] These philosophers cannot hear. They do not know what it means to say 'Speak that I may see Thee'. They can neither truly see nor hear. In their desperation to achieve rationalistic security they seek to say that the reality of the thing is re-expressed precisely in the written word, whereas not even the spoken word, which is so much more alive than the written word, can totally re-express the reality of the thing which is alive. Life for man always remains something of an inexpressible mystery.

Man must always seek to hear a little bit better, see better, speak better, and write better, within and among the myriad things of reality. The so-called nature of a known colour or the make-up of the particular structure of an eye help to make up a particular race.[55] Lips and tongues modify, change, and help create the manner in which people communicate with each other.[56] Life is a translation.

Two people can use the same word in the same language in the same way only to an extent, for their tongues and lips change the word in part while it is being spoken. No one can ever say that he knows precisely what a word means when it is uttered either by himself or someone else. Human life is not a certitude. Human life is a translation. Giordano Bruno had declared that the only rule for a creative poet was his manner of speaking.[57] Every poet must be true to his own manner of speaking if he hopes to begin to express the mysteries of his hidden personality. Every human being must be faithful to his manner of speaking if he hopes to express himself to other human beings. A man can never say that he is fully aware of his own speech, or of his own self, nor of the speech or the self of another. He can only begin to grasp his own self and the self of the other, his own speech and the speech of the other. Life is the beginning and never the ending of translation.

Hamann's great work, *Aesthetica in Nuce*, aims to teach mankind that senses and passions speak and seize upon images. Life is a series of sensations and passions and images which are spoken, expressed, revealed, seized but never contained and controlled. Enlightened reason too often only interferes with the human pulsations of sensing, passionately speaking, and imaging of reality which are perceived to

---

[54] *Golgotha and Scheblimini*, Ibid., III, p. 310.
[55] Nadler, II, p. 123.   [56] Ibid., p. 123.
[57] Bruno used rules very well when he was fighting the Pope about the temporal power of a pope.

be correct. But human life requires as absolutely necessary for its functioning 'Speech and writing',[58] and this speech and writing cannot be correct in the strictly enlightened fashion. Perhaps one could be very human without writing but one who was unable to speak would be a mere shadow of a fully creative human being.

Man learns to speak not only through observing animals, other humans, nature, and the promptings of his own self. He also learns to speak through the Muse, through Genius, through Mother Nature, through God, for thus man must listen to the promptings of God in his heart, for there lives within himself not only slumbering parts which have yet to be awakened and become greater and better, as Leibnitz had held in his *Discourse on Metaphysics*; there lives within himself not only 'Speech . . . the true existing spirit of this entire world of culture . . . ';[59] there also lives in man the manifestation of God Himself.[60] Man's inner self is not only influenced by slumbering human possibilities in a Leibnitzian sense. Man's inner self is not participating in a Hegelian type of absolute spirit influence. The transcendent God of the Jews and the Christians manifests Himself in the hearts of man by speaking to man. God loves us; He loves 'the breath which he has blown into us'.[61] Man speaks with his breath. His breath flows from his mouth in the spoken word to others. His breath symbolizes the life which God gave to us.

The 'breath'[62] of God gives union to body and soul.[63] Body and soul should not war against each other because they are a 'unity'[64] by the power of God's breath as He gives us our breath which flows forth from us in speech. Soul and body must always be together through the power of breath.[65] Since Hamann never strictly defines soul, it may appear at times that breath or the powers coming from the mouth are soul,[66] whereas at times breath controls and unites body and soul as aspects of existence differing from it. This tendency in Hamann arises from the fact that sometimes mind for him is like soul mixed with body, whereas at other times he wants to say that breath symbolizes the deepest power in man which controls both mind as a thinking process and body which is intermixed with mind. The question should not arise as to whether he could have been more precise in a rational sense. Perhaps he could have been, but he did not wish to be, for that would have been contrary to his view of reality.

[58] Nadler, III, p. 130.
[59] Hegel, *Phänomenologie des Geistes* in *Werke*, pp. 370 and 362-5.
[60] Nadler, III, p. 191.   [61] Ibid., II, p. 237.   [62] Nadler, I, p. 268
[63] Ibid., p. 268.   [64] Ibid., p. 268.
[65] Ibid., p. 15.   [66] Ibid., p. 15.

Hamann knows that the heart of man's life comes from God, from the breath of God which is His giving forth of life. The soul never exists nakedly as an entity in and of itself. Soul as soul is always 'a being that has His [God's] breath.'[67] Hamann is opposed to rationalistic distinctions concerning body and soul. Whatever the soul or life force in man is, it is revealed through the speaking power whose heart is the breath of God in us.

The enlightened rationalists who seek to explain speech without recourse to the breath of God interfere with God's manifestation to us through speech.[68] God speaks to us especially through His Son by day and night.[69] By this he could mean that the breath of God which becomes our breathing is the breath of His Son Jesus Christ, who is with us day and night as we breathe. He also means more completely that the Son of God, who is the Word of God, speaks to us day and night within our hearts as we breathe. God speaks and man speaks in ways that cannot be described in a rationalistically metaphysical sense with certitude. As Leibrecht says so well, 'He [Hamann] could never discourse about God as though God were a metaphysical thing.'[70]

Hamann did not agree with the experience of metaphysics itself if it implied an attempt to grasp or to understand fully a pulsing transcendent force—God. God was no 'thing' in the rationalistic sense which declared that He could be defined with certainty. Hamann could not think of the speaking God as a thing which was metaphysical, if the metaphysical was better than the physical because the physical was degenerate. Hamann was acquainted with neo-Platonism, but his love of the flesh which lived through the speaking power of the voicing breath of God was quite un-neo-Platonic. When he discoursed about God he discoursed about His loving condescension towards us in the sense that He gave us great powers to speak with His breath which becomes our breath communicatively.

God speaks to us through His Son who is the Word, the 'exegete of God'.[71] Hamann was interested in exegesis because of his language studies and because of Jesus Christ. He had learned that 'Criticism [in the aesthetic sense] helps to lead us to Christ . . . man judges and his taste (with faith) is more true than all the rules of philology and logic.'[72] The words of God were difficult to interpret, in spite of the fact that He condescended in love to speak words to us which were like human

---

[67] Ibid., p. 15.   [68] Nadler, III, p. 191.   [69] Ibid., II, p. 213.
[70] Walter Leibrecht, *God and Man in the Thought of Johann Georg Hamann*, translated by James H. Stam and Martin H. Bertram, Philadelphia, 1966, p. 84.
[71] Nadler, III, p. 315.   [72] Ziesemer-Henkel, II, p. 9.

words, precisely because the communication includes approaching a 'coincidence of opposites'. Man cannot successfully begin to interpret the spoken words of God without the help of His Son who is the Interpreter. True exegesis could not be accomplished in a purely rationalistic fashion. Human knowledge had to co-operate with the power of God in His Son in order to interpret the words of God as they are both written and spoken. Mendelssohn did a disservice to the Jewish sections of the Bible in so far as he sought to interpret rationalistically their meanings to the exclusion of allowing the powerful God Himself to help with the exegesis.[73] The human mind was not a *sui generis* entity of a Kantian kind. The mind's life, the mind's centre, was linked with the speaking breath of God. If one said that Hamann's position destroys the effort to make distinctions because it leaves reality in a confused condition, he would reply that he is interested in approaching the experience of making distinctions in the sense of seeing various open-ended levels or degrees in reality,[74] but he is not interested in distinctions if they kill life by slicing it into unreal sections of a pulsing reality. Just because he cannot make absolute distinctions Hamann refuses to abandon the search to know life experientially. He will wrestle with life as it is—a partial mystery. Only those who fear mystery force absolute distinctions upon a world which is not composed of absolute distinctions.

Those who seem to be omniscient are merely deceiving themselves. They are the ignorant 'public' of the *Socratic Memoirs*. God does speak to us, but not through definitions. God speaks to us 'through the corporeal and the sensible . . . '[75] We are corporeal and sensible creatures and God speaks to us according to our modes of apprehending His speeches. If we were minds alone, God might have spoken to us in the form of dogma, dependent upon whether the definition of our mind was 'that which grasps reality dogmatically'. Scripture which is the speech of God 'can speak to us men only in parables; all our knowledge is sensual and figurative . . . '[76] Man grasps parables because they are sensual and figurative. Man is always perceiving objects sensually and he creates images from these sensations which are still partially sensible. The rationalists praise abstract concepts because the abstraction frees man from the more grossly material or sensual aspects of reality. But this process of abstraction is a partial curse rather than a blessing if it takes man too much away from the sensible and the figurative, for

---

[73] *Golgotha and Scheblimini* in reference to Mendelssohn's *Jerusalem*.
[74] *Metakritik* in reference to Kant's *Pure Reason*.
[75] Nadler, I, p. 121.   [76] Ibid., p. 157.

man at the heart of his being is a sensible and figuratively speaking being.

In *Golgotha and Scheblimini* Hamann rejoices 'For He spoke, and it came to be ...'[77] God's speaking is the heart of creation. If the notion of soul is supposed to define the central power or force of a reality, then speaking is the central power or force of created reality because it comes from the Speech of God, the uncreated transcendent. Created human beings use their speaking to cry out to the universe their joys and their sorrows. God always hears the speech of His creatures. God is like 'a mother [who] understands the cry of a child ...'[78] Man is weak in comparison to God, but the heart of his life, his speaking, can reach out to God who is always there to hear. God could say to man 'Speak that I may see Thee'. One of Hamann's great consolations is that 'There is in the very ground of our hearts a voice which Satan himself is not allowed to hear as it is within us, but God hears it.'[79] The heart of our hearts is good; the speaking forth of our soul-power is good. Satan, who represents evil in his heart of hearts, cannot hear our good voice because like knows like; God, who is good, hears our heart of hearts, which is good.

Hamann is in love with the material of this world, with the flesh of this world, because its life force comes from God. He exclaims to Herder 'I stick to the letter, to what is visible and material ...'[80] That which is material is not evil; it ought to be clung to with resolute joy. Hamann respects his own materiality, his own body because it has so much power. His body helps him to grasp the power of life for good or sometimes for evil, which is more a power which deforms flesh than the meaning or nature of flesh itself. During his conversion experience in London, he watches the movements of his body carefully for signs of his inner life. He describes how 'I felt my heart thump, I heard a voice sigh in the depths and wail like the voice of blood ...'[81]

The heart of his life speaks out in communicative union with his body. Not only does he speak with the movements of his tongue and lips; his heart, his blood system speaks. Hamann could say 'I felt my heart swell and pour out in tears.'[82] His heart swam in tears as it was united consciously with other aspects of his body in seeing that he had been living a dissolute life, although Hamann is speaking here in typical

---

[77] *Golgotha and Scheblimini*, Nadler, III, p. 30.
[78] Ibid., I, p. 81.   [79] Ibid., p. 78.
[80] Ziesemer-Henkel, II, p. 416.
[81] Roth, I, pp. 212 and 213.   [82] Ibid., p. 212.

pietistic terms. But these passages cannot prove that he was a pietist or mystic. He always denied that he was by nature a pietist or a mystic. Perhaps he had pietistic strains in his younger days, as these passages suggest, but already in these young days he shows an admiration for the flesh which is not very pietistic. Perhaps he had mystical strains in later life, but he was not a mystic if being a mystic means being disinterested in the flesh which Hamann grew to love ever more deeply. When he calls himself a 'Spermologian' it is not because he has a Freudian fascination with sex. He truly loves the body and sees sexuality as a beautiful gift from God. As a Spermologian he loves the flesh and he also loves the Logos, the Word who became flesh. Even sexual organs are good,[83] because they express love and help generate children who are also children of God. Hamann could not generate his children with a dry definition. The source of evil comes as much from an incorrect use of mind as from the blood.[84] Both reason and God are related to sex.[85]

Hamann cannot accept the view that the soul is a good little thing, whereas the body is filthy flesh. 'The body preserves the soul'[86] is one of his great insights in the *Fragments*. People always see the body as dragging down the soul. They lament the fact that the soul is unfortunately caged in the wicked body. Only the soul could deserve to be immortal and the sooner it becomes so the better. But Hamann is certain that the body helps preserve the soul. As will become clear, he feels that the soul has no more right to immortality than the body.

Truth is also not some abstract nicety unrelated to flesh. There is a 'body of truth'.[87] Truth cannot exist in creation without body. Christ who is the truth became body. People cannot ultimately place their trust in abstract truths; people ultimately must place their trust in living embodied truth just as Thomas Aquinas, in a previous age, had seen that one only secondarily assents to conceptual truth, for man primarily assents to the person from whom conceptual truth flows through spoken or written words. The scholastics probably would not have assented to this particular view of Aquinas concerning the truth; Hamann assented with the whole of his pulsing heart. Truth flows from the mouth of man. Hamann wants to have all man's 'mouths'[88] of

---

[83] Nadler, III, p. 376.   [84] Ibid., II, p. 155.
[85] Ibid., III, pp. 31, 37, 100, 279, and 373.
[86] *Brocken*, Ibid., I, p. 309.   [87] Ziesemer-Henkel, I, p. 334.
[88] See Nadler, III, p. 279, Ziesemer-Henkel, III, p. 350, IV, pp. 51 and 143, Roth, VII, p. 142, and Gildemeister, V, p. 48.

communication inherently good. The head should always march with the heart, for in union they will both be good.[89]

If man seeks to live only with an intellect which is pure, with a 'pure reason', Hamann can only say 'our reason has flesh and blood, must have . . .'[90] He praises happily 'the fleshly intellect . . .'[91] He would have delighted in modern medicine as it explores how chemicals and energy currents affect the ideas of man. Indeed, man has a fleshly intellect. The body does not only hold the soul as a preserving force, nor does it merely help the mind which needs flesh in order to act. The body helps to hold man in bounds. Hamann states 'How horrifying man might be if the body did not hold him in bounds.'[92] It is the body that at leasts prevents some of man's evil ideas from being exerted upon others. The body often keeps man from killing at random.

The intellect can be evil if it plans the destruction of man. One soldier with his body alone could only kill one other soldier after a long bodily fight, but man creates machines through his intellect which today can not only kill many men, but which can destroy the entire world. Sometimes one gets the impression that Hamann wishes there was more flesh to man and less ability to hand for abstract ideas which can be used to destroy man.

Hamann had a great dislike for Frederick the Great because he controlled men so easily. Frederick's body, unfortunately, could not hold him in bounds; he used it to destroy people through his misguided intellect. That intellect would not allow his body to try and set up the conditions which would have helped prevent brutal death.[93] A poet uses his mind to create images which usually are in harmony with the flesh; many thinkers use their minds to destroy flesh and other minds. Hamann loves his flesh. His flesh and the flesh of other human beings is a living 'temple'.[94] The body is sacred, as are all its parts. As God the Son is the first-born of God, the Son of God, so a man's flesh is the 'first born . . .'[95] Man will never lose his body. In this life man is working to be ever more fully 'a bodily participation in the divine nature . . .'[96] Hamann will not give up his love for the flesh and the body in order to gain either an intellectual security or a spiritual safety. He will not search for a divinity unrelated to flesh—a kind of

---

[89] Schmitz-Kallenberg, p. 39. Thought is always dependent upon sense and life in order to be correct thought. See also Gildemeister V, pp. 56 and 505.
[90] Nadler, III, p. 164.　　　[91] Ibid., p. 165.　　　[92] Ibid., I, p. 309.
[93] See *Golgotha and Scheblimini*.
[94] Nadler, I, p. 288.　　　[95] Roth, VII, p. 201.
[96] Nadler, III, p. 224.

secure pure, abstraction. He is determined to be a bodily part of a divinity who communicates with and became flesh Himself. In *Krisis und Wende des Christlichen Geistes*, Kurt Leese says Hamann is very chthonic.[97] The word chthonic is difficult but yet, if it is understood in a non-pejorative sense that would be a compliment to Hamann. Hamann is chthonic in a sense reminiscent of the discussion of irrationality related to flesh in E. R. Dodds's book *The Greeks and the Irrational*. Happily, he had his Egyptian and Eastern influences which kept him from succumbing totally to the Winckelmannian Greek view of reality which dominated so much Germanic thought during his period of history. Leibrecht is opposed to Kurt Leese, whom he considers wrong in seeing Hamann as too Dionysian and chthonic.[98] Leibrecht implies that Leese does not think that Hamann is very Christian. This dilemma lies in the middle but not unimportant ground of reality. Hamann is both Christian and Dionysian, for the two notions although apparently antithetical can paradoxically live together in real life as a 'coincidence of opposites'.

Hamann is always concerned about his own body because it is precious; he would not consider this view of reality in relation to his body to be anti-Christian. Many people say he was an exceptional hypochondriac, but that depends on how one relates body to soul. Hamann may worry about his 'sick feet',[99] but that is because life for him is rooted in his body. If a person clings to his intellect and to his soul with the conviction that they are immortal then he will not be too concerned about the body. When such a person sees another human being much concerned about his body of course he can say 'what a hypochondriac'; but if that person loves his body as a great part of his life he is merely treating his life-sources sensibly.

Hamann knows that 'Naked and bare came I out of my Mother's body and naked will I return . . . '[100] Of one thing he is sure: he has a living body. He disdained Descartes' 'Cogito, ergo sum' because reality is 'Sum, ergo cogito'. Hamann knew that he was a body which feels and imagines and thinks and creates. He was a body which came from the earth, from his Mother, naked and bare. He knew that some day his living body would return to his Mother, Earth.

Man is a fool when he is always complaining about the activities of

[97] Kurt Leese, *Krisis und Wende des Christlichen Geistes*, Berlin, 1941, pp. 169–80.
[98] Walter Leibrecht, *God and Man in the Thought of Johann Georg Hamann*, translated by James H. Stam and Martin H. Bertram, Philadelphia, 1966.
[99] Nadler, I, p. 121.
[100] Nadler, I, p. 143.

the body. With indignation Hamann says 'How much man sins in his complaining about the body as a prison . . .'[101] Does the body always sin? Is not the body sinned against by the intellect, which in its unwillingness to admit the possibility of sin in itself, as a distinct thing, a Kantian organ for thinking, ascribes even its sins to the body? If sin exists, Hamann insists, body and mind sin together. If good exists, body and mind do good together. Life for man is an embodied life.

Man does not only *have* body while he *is* mind. Man *is* both body and mind. Fritz Lieb may say of Hamann that Hamann feels man's body is good only in grace,[102] but one has a sneaking suspicion that somehow Lieb wants to see mind as more capable of good, without grace, than body could ever hope to be, without grace. Hamann would insist not! There is a sense in his view of life that both body and mind can be quite sinful without grace, but he insists that mind can be just as sinful as body. With grace both body and mind are good. Within this view of creation Hamann always insists that God first created not only mind to be good, but He also created body to be good in the beginning. Hamann glories in the reality of his body and in all materiality. He can even glory in death in so far as the body changes into other good materials. 'We will become these three things, dust, earth, and ashes, and it is beautiful. I die daily . . .'[103]

Hamann wants to live dynamically, but he does not greatly fear death for the body remains in other material forms after death. This will be beautiful. One can perhaps be more certain of the immortality of matter at least in an indefinite sense by playing with the 'coincidence of opposites' in relation to the notion of immortality. As Hamann lives he will concern himself for the health of his body every day, not because he is afraid to die, but because a healthy body positively helps him to live more dynamically. When he dies he will die without dread, as the circle in Münster realized when they saw him dying. 'I die daily— it is beautiful.' With his student, Herder, he sought always to express the fact that primitive enfleshed man was poet, thinker, musician, historian, and priest within one person.[104] Many modern anthropologists, such as Malinowski and Mircea Eliade, agree that among primitive peoples music and poetry are always associated within a primitive creativity. Hamann did not think of primitives in a pejorative sense.

---

[101] Ibid., p. 299.
[102] Lieb does not seem to believe that spiritual grace can really mix with body.
[103] Ziesemer-Henkel, I, p. 309.
[104] See W. Nufer, *Herders Ideen zur Verbindung von Poesie, Musik, and Tanz*, Berlin, 1927, pp. 18 ff. and *Aesthetica in Nuce*.

Some people disdained the Egyptians because they came before the Greeks: what had they done except build tombs? Hamann insisted that for a particular man to be fully alive he must be an enfleshed poet, thinker, musician, historian, and priest.

The flight into abstraction could mask itself as progress away from the past, but did it not take more creative energy to have vast diverse talents unified within one man? Malinowski, Eliade, and Lévi-Strauss saw the great creative genius of the primitive. Lévi-Strauss, in *The Savage Mind*, claims that the primitive's mind was not savagely simplistic. Hamann and Herder could see that the writings of Descartes and the Cartesians, which spoke of a separate 'faculty' of mind or Kant's 'organ of mind', simply avoided the effort to write more complexly in such a manner that the writing would truly reflect the complexities of enfleshed man. Abstract thought was complex but in the wrong manner of complexity; paradoxically, it was too simplistically complex!

Man has 'symbolical . . . handwriting'.[105] Man's writing is always partially enfleshed if it is to be human. How can man pretend that that which is written escapes the flesh totally? Can he not see that the very shape of the letters in an abstract word is still a concession to the material and that the words are produced by an enfleshed being? Hamann insists that words are always very dependent upon images.[106] Is not even one letter a form of image?[107] The primary purpose of language is to reveal the self symbolically and actively.[108] The self is enfleshed. The body preserves the soul. The self is not an abstract spirit; it is concrete spirit.

Man seeks to express the living truth in language, and truth at its heart is not abstract; 'truth is like a seed . . . '[109] Seeds grow and have life. Truth is a living experience in this world of corporeality. Man expresses 'self [to others] according to the taste of each one . . . '[110] Matter is alive, writing is alive and changing according to how readers perceive it and according to how the author wishes to re-express his lived truth in new words, just as an enfleshed person presents himself to different people in myriad shapes to fit both their taste and his own taste. Just as flesh itself works more towards that which is good and perhaps beautiful so 'According to Augustine's thoughts on style one

---

[105] Nadler, III, p. 240.
[106] Ibid., I, p. 12.
[107] See *Metakritik, New Apology for the Letter H*, and *Socratic Memoirs*.
[108] Ziesemer-Henkel, I, p. 396.
[109] Ziesemer-Henkel, I, pp. 335-6.
[110] Ibid., p. 336.

could wait for the transformation of the biggest mistakes into something beautiful . . .'[111] As Shaftesbury had seen, that which is held to be beautiful by some is simultaneously held to be ugly by others because of different tastes. Life is a constant enfleshed translation.

Since Hamann knows that language has body, he can always say of intellectual questions 'For me it is a question neither of physics nor theology, it is a question of language which is the mother of both reason and revelation—their Alpha and Omega.'[112] Hamann knew that enlightened physics would become less and less physical as its thought patterns became more and more abstract. Einstein paradoxically fought a battle against 'classical' physics which had become quite conceptualistic in a dogmatic sense. Hamann would have agreed, just as he disdained his contemporaries, theology because it refused to give Jesus His flesh; theology preferred to play with concepts. Hamann was a lover of Christ, but he was no theologian. He loved the creatively condescending and loving God, but he was no theologian, for his God revealed Himself in nature, in enfleshed Scripture, and within Hamann's own thumping heart. Every intellectual question must realize that language is the heart of any question because language is the Mother, the womb of reason. Reason is enfleshed because it has an enfleshed Mother—language. The beginning and end of reason is enfleshed language; there is no way in which reason can completely escape all corporeality.[113] Words which are written are always in time and space which help make up materiality. The most abstract propositions are still faced with the fact that 'Words receive their value just like numbers from the position in which they stand . . . their concepts . . . are changeable according to time and place . . .'[114] Words have physical positions. They stand somewhere in space. Time and place, tradition, as a flowing experience, will always influence the enfleshed meaning of words. Even numbers have a position.

If an enlightened person wished to say that written words may have some materiality but yet claim that numbers are really abstract and actually control both time and space, Hamann would insist that numbers too have some kind of body. If they are being thought of by a human being, they are being thought of by an enfleshed being. If numbers are written down they have position. Mathematics is a special type of language because mathematics is a kind of communication. Hamann insists that 'the entire certainty of mathematics is dependent upon the

---

[111] Ibid., p. 337.   [112] Gildemeister, V, p. 124.
[113] See *Aesthetica in Nuce, Golgotha and Scheblimini*, and *Metakritik*.
[114] Nadler, II, p. 71.

nature of its language . . . '[115] There are different kinds of language but they all have some form of materiality. The 'everlasting strife on the boundaries (between various types of languages) will go on until languages proceed towards prophecies . . . '[116] Prophecies always deal with concrete/spiritual events.

Languages cannot purify themselves from corporeality and thus achieve certitude. Languages, if they are to be true to human beings, must become even more prophetic in nature. Languages must become symbolically alive, revealing events of human experience. Language must be able to change in order to express more fully the changeableness of man's world. The Latin language is good precisely because it can change according to its various parts so as to give new revelations.[117] Speech and language must always try to express more fully human experience not by escaping into abstraction, but by seeking to reveal human sensations of reality. This is a never-ending task because even hyperboles of speech cannot reveal the sheer intensity of human sensations of reality.[118] Human experience is an intensely sensual experience which can be almost overpowering for those human beings who can see and hear reality to the full. Man must seize the moment and live with intensity. He must not waste most of the moments of his life thinking about an abstract immortality. How does one begin to build up an abstract notion of immortality? One does so through 'a sly binding of word and word, speech and speech, perceptions and judgement . . . '[119] Words are dependent upon speaking which is dependent upon perceptions and judgement which take place in a concrete/spiritual human experience. Those nice abstract words about immortality are still embodied. Seize the moment and live life with intensity. Hamann continues 'must not the end-point be the measure of the middle?'[120] The middle is enfleshed spirit, not unenfleshed spirit. The middle is speech, not a kind of abstract experience which gives mere words power over mortality. The middle is the enfleshed word.

Man lives in a concrete/spiritual world. Hamann knows there is power at the heart of his life which has more power than dirt for instance, but this inferior power is still rooted in and intermingled with dirt. A given human reality is at its heart greater than the power by which it comes into being or appears visibly outside itself to others. Man seeks to reveal his heart; it is difficult for the subject to reveal, and the receiver too must be very intensely alive to receive the revelations.

[115] Ziesemer-Henkel, V, p. 359.
[116] Ibid., p. 360.
[117] Roth, II, p. 138.
[118] Roth, V, p. 258.
[119] Nadler, III, p. 10.
[120] Ibid., p. 11.

Hamann remarks to his close friend, Herder, 'The inner or more hidden sections of my few writings may most likely remain for ever the most excellent part . . .'[121] Hamann does not make this statement because he disdains the material or that which can be seen. There are paradoxical levels of seeing and Hamann seeks to reveal the most complex wonders of corporeality to those who have the complex eyes to see and the hands to grasp that bodily enveloping spirit.

As Unger mentions, when Hamann interpreted the poetry of other writers, he followed the instructions of Francke's *Praelectiones* and Rambach's *Institutions* which told the interpreter to look at the grammar, the literal or real, and the spiritual.[122] Hamann also used this method for reading the Bible which was written by the poet, God. All good poetry flows from God and is in a sense an 'obscure theology'.[123] But in following Francke and Rambach it is clear that Hamann refused to discard the grammatical and the literal to grasp spirit. Grammar, literal reality, and spirit are always intermixed. Spirit and matter in Hamann are always fused.[124] Man has spirit or soul, but it is always intermingled with the preserving body. When Hamann writes language he is seeking to put into writing his bodily spirit. His writings become bodily spiritual experiences. Thus Hegel was correct in observing of Hamann's writings that they 'do not *have* a characteristic style as much as the reality that they *are* style . . .'[125] The style *is* the creative act of the body/spirit; whenever one speaks of soul or mind in reference to Hamann one must implicitly at least link it to body.

Through sin there exists a 'leprosy of the soul . . .'[126] The soul as linked with the body can have sickness. Of course this passage is metaphorical, but although Hamann uses the word 'soul' as a concept he constantly refers it to some type of corporeality. 'The soul of the sinner'[127] participates in the sin. It is not only the body which sins. The soul has relations with Satan himself.[128] Satan himself was an angel but he became evil just as the soul of man becomes evil as well as his body. Faith brings a new life to the soul of man.[129] The soul without faith is just as dead on one level as the body without

---

[121] Ziesemer-Henkel, III, p. 40.
[122] R. Unger, *Hamanns Sprachtheorie im Zusammenhang seines Denkens*, München, 1905, p. 50.
[123] Ziesemer-Henkel, I, p. 438. See also Nadler, II, p. 365, and Nadler, I, p. 241.
[124] See R. Unger, *Hamann und die Aufklärung*, Jena, 1911.
[125] Hegel, *Hamanns Schriften*, in *Sämtliche Werke*, XI, p. 226.
[126] Nadler, I, p. 156. [127] Ibid., p. 197.
[128] Ibid., p. 197. [129] Ibid., p. 291.

faith.[130] Christians are correct when they see themselves as dead, in a sense, without faith, even though they are alive on earth, but they are incorrect if they think that faith gives a new life to the soul alone while the body remains evil and dead.

The whole man receives a new life in faith. Grace, and faith as grace, creates a new enfleshed man.[131] Hamann does not glory in his soul as soul. He can speak of it as the 'poor soul',[132] just as easily as he can speak of weakness in the health of the body. With God the soul 'will eat and will become fat,'[133] Hamann does not mean this merely in a metaphorical sense because God always tells him as a human being to eat and drink in order to enjoy good health. Without God 'the soul is like a dead wick.'[134] Man cannot egoistically place his strength in a soul of great power. The power of the soul, as well as that of the body, comes from God. The arrogant enlightened man may think that his soul gives him the light of the world *sui generis*, but the soul without God actually gives no light at all; it is a dead wick.

The soul alone is not the light of the world; God in Jesus Christ is the light of the world. If the soul as soul is said to continue to exist after the death of a particular human, Hamann supposes that this could be true if, as in sections of the Old Testament, the soul continues to exist in a person's children.[135] Hamann was deeply influenced by various strands of the Old Testament. He was not exceptionally concerned over the question of how the same soul could exist simultaneously in a parent and in one of his children'. Would not the child have to receive a new shiny soul as a *creatio ex nihilo*?'

[130] Ibid., p. 292.
[132] Ibid., p. 86.
[134] Ibid., p. 288.
[131] Nadler, I, p. 294.
[133] Ibid., p. 87.
[135] Schmitz-Kallenberg, p. 103.

III

CONTINUATION OF HAMANN'S VIEWS CONCERNING HUMAN CREATIVITY

Creativity, body, mind, soul, spirit run together for Hamann not because he is lazy in making distinctions, but because that is reality, for it is true that reality is a constant activity for human beings on several levels with all those levels working together. Hamann says 'Our spirit is to be thought of as awake only when it is conscious *of God* when it *thinks* and *perceives* Him . . .'[1] This activity of consciously thinking of and perceiving God can often be done by communicating with all levels of human consciousness, with Him directly, with oneself properly, with others, nature, and the Muses. Many people are simply too lazy to exercise their options. If man uses his soul correctly in union with body 'it can be a stage for the world, men, and even angels.'[2] Human souls can even reach out to Christ and be touched by Christ because Christ is the 'soul of faith.'[3] Christ is the enfleshed soul of faith, the Incarnate soul. The human soul can also be touched by Satan and one must always 'fear the enemy of your soul . . . '[4] Man must beware of 'the sinful air in your soul'.[5] Thus one can refer to soul as a reality in Hamann's thought but one must always connect it not with pure air of immortal power but with possible evil air and with the good body which preserves it.

Although Hamann rarely speaks of soul alone, as has been apparent in some of the previous quotations from his early writings where soul appears to be more or less unrelated to body, he does see that there is some kind of power in man. He speaks of body alone more often because of his love for the flesh which he knows also has power. He often refers to body and soul simultaneously because they exist together simultaneously. He knows that the relationship between body and soul is a 'great mystery'.[6] But he knows that body and soul are always related. In another fashion he insists that the material and

---

[1] Ziesemer-Henkel, V, p. 369. [2] Nadler, I, p. 274.
[3] Ibid., p. 274. [4] Ibid., p. 205.
[5] Ibid., p. 206.
[6] *Philologische Einfälle und Zweifel*, Nadler, III, p. 40.

intellectual worlds are always intermixed.[7] Unlike Philo[8] Hamann does not pine for the basically static security of essentialist eternity.

Body and soul must always be together. Hamann even insists that that which is good is good because it keeps body and soul together whereas that which is evil seeks to destroy the union of body and soul.[9] For this reason he saw the Berlin Circle headed in the direction of evil because they sought to abstract mind from its union with the body.[10] Asceticism was not Hamann's way, because eating and drinking helped to preserve the union of body and soul. God Himself told Hamann to eat and drink with joy. Body and soul must always be related in operations of intellect, sensation, passion, and love.[11]

Certain fashions of thought make body and soul appear to be contraries. In reality they are united: a reality larger than the powers of rational thought. Thought, in order to conquer its own narrowness, must know when to perceive a 'coincidence of opposites'. People who say that Hamann solves all difficult questions by crying 'coincidence of opposites' are reading him superficially. He was very adept at distinguishing; Hamann had the true scientific unrationalistic spirit of seeking to analyse, and yet admit mystery where mystery existed. The key to the notion of the 'coincidence of opposites' is to know when to use it, just as the key to recognizing contraries consists in knowing when to use them, while it is true that both can be perverted.

It is easier in a sense to seek security in soul, but one must paradoxically see that the body 'covers the evil and shame of [the soul] . . .'[12] Hamann always seeks to keep body and soul together and metaphorically exclaims that 'My method consists in this . . . to bring the feet and the body [proper] into symmetry with the inner man—that has been my work.'[13] He always seeks in his life to have body and soul work creatively together.[14] He glories in his corporeality because his contemporaries seek to destroy the glory of body. He often insists that man 'was not created out of the air.'[15] He tells his contemporaries

---

[7] Ibid., III, p. 255.
[8] Philo wrote quite often in an allegorical fashion concerning Scripture, but, whereas Hamann was quite interested in a dynamic flesh-and-blood type of allegory, Philo was interested in concepts of an abstract nature within given sets of categories although he is not excessively systematic in his style.
[9] Roth, VIII, p. 394.
[10] The Berlin Circle is part of the 'Public' constantly derided in *Socratic Memoirs*.
[11] Nadler, I, pp. 162 and 301, III, pp. 29, 40, 41, Ziesemer-Henkel, I, p. 55, and Nadler, V, p. 326.
[12] Nadler, I, p. 309.   [13] Ziesemer-Henkel, V, p. 44.
[14] Gildemeister, IV, p. 497.   [15] Nadler, I, p. 309.

'We are earth . . . '[16] He rejoices because 'the earth is my Mother . . . '[17] He can take comfort in the fact that the worms of the earth are my brothers'[18] Man is a 'God of the earth.'[19] The earth helps us be gods. The Son of God came from the earth. Man can rule the earth lovingly because he is earth.[20] A man will become a greater man not by escaping into a world of airy abstractions like the members of the Berlin Circle. A man will become a greater man by grasping more creatively that his power comes from 'the earth.'[21] When man says with all his heart 'yes' to the reality that he comes from earth, then he will create ever more powerfully as a living human being.[22] Just as God the Son came from earth, so 'gods mount upwards from the earth'.[23] God enabled man to become a god by making him out of earth.[24]

It is somewhat difficult to trace why Hamann was so devoted to corporeality of Spirit, but he was influenced by those who preceded him in history. We have already noticed his love for the Egyptians and other eastern peoples.[25] He loved Heraclitus who was his favourite Greek philosopher just as Homer was his favourite Greek poet. It is difficult to grasp either who Heraclitus was or what his views concerning reality were, except in a piecemeal fashion, which is probably one of the reasons why Hamann liked him so much. He was called 'the obscure' because of his style of writing which was sibylline in character. Aristotle, whom Hamann disdained, said Heraclitus was quite incapable of reasoning correctly. Heraclitus preferred poetical words to abstract words. Part of the essence of his view of reality was the unity of opposites which was also part of the essence of Hamann's view of reality, although Heraclitus' view emphasized conflict, whereas Hamann's was more peaceful. Heraclitus' Logos is a word which must be heard and listened to, which is somewhat similar to Hamann's insistence that a person must ask another person 'Speak that I may see Thee' in order really to hear and listen to him well. He never thought of existing spirit as being separate from physicality. His soul was inserted into a fiery flux. It was better for soul to be intermingled with fire than with water.[26] Heraclitus had said that the world was an 'ever-

[16] Ibid., p. 72.
[17] Ibid., II, p. 332.
[18] Ziesemer-Henkel, II, p. 157.
[19] Nadler, III, p. 199.
[20] Ibid., p. 310, and IV, p. 425.
[21] Roth, VI, p. 257.
[22] Ibid., p. 257.
[23] Nadler, II, p. 365.
[24] Ibid., p. 200.
[25] Ibid., p. 22. See also O. Mann, *Hamann: Magus des Nordens, Hauptschriften*, Leipzig, 1937, p. 112.
[26] See O. Gigon, *Untersuchungen zu Heraklit*, Leipzig, 1936.

lasting living fire'.²⁷ Fire was an energetic material, dynamically alive in a way that pleased Hamann. Hamann liked sections of Plato in which he was lively and Cratylian, but since Plato thought of soul as enveloping body,²⁸ it is safe to say Hamann was not too Platonic in his views, since in the *Fragments* he saw body as preserving the soul. He liked the Judaic respect for corporeality. Aristotle, of course, had a somewhat complex view concerning the reality of soul, in so far as he seems to say that soul is mortal in so far as it is the subsistent form of the body, but Hamann disliked Aristotle's rationalism which, in discussing the notion of soul, insisted that soul as intellect was immortal. Aristotle claimed that 'This intelligence is separate from the other [soul as subsistent form of the body] . . . . Once separated from the body this intellect is immortal, yea, eternal.'²⁹ Hamann could not stand this kind of rationalism.³⁰

He had also read sections of Arabian thought. Averroes seems to believe in the immortality of the soul theologically but not philosophically. In this he was to some extent following the philosophical views of Aristotle, although by switching around his own philosophical views concerning the soul he can at least say that the possibility of an impersonal immortality exists.³¹ Hamann disliked simplistic distinctions between theology and philosophy; he found himself in agreement with Averroes's tendency to deny immortality of the soul. There were also the early Church Fathers, some of whom he loved. Although he liked some of Augustine's views on language, he does not seem to have been impressed with his intellectualist approach to soul, but he loved Tertullian. Tertullian had said 'flesh is of God'.³² He wrote in a very singular style, loving paradox. He thought that philosophy was sometimes the enemy of religion. Although he was interested in matter because of the Incarnation, he did not accept the belief that God was limited by matter in his activity. He was quite anti-Platonic. His most significant anti-Platonic view maintained that the soul is in some sense

---

[27] See G. Griffith, *Interpreters of Reality*, London, p. 53.
[28] See John G. Callahan, *Four Views of Time in Ancient Philosophy*, Cambridge, Mass., 1948, p. 11.
[29] Aristotle, *De Anima*, translated by David Knowles in *The Evolution of Medieval Thought*, New York, 1964, p. 210.
[30] See Aristotle's *De Generatione Animalium*, 336b, in *The Basic Works of Aristotle*, R. McKeon, New York, 1941, pp. 526-7.
[31] See G. F. Hourani, *Averroes on the Harmony of Religion and Philosophy*, London, 1961.
[32] Tertullian, *Concerning the Resurrection of the Flesh*, translated by A. Souter, London, 1922, p. 12.

physical.³³ He was always interested that Jesus was 'possessed of flesh and body',³⁴ and he held that in reference to the flesh 'the entire Godhead has been taken and surrendered to it . . . what good does it do now . . . to air the name of earth, as a mean and humble element? . . .'³⁵ Hamann always gloried in the flesh of Christ and His cross. He had also read Athanasius,³⁶ who had held that God was the best sculptor because He mirrored Himself in the creation of the world.³⁷

Even within the scholastic tradition Hamann had read sections of Bonaventure, just as he had read Heraclitus in the Greek tradition. Bonaventure had seen Christ as the great art and artist of God; He was rooted in creative corporeality. Hamann saw Christ as both poet and artist. He always seemed to be able to ferret out of tradition elements which praised matter, body, life, and creativity as enfleshed spirit. After the period of the scholastics Bonaventure, Aquinas, and Ockham,³⁸ Hamann had read some Pompanazzi, and all of Luther. Pompanazzi held that men's knowledge deals only with phantasms, succession, time, discursiveness, and obscurity.³⁹ Hamann could say the same wholeheartedly. Although he had been taught in the Aristotelian tradition, Pompanazzi placed much more emphasis in his philosophy on sense experience. He developed a notion of 'double truth' which could be viewed on another level as an implicit 'coincidence of opposites'.⁴⁰ He insisted that the soul was mortal,⁴¹ in so far as one could know it. The immortality of the soul was merely a question of faith. He said that

---

[33] See J. H. Waszink, *Tertullian, De Anima*, Amsterdam, 1947.

[34] J. H. Waszink, *Tertullian, De Anima*, p. 4.

[35] Ibid., p. 15.

[36] The writings of Athanasius are usually quite spirited and combative. He did not care for philosophy. He constantly insisted upon the centrality of the Incarnation of Jesus Christ for Christianity which is quite similar to Hamann's view. See L. Bouyer, *L'Incarnation et l'Église—Corps du Christ dans la théologie de S. Athanase*, Paris, 1943. See also R. Bernard, *L'Image de Dieu d'après S. Athanase*, Paris, 1952.

[37] The *Oratio contra gentes* is not one of the most fascinating works by Athanasius, but the notion of God as sculptor is original.

[38] Ockham insisted that one must have direct rather than indirect experience of individual objects. His view of matter insisted that it be powerful and actual as a physical entity. Form was also a physical entity for him. He disliked excessive abstraction which would have pleased Hamann as it previously had pleased Hume. The creative power of God resided at the heart of his so-called theological view of reality. See Herman Shapiro, *Motion, Time and Place According to William Ockham*, New York, 1957.

[39] He was quite enthralled by the problem of obscurity.

[40] A. H. Douglas, *The Philosophy and Psychology of Pietro Pompanazzi*, ed. by C. Douglas and R. P. Hardie, Cambridge, 1910.

[41] Ibid., pp. 304 and 378.

the soul always operates only with the body.[42] Hamann could agree absolutely. Hamann loved the body of reality. Giordano Bruno had influenced him very greatly.[43] Many people say Bruno was pantheistic, as his being burnt in the square in Rome would suggest. Was Hamann pantheistic? Perhaps panentheistic?[44] If asked, Hamann might have said that, in the manner of Bruno, God could achieve a 'coincidence of opposites'. Why not? God 'semper facit nova'. Hamann loves materiality. He had read Paracelsus[45] and was fascinated by his new insights into the body. Paracelsus had influenced many ideas about body in the time of Hamann.[46]

In Hamann's time the body was being taken more seriously by some people. Although the 'public' did not care much about the body, fewer people were spending all their time wondering about grades of visible souls. The scientist Boerhaave showed a connection between a kind of energy in elements with vital processes.[47] He was the greatest physician of his time. He wrote in an exquisite Latin style. One of his interests involved aphorisms about diseases.

Hamann did not like Newton. He disliked his slavish devotion to mathematics. Newton found it difficult to communicate through speech. Hamann would have thought that part of the reason for this

---

[42] Ibid., pp. 305 and 321.

[43] See Nadler, II, pp. 98 and 105, Nadler, III, p. 107, Ziesemer-Henkel, IV, p. 27, Roth, VI, p. 183, and Gildemeister, V, pp. 49 and 619.

[44] Panentheism insists that although all things are in God, the energies of God are not exhausted in this process. In a sense, God is dependent upon the world, but not totally dependent. Friedrich Jacobi, who was influenced by Hamann, used the term. The theory attempts to deal with the problem of how God can be both temporal and eternal which is a central question in Hamann's view of reality in a fashion similar to Hegel. Panentheism appears to need the notion of a 'coincidence of opposites' to help make it work especially in the theology of Nicholas of Cusa. The most noted modern panentheist is perhaps Charles Hartshorne. See J. D. Collins, *God in Modern Philosophy*, Chicago, 1959. See also P. Weiss, *Modes of Being*, Carbondale, Illinois, 1958.

[45] Philippus Theophrastus Bombastus von Hohenheim, called Paracelsus, was an alchemist, which profession demanded some magical views of reality in the sixteenth century. Like Hamann, he was never allowed to be a professor although he had a profound impact on many students whom he met in his travels. He disliked the Scholastic traditions of theology intensely, although he was indebted to Duns Scotus. See C. G. Jung, *Paracelsica*, Zurich, 1942.

[46] See Erwin Metzke, 'Erfahrung und Natur in der Gedankenwelt Paracelsus', in *Coincidentia Oppositorum, Forschungen und Berichte de. evang. Studiengemeinschaft*, Bd. 19, Witten, 1961.

[47] Hermann Boerhaave, *The Modern Practice of Physic*, translated by R. James, London, 1766, vol. I, pp. 1–6 and 278–9. See also *A New Method of Chemistry*, translated by Peter Shaw, London, 1753, Vol. I, pp. 8–11 and p. 39; third edition, vol. II, pp. 345–7.

malady was that he thought too much. He had difficulty with friendships because of his tendency to destroy people who disagreed with him in any way. He was anti-Trinitarian, although Hamann was not aware of this fact. He gave God a small place in relation to the universe after the first great act of creation, because creation was one big machine, whereas Hamann gave God a continuous central position within ongoing creation that was not essentially mechanistic.[48]

The non-scientist, J. Boehme, influenced Hamann; he held that God was somehow partially 'Leib'.[49] Hamann never succumbed too deeply to Boehme, just as he most certainly never succumbed to Spinoza, although he read vast sections of his works. Hamann especially disliked the excessive rationalism of his metaphysics and the lack of personality evidenced in his philosophical writings. Spinoza did not like contingent uncertainty so he sought to find an object for his mind which would give him uncertainty, which is somewhat similar to Kierkegaard's mental quest. The fact that God and/or Nature is a system to Spinoza is repellent to Hamann. Hamann's beloved Holy Scripture was not very important to Spinoza because he believed that the lessons from Scripture were out of date. As for religion Spinoza in certain respects adhered to a type of rationalistic mystical cabbalism, a kind of mysticism which Hamann had always disliked.[50] Spinoza had held that 'imagination was the cause of error.'[51] Hamann loved the imagination. It could err if man thought too much, which was perhaps Spinoza's problem. Giordano Bruno had argued for identical matter in God and man in his *De Immenso et Innumerabilibus*, IV, 1 and 2 in *Opera, Latina Conscripta*, ed. by F. Fiorentino, Neapoli, 1879-84, but he favoured the corporeality of matter whereas, when Spinoza brings God and man under the rule of Nature, Nature is not applauded for its corporeality.

Spinoza seems to give some credit to body when he says that 'The mind is fitted to perceive adequately more things in proportion as its body has more in common with other bodies . . . ',[52] but the body is weak in its ability to relate to other bodies. It is the fault of the body

---

[48] See G. Buchdahl, *The Image of Newton and Locke in the Age of Reason*, London, 1961.

[49] J. Boehme, *Morgenröte*, in *Sämtliche Schriften*, Stuttgart, 1955, Bd. I. See also *The Signature of All Things and other writings*, London, 1969.

[50] Leon Roth, *Spinoza, Descartes and Maimonides*, Oxford, 1924. See also L. Strauss, *Die Religionskritik Spinoza als Grundlage seiner Bibelwissenschaft*, Berlin, 1930.

[51] Spinoza, *Ethics* II, S, XXXV in *Opera*, ed. by Carl Gebhardt, Heidelberg, 1925, vol. II, p. 117.

[52] Ibid., *Ethics*, II, XXXIX, Corollarium, in *Opera*, vol. II. pp. 119-20.

that mind cannot perceive more perfectly. Hamann begins with the humbling but realistic fact that he is body; he is from the earth. He is not strictly mind. Love the body and be grateful for the body rather than curse it for its weakness. Is not the spirit weak? How can one suppose the mind capable of perfection? Does not the body help preserve the spirit? Spinoza is very impressed with mind for he says that 'the idea of the mind and the mind itself are one and the same thing.'[53] But Hamann knows that ideas flow from body and mind acting together in this world.

Although Spinoza is not excessively Cartesian, it is clear that he could not help but be influenced by Descartes historically.[54] Just as Hamann had noted that without a Berkeley[55] there would have been no Hume, so without a Descartes there would have been no Spinoza, as he developed in the concrete world historically. Spinoza is so impressed with mind in relation to body that he says 'the human mind has no knowledge of the body and does not know that it exists except through the ideas of the modifications by which the body is affected.'[56]

Hamann experiences that he is body/mind always acting together. If the mind does not know the body, the human being who possesses this mind is not being very human; he is not fully, creatively alive as an enfleshed spirit. Spinoza's *Short Treatise on God, Man, and His Well-Being* appears more human in the Hamannian sense, but Hamann could never call himself a Spinozist on the question of the relation of body/mind/soul/spirit. Man is enfleshed spirit.

As a philosopher, Leibnitz was more congenial to Hamann than Spinoza[57] though he could also be critical of Leibnitz on occasion.[58] He had read Leibnitz while he was in Riga.[59] Hamann thought that body was essentially an organic whole with soul as its dominant monad, whereas in an existential sense body/soul was a kind of aggregate entity. Leibnitz saw body and soul as more closely intertwined than Spinoza,

---

[53] Spinoza, *Ethics*, XXI, Scholis, *Opera*, vol. II, p. 109.
[54] See Norman Kemp Smith, *New Studies in the Philosophy of Descartes*, London, 1952, pp. 129 ff.
[55] Berkeley's immaterialist philosophy helped force Hume to think about the problem of psychological belief. Although Berkeley did not favour materialism in a vein similar to Hamann because materialism led to scepticism, he became excessively idealistic which is quite un-Hamannian. See A. A. Luce, *Berkeley and Malebranche*, London, 1934. See also H. M. Bracken, 'Berkeley on the Immortality of the Soul,' in *The Modern Schoolman*, vol. 38, 1960-1.
[56] Spinoza, *Ethics*, II, XIX *Opera*, Vol. II, p. 64.
[57] Ziesemer-Henkel II, p. 37, I, pp. 198, 228, II, p. 205, and Nadler III, p. 23.
[58] Ibid., II, p. 229, and IV, p. 316.
[59] Ibid, V, p. 56.

which is one of the reasons why Hamann liked Leibnitz better. In *The Horizon of Human Doctrine*[60] Leibnitz had praised the 'art of combinations'. He saw the world as a series of changing interrelationships which was like Hamann's view of the creative activity of the world. He mused about the soul that 'We have demonstrations about the circle, but only conjectures about the soul . . . research on the secrets of thinking.'[61] Leibnitz was deeply interested in Nicholas of Cusa[62] and in Bruno who gave Hamann his central view concerning 'coincidence of opposites'.[63] In his *New System of Nature*,[64] Leibnitz says that if anything exists after the death of a human being it would have to be a combination of body and soul because the two are so intertwined in this life. Body and soul work together to change roots of words.[65] Although Hamann is not excessively concerned about the question of immortality, the methodology accompanying his living view of reality demands that if man were immortal, immortality would have to include both body and soul.

Ernst Cassirer points out that Leibnitz thought that taste, in a cultural sense, approached instinct. Leibnitz always held that body and soul acted as if they were influencing each other. Hamann insisted that they *are* influencing each other, but it is better for Leibnitz to say that they act *as if* they are influencing each other than to say that they do not influence each other either in the world of observable reality or in the world of *as if* reality. In speaking of an entelechy he says that it is 'either a soul, or something analogous to soul, and always naturally actuates some organic body, which is not one substance.'[66] Leibnitz is hesitant as to what a strict systematic definition of soul could be in relation to real things, but he knows that real things cause various

[60] *Leibnitz: Selections*, ed. by Philip P. Wiener, New York, 1951, p. 73.
[61] Ibid., p. 92.
[62] Nicholas of Cusa had an unquenchable interest in collecting ancient manuscripts. His view that 'our intellect, which is not the truth, never grasps the truth with such precision that it could not be comprehended with infinitely greater precision' [*De Docta Ignorantia*, I, 3, in *Opera*, 3 vols., Frankfurt am Main, 1962] would please Hamann because this view stops the enlightened ones in their tracks as they hope to arrive at the truth with certainty. Knowledge of the truth is true to a degree, which was Hamann's viewpoint concerning man's ability to know the truths of reality. Cusa was contemptuous of Aristotle because he would never be able to accept the notion of 'coincidentia oppositorum'. See J. Koch, *Nikolaus von Cues und seine Umwelt*, Heidelberg, 1948.
[63] See Anna Simonovits, *Dialektisches Denken in der Philosophy von G. W. Leibniz*, Berlin, 1968, p. 85, and Gerhardt edition, IV, p. 357, I, pp. 1, 4, and 10, and V, pp. 68 and 78.
[64] *Leibnitz: Selections*, p. 119.
[65] Sigrid von der Schulenburg, *Leibnitz*, Frankfurt am Main, 1973, pp. 40–3.
[66] *Leibnitz*, Gerhardt, IV, pp. 395–6.

intellectual analogies which could coalesce into some form of a definition of soul. Hamann knows of a soul/mind/spirit something. This soul-like something for Leibnitz actuates an organic body.

Hamann knows that body and soul act in an intermingling fashion. He would not either actually or epistemologically separate the two enough to say that one *de jure* actuates the other in a definitive sense of actuation. Even when Leibnitz is being metaphysical, he does not seek to escape into a 'soul world'. He readily states that there is 'a certain metaphysical union of soul and organic body'.[67] Leibnitz never thinks of soul as 'entirely separate'.[68] He does think that the soul is 'immaterial' in relation to 'an organic body',[69] but the two always interact. In *The Horizon of Human Doctrine* he states honestly that 'We have demonstrations about the circle, but only conjectures about the soul . . . research on the secrets of thinking . . .'[70] Leibnitz may conjecture that the soul is immaterial. He researches the secrets of thinking just as Hamann always sought to penetrate the mystery of reason more deeply without exhausting the mystery. Leibnitz respected soul or spirit but he never succumbed totally to its charm in such a way as to dislike body or matter. Somehow all spirits, other than God Himself, must have matter of some type, and that is by nature good.[71] For Hamann, even God became flesh in Jesus Christ. Leibnitz knew that angels, who are other than God, must definitely have bodies of some kind.[72] Hamann sought to turn angel speech coming from the tongues of angels into human speech coming from the tongues of men. Leibnitz often appears to present irreconcilable views as is stated by Russell,[73] but could this not be caused by the fact that he was very often moving in the direction of paradoxes and the 'coincidence of opposites' which Hamann loved so much?

Wolff merely popularized Leibnitz by shaving off his more difficult or paradoxical corners. Hamann was more faithful to Leibnitz *per se* than to Wolff. Hamann will not and cannot forsake body. Perhaps C. F. Oetinger helped Hamann even more completely to embrace the wonders of the body.[74] Oetinger held that God always worked to make body

---

[67] *Leibnitz*, Gerhardt, II, p. 371.   [68] Ibid., VI, p. 619.
[69] Ibid., II, p. 657.
[70] *The Horizon of Human Doctrine* in *Leibnitz: Selections*, p. 59.
[71] George Martin Duncan, *The Philosophical Works of Leibnitz*, New Haven, Connecticut, 1890, p. 169.
[72] *Leibnitz*, Gerhardt, II, p. 324.
[73] See B. Russell, *A Critical Exposition of the Philosophy of Leibnitz*, London, 1937, p. 147.
[74] P. Ernst, *Hamann und Bengel*, Königsberg, 1935, p. 38.

better.[75] He explains his indebtedness to Tertullian when he writes 'It is known from Tertullian that as he taught, "all substance is bodily, also God, and the human soul." '[76]

Zinzendorf also influenced Hamann. Zinzendorf helped create the Moravian Church, and was deeply influenced by Lutheran pietism. He was riveted in his religious experience to a kind of Christocentrism.[77] Hamann was interested in his views on Socrates.[78] He appreciated the fact that Zinzendorf felt that there was a form of sensualism at the heart of life and writing.[79] Zinzendorf had received private instruction from Oetinger who talked to him of the corporeality of God.[80] Any effort to link Hamann too closely with Oetinger and Zinzendorf, especially in an attempt to make him appear excessively bizarre, is to be discounted. Hamann evolved his views on body/flesh/mind/soul/spirit from a vast source of readings. He loved body and soul as they creatively interacted, making human beings more fully alive communicatively.

The English influence upon Hamann was great, and he was especially fascinated with Hume, although he had read many other English writers, including Locke. In his letters, Locke, in his matter-of-fact way, says that substance which thinks is spirit and substance which has solidity is body.[81] Locke disliked Scholasticism so he decided to develop a philosophy of his own. He was an exceptionally reasonable man, publishing not only *Reasonableness of Christianity* but also *A Vindication of the Reasonableness of Christianity* as well as a second *Vindication*.[82] Hamann thought Locke somewhat simplistic. Locke had begun to think that God possibly gave matter the power to think.[83] Hamann knew that matter was part of the human creative act of thinking communicatively.

Berkeley in his *Commonplace Book* gave his view that 'bodies, etc.,

---

[75] C. A. Auberlan, *Die Theosophie Friedrich Christoph Oestingers nach ihren Grundzügen*, Tübingen, 1847, pp. 446–52.

[76] Oetinger, *Biblisches Wörterbuch*, Hildesheim, 1969, p. 219.

[77] See O. Pfister, *Die Frömmigkeit des Grafen Ludwig von Zinzendorf*, Vienna, 1925.

[78] Nadler, III, p. 417.

[79] Wilhelm Bettermann, *Theologie und Sprache bei Zinzendorf*, Gotha, 1935, pp. 9–11.

[80] Erich Beyreuther, *Zinzendorf und die Christenheit*, Marburg, 1961, pp. 57–63.

[81] John Locke, *Letter I* in *Works of John Locke*, London, 4 vols., 1823, IV, p. 33.

[82] See D. G. James, *The English Augustans: The Life of Reason*, London, 1949. See also T. E. Webb, *The Intellectualism of Locke: An Essay*, Dublin, 1857.

[83] John Locke, *Essay Concerning Human Understanding*, Oxford, 1924, p. 267.

do not exist even when not perceived—they being powers in the active being . . . '[84] Hamann was interested in the activity of beings, but beings made up of really existing bodies. Hamann may not have been Berkeleian but he admired Berkeley in so far as it was true that, without Berkeley, there would have been no Hume, just as Berkeley had remarked in *Original Composition* that, without a Herodotus, there might have been no Thucydides. Berkeley felt that one must speak 'of the world as contained by the soul, and not the soul by the world . . .'[85] Hamann knew that the world and the soul interpenetrated and helped contain each other. In his *Three Dialogues Between Hylas and Philonous*, Berkeley explains beautifully how God is pure spirit. Hamann preferred the bizarre beauty of the crucified Christ. Ideas were to be admired and in fact 'the very existence of ideas constitutes the soul as perceiving.'[86] Hamann knows that the ideas a man thinks proceed from his feet and from his so-called soul.

Hume loved matter more than Berkeley loved matter and was sceptical especially of spiritual happenings. Hume held that 'a miracle is a violation of the laws of nature.'[87] Hamann believed in miracles but he appreciated Hume's respect for nature. He also doubted the subjectivist miracles of the mystics and excessive pietists. Hume had a kind of psychological belief in body. Hamann saw that Hume really had an affirmative attitude towards the body and this world. He had read Hutcheson who could claim that perception was a 'sensuous' [88] experience. There was something in Hume, Hutcheson, and Shaftesbury that appealed to Hamann's love of matter and his love of the act of creating beauty.

Hamann had lived with and taught Herder, who loved creative concrete living, perhaps by being influenced deeply by Hamann himself. In one of his works Herder says 'Is the soul then material? or have we so many immaterial souls? . . . I do not know what material and immaterial is . . .'[89] For Herder the notions of soul, material, immaterial were

---

[84] Berkeley, *Commonplace Book*, in *The Works of George Berkeley*, ed. by Fraser, vol. I, Oxford, 1871, p. 52.

[85] *The Works of George Berkeley*, Edinburgh, 1948, Section 285.

[86] Berkeley, *Principles* in *The Works of George Berkeley*, ed. by Fraser, vol. I, pp. 156-7.

[87] David Hume, *Treatise on Human Nature*, ed. by L. A. Selby-Bigge, Oxford, 1958, pp. 474-5.

[88] Frances Hutcheson, *An Inquiry into the Original of our Ideas of Beauty and Virtue*, London, 1725, p. 10, (Sec. I, par. 13).

[89] J. G. Herder, *Vom Erkennen* in *Ausgabe von Herders Werke*, Berlin, 1877, Bd. VIII, p. 93.

immaterial notions in a metaphorical sense. From Hamann he knew that he was alive, embodied, and capable of creating beauty. Herder was becoming a fully alive communicating human being in this world. When Hamann died, Herder wrote 'A great band in my life is torn . . .'[90] Herder wholeheartedly meant this in a physical/spiritual sense.

Hamann had helped teach Herder to live in this enfleshed spiritual world through his own life. Herder was certain that in a sense Hamann 'remains a phenomenon for ever'.[91] Hamann would live for ever as a phenomenon in his physical/spiritual creations. The early Herder always sought to follow Hamann's interest in the material, in images, by putting more and more images into his writings so that they would not be abstract;[92] Hamann taught his pupil to love the concrete world well. Walz claims that Herder accepted Leibnitz's concept of the monads through the advice of his teacher, Hamann. As Hamann saw it, Leibnitz's concept of monads was one of the touchstones for individual romantic creations.[93] Leibnitz had expressed this possible view of his monads implicitly in *Nouveaux essais sur l'entendement*.

If body and soul really do exist then Herder knows they exist in such a way that 'our whole body is filled with soul.'[94] Hamann has successfully implanted his views on body and soul into Herder. Hamann loved Klopstock's poetry because it was so sensuous, so rooted in bodily existence. Herder's *Of the Language of Poetry* praises Klopstock's sensual and non-rational creation of poetry.[95] Hamann chose friends who believed in the value of the body. It is no wonder that, besides Herder, one of his better friends was Lavater, who believed strongly that qualities cannot exist, unless they belong to a physical substratum.[96] Hamann believed that human beings were a matter/body/flesh/mind/soul/spirit intermingling reality constantly communicating through creative activity in order to be fully alive with self, others, the world, the Muses, and God.

It is already clear how Hamann influenced the *Sturm und Drang* writers because of his beliefs in individualistic concrete creative activity. One of Herder's works, *Ist die Schönheit des Körpers ein Bote von der*

---

[90] R. Burkner, *Herder: Sein Leben und Wirken*, Berlin, 1904, p. 216.
[91] Herder, *Ausgabe*, I, p. 226.
[92] Edgar B. Schick, *Metaphorical Organicism in Herder's Early Work*, Paris, 1971, p. 30.
[93] Gustav A. Walz, *Die Stadtsidee des Rationalismus und der Romantic und die Stadtsphilosophie Fichtes*, Berlin, 1928, p. 247.
[94] Herder, *Vom Erkennen* in *Ausgabe*, VIII, pp. 185-93.
[95] Frederick Henry Adler, 'Herder und Klopstock', Diss., Illinois, 1913, p. 5.
[96] Lavater, *Physiognomische Fragmente*, Leipzig, 1775-8, I, 132.

Schönheit der Seele,⁹⁷ puzzled over intermingling activities of body and soul. His *Über den Ursprung der Sprache*⁹⁸ gives earth its due place in reality. A near contemporary of Hamann's, Platner, adopts the minor sexual theme in Hamann's works as one of his major themes in *Neue Anthropologie* in the sense that there was high aesthetic value in sexual pleasure.⁹⁹ As Hamann claimed that through symbolic creative activity his inner heart or soul could be revealed to other persons, so Goethe wrote that 'Happiness of the soul and heroism are as communicable as electricity.'¹⁰⁰ Hamann had been intrigued by the communicative powers of electricity. Electricity was one of those new scientific discoveries which communicated a new kind of relationship.¹⁰¹ Goethe re-expressed the powers of his soul to other persons with exquisite zeal. He not only expressed happiness with great electric force, but he also expressed sorrow in *The Sorrows of Werther* with such force that many people who read it in Europe were moved to commit suicide.

Like Platner, the German aesthete Heinse decided that there was great beauty in sexual pleasure.¹⁰² Johann Christoph Friedrich Schiller, who was a medical doctor like Paracelsus, and who had also been influenced by Hamann, wrote an interesting book, *Versuch über den Zusammenhang der thierischen Natur des Menschen*.¹⁰³ This is reminiscent of Hamann's interest in listening to the voices of animals in order to understand more fully how man speaks creatively. The great theologian, Schleiermacher, was interested in Hemsterhuis who had influenced Hamann so some extent concerning the notion of God's humanity.¹⁰⁴

Hamann knows he is body and soul on earth and that the spiritual power of God, who is from heaven, is in him; since he loves the earth he concentrates on God's revelation to him on earth: God is in this world.¹⁰⁵ This experience is the heart of Hamann's faith.¹⁰⁶ He believes in a transcendent God, but the transcendent God comes into the world in a 'coincidence of opposites' so that man can concentrate upon loving God in the world. Hamann can exclaim that 'all that God has is

---

⁹⁷ Herder, *Ausgabe*, I, 43 ff.   ⁹⁸ Ibid., pp. 1 ff.
⁹⁹ Ernst Platner, *Neue Anthropologie*, Leipzig, 1790, pp. 814 ff.
¹⁰⁰ *Alles um Liebe: Goethes Briefe*, München, 1948, pp. 52 and 53.
¹⁰¹ J. A. Fabricius, *Hydrothéologie*, Hamburg, 1734. See also J. G. Hoffman, *Kurtze Fragen von den Natürlichen Dingen, oder Geschöpfen und Werken Gottes*, Halle, 1770. Hamann was looking for a 'Geisterphysik', Nadler, II, p. 192.
¹⁰² J. J. Wilhelm Heinse, *Werke*, ed. by H. Laube, Leipzig, 1838, VIII, p. 587.
¹⁰³ J. C. Schiller, *Versuch über den Zusammenhang der thierischen Natur des Menschen*, Stuttgart, 1862.
¹⁰⁴ See Wilhelm Dilthey, *Leben Schleiermachers*, Berlin, 1966, p. 25.
¹⁰⁵ Nadler, II, p. 213.   ¹⁰⁶ Ibid., p. 132.

mine'[107] This is strictly a partial exaggeration because *to be all that God is, is to become God*, whereas Hamann only becomes *godly*, but he does know that God is communicating with him paradoxically.[108] He is so overcome with God's communication[109] that he exclaims once more that 'All that is godly is also human . . .'[110] Yet he knows that our relationship with God is creaturely.[111]

Hamann has no restrictive belief that God only communicates with Lutherans or other Christians or Jews. He communicates with all men everywhere.[112] It is true that Hamann loves the Bible very much because it is a very helpful and special form of communication from God,[113] but that does not prevent God from communicating creatively in various fashions[114] according to Hamann.

Since Hamann has great respect for analogies and paradoxes he can claim that there are strong analogies between Christianity and paganism.[115] Because *Konxompax* includes an implicit study of Tibetan beliefs, this is a quite serious statement on his part. This relationship between Christianity and paganism is a real 'coincidence'.[116] Human nature is a confused knot made up of various peoples who communicate on various levels, but God is able in condescending love to communicate with all kinds of people. Thus all men are images in His communication.[117]

Hamann can indeed, as a particular individual one of many different kinds of individuals, exclaim 'I am God's image and heir . . .'[118] As God communicates with us, with our body and soul, He knows each hair of our head.[119] Man can and must use his sensual body also to search out God communicatively. 'Our eyes have the sharpness of eagles, . . . if we in your word see all . . .'[120]

The word is the Logos, God, the Son made Flesh. Man's eyes were not strong enough to grasp the sight of God without His help so He came to us.[121] He came to us as 'man.'[122] Hamann is deeply interested in Jewish history because it is all a tasting of a coming Christ who 'remains.'[123] The story of Jacob is special in the sense that Jacob's ladder refers to 'human deification and godly Incarnation.'[124] The

[107] Nadler, I, p. 253.
[108] Ibid., III, p. 271.
[109] Roth, IV, p. 23.
[110] Ibid., p. 23.
[111] *Konxompax*, Nadler, III, p. 227.
[112] Roth, VII, p. 61.
[113] Nadler, I, p. 78.
[114] Roth, VII, p. 61.
[115] *Konxompax*, Nadler, III, p. 223.
[116] Ibid., p. 224.
[117] Ibid., II, p. 198.
[118] Ibid., I, pp. 250 and 251.
[119] Ibid., III, p. 240.
[120] Ibid., I, p. 71.
[121] Ibid., p. 265.
[122] Nadler, III, p. 308.
[123] Ibid., p. 286.
[124] Ibid., p. 287.

ladder is a special symbol of the communication of God to man and man to God.

The Incarnation of God is for Hamann the most important event of all time, for through it God communicates unitively with man, with flesh, and becomes flesh. This event is the heart of the 'magical and logical circle of human deification and godly Incarnation . . .'[125] This event is so powerful and all-encompassing that it can begin to be grasped in a logical circularity as well as a magical circularity. It encompasses all imaginable means by which man could begin to grasp its significance. Hamann believes that 'the manifestation in the flesh is the middle point for all . . .'[126] Nothing is more central to man that that God became flesh because man is flesh.

The world has many mysteries, many unknown symbols, but the word Incarnate becomes the apogee of all the mysteries of the world.[127] Hamann loved nothing more than creatively interacting with the symbolic mysteries of this world because the Incarnate Word was the biggest symbolic mystery in this world. Christ has become flesh so thoroughly that Hamann wishes to impress upon himself that 'He has come so near to us that we cannot cut ourselves away from Him. He is bone of our bone and flesh of our flesh . . .'[128] Christ's becoming flesh has happened once and for all and will continue to exert its power. Even if mankind wanted to escape the Incarnation of Christ it could not because He has become bone of our bone and flesh of our flesh. Hamann likes saying that Jesus is from 'woman born'.[129] He comes from a woman's flesh.

Hamann exclaims 'The one becomes all; the word becomes flesh, the Spirit becomes the letter.'[130] The spoken and written word is flesh just as the Word and *Geist* become flesh in different ways; Hamann rejoices that Word becomes flesh and Spirit becomes letter. Language is always involved with the flesh and the material. Christ is indeed all in all.[131]

There is no strictly rational religion revealed in the mysteries of the world as Starck and Lessing held, for those mysteries reveal that Christ is their centre.[132] *Aesthetica in Nuce* irrevocably combines Hamann's views concerning symbolic communication as a creative human activity by having as the centre of its message the middle point of all reality,

---

[125] Ibid., p. 287.
[126] Ibid., I, p. 242.
[127] Ibid., VI, p. 117.
[128] Nadler, I, p. 212.
[129] Ibid., III, p. 393.
[130] Gildemeister, V, p. 246.
[131] *Konxompax*, Nadler, III, p. 226.
[132] *Konxompax*, Nadler, III, p. 222.

the active coming-to-be flesh of the Word of God.[133] The coming-to-be flesh is not only the great event of the earth, but also of heaven, for as will become clear, Hamann views heaven mostly in its relationship to earth.[134] Men ought not always to be looking up to God in heaven, but rather, men should gratefully concentrate on the fact that God speaks to man on earth through His Son day and night, creatively communicating with those men who can hear,[135] who can gratefully say to God 'Speak that I may see Thee!'

Heinrich von Stein in his *Geschichte des Platonismus* is correct in saying that Hamann had the Incarnation as the middle point of his works, but Hamann believed in the Incarnation not in a Platonic sense, for God was always and is always existentially active in His Incarnation. Fritz Lieb in his *Glaube und Offenbarung bei J. G. Hamann* agrees that the centre of Hamann's thought is the Incarnation, but he interprets this too strongly to mean that Hamann differed extensively from Schleiermacher. They did differ, but Hamann's view of the Incarnation is not a conservative Christian view. Karl Rosenkranz in *Geschichte der Kantischen Philosophie* says that Hamann opposes Kant because the universal schema of his (Hamann's) work is the Incarnation, but Hamann could not stress too much that he was dealing with schemata in a very rationalistic sense.

Thus Hamann embraces the Incarnation and exclaims to God '—you come to me? Oh! God and His son are so gracious that They come to us.'[136] He now knows that the 'whole riddle' of human existence is the coming-to-be flesh of God,[137] for now he can truly believe that God actively communicates with us in the flesh and because of this fact we can actively communicate with God creatively in the flesh.[138] Hamann rejoices in God: 'He Himself became a man so that He could make us become gods. He gives us all that He has . . . All that God has, is mine . . . '[139] Through Christ, man is moved from blindness and foolishness into a new happy life.[140] With Christ, man can live like Christ; man can be a Christian, an enfleshed God.

Hamann rejoices that 'My whole Christianity is a taste for tokens . . . '[141] As an enfleshed Christian, Hamann spends his days creatively tasting the tokens of communication with God in this world. Life is a series of creative communicative translations. Man and woman unite

[133] Ibid., II, p. 212.
[135] Ibid., II, p. 213.
[137] Ibid., III, p. 192.
[139] Ibid., I, p. 253.
[141] Roth, V, p. 278.

[134] Ibid., III, p. 308.
[136] Nadler, I, pp. 30, 195, and 202.
[138] Ibid., p. 192.
[140] Ibid., II, p. 40.

communicatively just as God and man unite communicatively in mutual creation.[142] God is now miraculously flesh so that, even when man has intercourse with his wife, he not only knows that he comes from earth as earth, he knows that he comes from God who has become flesh.[143] Nothing that is flesh is shameful simply because it is flesh. Even pudenda are not shameful.[144] Is not God flesh?[145] Indeed, man's destination is to become creatively and communicatively 'a bodily participation in the divine nature'.[146] God has become flesh. That He has become flesh helps Hamann to glory in being human, even creatively human as God is both creative and human.

Hamann is in love with life, with his matter/body/flesh/mind/soul/spirit self. Did he think of death very much? Yes, but not with particular fear; his lack of fear of death did not come from a blind clinging to notions of either immortality or resurrection. He did not greatly fear death precisely because he was deeply involved with living creatively.

Hamann can say 'I must die . . . ',[147] but he does not spend a great deal of time lamenting the fact. He has learned to accept that death is 'the common lot of nature . . . '[148] He is an existential realist. Every man must be able to say to himself 'Your end has come . . . '[149] That breath and spirit which helped make man a living, creative being 'goes out . . . '[150] In this passage, which comes from Hamann's mature period of writing, he does not say that his spirit or breath goes out to a heaven or that it is immortal; he merely says it goes out.[151] He knows that '. . . the angel of death . . . calls you by name . . . '[152] The angel of death speaks, the most powerful creative act of any being, and his speaking names the one who must die.

Man can sometimes be sad as he recognizes in the midst of his daily living that he will die.[153] 'What is more certain than the end of man . . . '[154] His *Biblical Reflections* show awareness of the fact: 'what law of nature is more complete and more certain than the law that man must die . . . '[155] Man is to a large extent a physical creature who has a

---

[142] Nadler, III, p. 199.   [143] Ibid., p. 202.
[144] Ibid., p. 279.
[145] See Ziesemer-Henkel III, p. 350, IV, pp. 51, 139, and 143, Roth VII, p. 142, and Gildemeister V, p. 48.
[146] Nadler, III, p. 224.   [147] Nadler, III, p. 49.
[148] Ibid., p. 395. See also Nadler, II, pp. 235 and 174, and Schmitz-Kahlenberg, p. 148.
[149] Ibid., III, p. 299.   [150] Ibid., p. 299.
[151] See Ziesemer-Henkel, I, p. 336. Nadler, III, pp. 185 and 217, and Roth, III, pp. 10 and VI, pp. 260–2.
[152] Nadler, III, p. 52.   [153] Ibid., p. 201.
[154] Ibid., II, p. 73.   [155] Nadler, I, p. 24.

'conception and a ceasing to be . . . '[156] As a man Hamann is 'a mortal *Individuum* . . . '[157] But he is an individual person creatively alive; that is his glory in this world. This concept differs quite drastically from Kierkegaard's existential individuality thirsting for eternity.

Hamann had seen how Job in his period of suffering grasped the insight that living man always has a 'certain premonition of the grave . . . '[158] He recognizes this fact but revels in his living existence. Ironically he can exclaim 'I feel the presentiment of a vengeance, . . . Death! King of fearfulness!'[159] His favourite student and friend, Herder, can write 'the Styx flows in this world . . . ',[160] but Herder too, in spite of his own fears and the many sufferings of his wife, sees life as Hamann saw it—a time for creative communication.

Even when the world was new and fresh, death was announced so that man could know his end: 'the fixed rule of all death, more than any other, was the strong prophetic secret for an ever new-creating earth . . . '[161] The newly created earth proclaimed both the life and death of man so that man, knowing that some day he would die, would live life intensely in creative communication. Death is not something that cheats man; death is not evil and sinful. Death is part of the reality of being human. Death is part of earthly creation. Death did not steal into the world in the middle of its existence. Death was with the world in the beginning. The theological notion that death became a human experience only on the occasion of the original sin is false.

The living, upon recognizing the inevitability of death, have usually had two choices: they could either spend most of their lives fearing death and bemoaning the fact that they must die or they could accept death and live life intensely. Hamann chose the second course. He can thus exclaim, 'We will become these three, dust, earth, and ashes, and it is beautiful. I die daily . . . '[162] Part of the key to self[163] is to accept death and then to live with joy.

A man gains in stature when he sees that he derives from earth and says 'Yes'[164] to earth including death, and then uses earth to communicate his life to and with other living earthlings. It is in this joyful sense that Hamann can say 'I know that the earth is my Mother and the worms are my brothers . . . '[165] If man communicates creatively with

---

[156] Ibid., p. 228.
[158] Ibid., I, p. 147.
[160] *Herders Briefe*, p. 217.
[162] Ziesemer-Henkel, I, p. 309.
[164] Roth, VI, p. 257.

[157] Ibid., II, p. 344.
[159] Ibid., II, p. 236.
[161] Nadler, III, p. 224.
[163] Nadler, I, p. 228.
[165] Ziesemer-Henkel, II, p. 15.

earth then he gains stature; man becomes a 'God of the earth'.[166] Man knows that what came from the earth goes back to the earth,[167] but still he creates with the earth.[168] This earth, which Hamann loves because he comes from it, is like the Judaic earth which is mortal, rather than the Hellenic earth which could be eternal. Both earth and man are here 'for a time'. God can always create new men and new earths.

When Hamann died Herder exclaimed 'A great band in my life is torn,'[169] but I am certain that if Hamann could have spoken to Herder after his death he would have told him not to waste time in sorrowful mourning over him but rather to spend his time creatively communicating life. This was one of Hamann's mottos: men should mourn the dead by living as they desire.[170] Edward Young's *Night Thoughts* has a central theme: the fact that man must die.[171] Hamann recognizes that people usually do not speak as if they are mortal, as if they will die,[172] but he knows that he will die and that he is mortal like his Mother, Earth. Man is not properly equipped to feel an understanding of death,[173] because death is the end of life and feelings are for living, so that, when man uses his feelings for living to try to understand death, especially in a very intellectual way, he is merely perverting his feelings.

If death is understood correctly it becomes a 'teacher of wisdom'.[174] The wisdom that death teaches is, 'accept me and live life intensely'. Death is paradoxically one of our greatest and best teachers[175] because it teaches us to love life ever more completely and not to waste our living moments foolishly. Thus Hamann can say, paradoxically, that 'the best beginning of education is to love death.'[176] Man's creative powers in the world may be 'as the flowers of the fields',[177] but at least they are flowers; they are, for a time, living beauty. Since Hamann lives today with joy he can exclaim 'Let us be merry and joyful, because in the morning we shall be dead . . . ' On his deathbed he said cheerfully to Amalia von Gallitzin 'all is wasted away'.[178] His great friend by reading, Edward Young, had written 'It is with thoughts, as

---

[166] Ibid., p. 276. [167] Ziesemer-Henkel, II, p. 276.
[168] Nadler, III, p. 310, and IV, p. 425.
[169] R. Burkner, *Herder: Sein Leben und Werken*, Berlin, 1904, p. 216.
[170] Mann, Otto, *Hamann: Magus des Nordens*, p. 186.
[171] See C. V. Wicker, *Edward Young and the Fear of Death*, Albuquerque, New Mexico, 1952, pp. 66–79.
[172] Nadler, II, p. 336. [173] Ibid., I, p. 171.
[174] Roth, VIII, p. 334. [175] Ziesemer-Henkel, II, p. 73.
[176] Roth, VI, p. 247. [177] Ibid., VII, p. 287.
[178] *Mittheilungen aus dem Tagebuch und Briefwechsel der Fürstin Adelheid Amalia von Gallitzin*, Stuttgart, 1868, p. 29.

it is with words; and with both, as with men, they may grow old and die . . .'[179] Hamann knew that he would die.

Nietzsche sometimes chided Schopenhauer for *willing* to live, because if one were already alive how could one will to live more? Perhaps Hamann and Schopenhauer are much more perceptive, for they saw that the living during their lives could always will to be more alive, more creative, more communicative. But whereas Schopenhauer became pessimistic, Hamann was quite optimistic, because he had gladly accepted the fact of death within the greater event of living.

Hamann somehow sensed that there was another death, worse, in a fashion, than the death which comes to all men. This was to be dead to creative living, a gift bestowed most fully by God upon those who were communicating in a lively way in this world. There were many enlightened people in the world who appeared to be alive, to be breathing, but they were creatively dead. They were dead, unenlightened wicks,[180] unreceptive to the creativity of God. Many were dying of a kind of leprosy in their life.[181] It is this kind of death or dying which Hamann laments in his *Socratic Memoirs* in reference to his two enlightened friends, Berens and Kant, and 'the public' in general.

He laments to the enlightened ones 'God is not a God of those who are dead, but a God of the living. But you are dead in your lives . . .'[182] He would like to find a way of raising these people from their living death. He laments that there is 'the death and the hell of living worldly wisdom.'[183] There is a sense in which man can be dead and in hell in this life. Hamann wishes to save those who are in a 'living hell' and a 'living death' because God is a God of those who are truly living.[184] He laments that lack of faith is the look of death on the faces of living persons.[185] God has said 'let the dead bury their dead',[186] for God is a God of the living and not of the dead.[187] It is Christ, who is God, who can ultimately call us from death to a new life.[188]

New belief can cause the death of death.[189] People can be born again in the baptism of Christ.[190] Our baptism is linked with the baptism of Christ by John which helped Jesus of Nazareth to be ever more alive[191] as a human being. With the word of God in us we cannot

---

[179] Edward Young, *Original Composition* in *The Complete Works, Poetry and Prose*, London, 1854, vol. II, p. 13.
[180] Nadler, I, p. 288.   [181] Ibid., p. 156.
[182] *New Apology for the Letter H*, in Nadler, III, p. 94.
[183] Ibid., II, p. 103.
[184] Ibid., III, p. 107.   [185] Nadler, III, p. 306.
[186] Ibid., p. 395.   [187] Ibid., p. 395.
[188] Ibid., I, p. 297.   [189] Ibid., p. 266.
[190] Ibid., p. 254.   [191] Ibid., p. 245.

experience 'living death' in this world, and that is a great gift. This new man living in God is very different from the natural man. The natural man in relation to him is like a man in a deep sleep in relation to one fully awake.[192] Thus baptism in Christ is an awakening of the natural man from a deep sleep, a raising of a man from a kind of death; it is a rebirth now.

Hamann's early writings concerning his own life show a form of belief in a resurrection after his life which is like the Lutheran or Christian notion of resurrection.[193] However, even in these writings there are signs that Hamann is mostly concerned about the manner in which man lives his life now in the world; how does one allow oneself to be converted by God at various moments in order to live a more creatively vital life now?

Hamann experiences that Christ raises man from sin now into a new relationship with God.[194] In a special way, the rebirth of man now is the work of the Holy Spirit.[195] Gildemeister points out that, since there is no notion of absolute creation in Hamann, the notion of the resurrection of individual humans into a form of living which will go on for ever is somewhat foreign to Hamann's thought.[196]

He is concerned about being alive now, being risen from a living death now. He does not waste much time wondering what a risen life after man's natural death would be like; he rejoices more in the fact that Christ can come to awaken persons from their night of living death in this world.[197] Christ can help redeem us from our sins now, so that we can live a more creative life now.

During Hamann's life, the notion of resurrection was under discussion by Reimarus and his opponents, but it did not become a burning issue for Hamann. Reimarus' views were heavily influenced by the fact that he was an exegetically-oriented deist. A section of his great work *Apologie oder Schutzschrift für die vernunftigen Verehrer Gottes* insisted that the Resurrection of Jesus Christ was a mere story made up by the apostles. He had a deep influence on Lessing.[198] He would not have made this the central statement of his religion: 'without the bodily

---

[192] Roth, I, p. 417.
[193] Nadler, I, pp. 61, 248, and 262.
[194] Ibid., II, p. 168 and III, pp. 149, 304, and 308, and Ziesemer-Henkel, II, p. 157.
[195] Ziesemer-Henkel, I, p. 385, Nadler, IV, p. 282, and III, p. 227.
[196] Gildemeister, VI, p. 514.
[197] Nadler, III, p. 303.
[198] See A. C. Lundsteen, *Hermann Samuel Reimaries und die Anfänge der Leben-Jesu-Forschung*, Copenhagen, 1939.

resurrection the Christian message is simply discredited.'[199] In so far as Hamann is Christian in his religious beliefs, it helps him to live more fully in the present. In a confusing and somewhat paradoxical way, Lessing and Kierkegaard work within the Reimarus framework so far as concerns the Resurrection, but Hamann rejoices that he rises now from the living death of the enlightened ones and grasps life creatively now.

Locke's great quandary as to whether man experiences resurrection immediately after the moment of death was of slight interest to Hamann,[200] although he is not uninterested in the moment as moment, for Hamann is creatively alive in the present. Lazarus may have been asleep,[201] but it is the awakening from sleep *in this life* which is the gift of Jesus Christ. Goethe implies a kind of resurrection now in Faust.[202] Let men rejoice that they are reborn again now in Christ.[203] The Holy Spirit also reinvigorates man, giving him a new life now.[204] Man is indeed raised from sin into a new living relationship with God.[205]

Indeed, Hamann believes in a heaven that represents the living power of God.[206] Christ, as Son of God, participates in the power of God which is where heaven is. One can say in a sense that heaven is here in this world in so far as the power of God creatively enters into this world. In his earlier writings, heaven seems more to be a 'place out there'. In a special fashion, the power of God in Christ is made manifest so that Christ is a powerful King in heaven and on earth.[207] Hamann refers to heaven in various ways. People there and on earth should bend their knees honouring the power of Jesus Christ,[208] because Christ reigns in heaven and on earth.[209] Christ brings the best part of heaven into this world when His Father, who is God, sends Christ into this world as enfleshed creative power.[210]

The Incarnation of Christ becomes the great event of both heaven and earth.[211] In Hamann's later writings, this beloved earth of his

---

[199] 'The Works of Clark H. Pinnock' in *Jesus of Nazareth: Saviour and Lord*, ed. by Carl F. H. Henry, Grand Rapids, 1966, p. 148.
[200] John Locke, *Works of John Locke*, London, 1823, vol. II, p. 293.
[201] Nadler, II, p. 353.
[202] Goethe, *Faust: Vor dem Tor*, V, pp. 168-79.
[203] Nadler, I, pp. 132, 150, and 242.
[204] Nadler, III, p. 227, and IV, p. 282.
[205] Ibid., II, pp. 11 and 68., III, pp. 149, 304, and 308, and Ziesemer-Henkel, II, p. 157.
[206] Ibid., I, p. 246.
[207] Ibid., p. 226.
[208] Ibid., p. 271.
[209] Ibid., p. 272.
[210] Ibid., p. 263.
[211] Ibid., III, p. 308.

becomes ever more important as God's power becomes more fully visible in it through Christ, Scripture, and Nature, in conjunction with the creating Spirits, the Muses, and Genius. The great mystery of the power of heaven is in this world, in Christ, as its central event.[212] God, in giving us Christ, is overcome with the experience of giving: 'He gives us all that He has—. . . All that God has, is in me—. . .'[213] Earth receives the power of God and becomes important, just like heaven.[214] In a sense, God left the old heaven and brought his power into the world.[215] Hamann can truly exclaim '—you come to me? Oh! God and His son are so gracious that they come to us.'[216]

Heaven has come to earth so that man need not worry about finding a way to get to his old conception of heaven as the place where God is. The power of heaven had spoken of Jesus 'This is my beloved Son in whom I am well-pleased . . . '[217] God is somehow still transcendently powerful, but God has also come into this world. There has been a 'coincidence of opposites'. Philosophy may either seek to explain this event rationally, or explain it away, but total attempts at explanation exasperate Hamann because total explanation is impossible. How does he know it is real as an event if it cannot be totally explained as an event? It can begin to be explained—the rest is experienced. Hamann is not against beginning explanation of an event, but he knows that, when one claims to have explained an event totally, the event has been perverted. The event is more important than total explanation because any form of explanation flows from the event in the first place.

It is here in this world that 'Our nature will be made new . . . '[218] This world will become a 'showplace . . . '[219] Our new birthday takes place in the enfleshment of Christ.[220] Hamann can state 'Unbelief in the most actual and temporally historical type of that word is the only sin really against the spirit of true religion.'[221] Hamann in his later life is in love with his life in this world as he creatively communicates with other humans, nature, and God who is with us.

In *Golgotha and Scheblimini*, Hamann is angry with Mendelssohn because he seems to say that man lives in this world and that God is in His heaven. But Hamann knows that God creatively communicates with us here in this world.[222] Heaven and earth are not completely

---

[212] Nadler, I, p. 261.
[213] Ibid., p. 253.
[214] Ibid., p. 254.
[215] Ibid., p. 254.
[216] Ibid., p. 195.
[217] Ibid., p. 196.
[218] Nadler, I, p. 271.
[219] Ibid., p. 271.
[220] Ibid., p. 151.
[221] *Golgotha and Scheblimini*, Nadler, III, p. 309.
[222] Nadler, III, p. 226.

separated because God and man are not completely separated. A secular world, which Hamann felt Mendelssohn was proposing, would become a world of misrelationships in the order of communication,[223] because men are expected to be creatively related to each other in relation to the communication man has with God Himself. Although some people have attempted to show that Hamann was anti-Jewish because of his criticisms of Moses Mendelssohn, the paradox consists in the fact that he was criticizing Mendelssohn precisely because he was secularizing the Jewish religious experience which Hamann admired. Without God's communication, we certainly cannot have deep conceptions of God.[224] It is through God's deep communicating with us that we get to know better 'the secrets ... of the depths of our hearts ...'[225] God 'leaves heaven, He makes himself solitary and empty, and comes into our hearts ...'[226] Christ also comes into our hearts and creatively gives us 'the key to God's heart ...'[227]

There is always a 'human deification and a godly Incarnation ...'[228] Indeed, all of heaven, all of God's creative living is ours.[229] 'Heaven is in us.'[230] When Hamann says that 'Our philosphy must begin in heaven ...'[231] he is speaking of the fact that the power of God is the heart of reality, so that if philosophy wants to know the heart of reality it must begin with the creative communicative power of God. There is a 'heavenly wisdom' which helps man to know creatively and love himself.[232] Man now can know that 'We live, grow, and are in God ...'[233] As a creative writer Hamann can put ideas together that come both from heaven and earth.[234] Old notions of heaven and earth may pass away but the creative word of God remains.[235]

Heaven will always be related to this world. Persons should not waste too much of their time questing for an immortality in a heaven unrelated to this world. Hamann can reflect 'How many strong spirits [human], like Herostratus have sought with a kind of total courage to find a kind of immortality but because of their fear of death have pleaded and wept for a better type.'[236] But Hamann does not fear death; why spend so much of human life screaming and pleading for a strong form of immortality? Hamann knows that he dies daily and it is

---

[223] Ibid., pp. 224, 225, and 313.   [224] Ibid., I, p. 248.
[225] Ibid., p. 236.   [226] Ibid., p. 64.
[227] Ibid., p. 257.   [228] Nadler, III, p. 287.   [229] Ibid., I, p. 242.
[230] *Neue Hamanniana, Briefe und andere Dokumente*, München, 1905, p. 117.
[231] Nadler, VII, p. 48.
[232] Ibid., I, p. 131.   [233] Ibid., p. 255.   [234] Ibid., II, p. 349
[235] Gildemeister, V, p. 26.   [236] Nadler, I, p. 9.

beautiful.[237] The angel of death[238] will call: 'Your end is come'[239] and Hamann will say 'So be it' without screaming. Immortality! Immortality! Please! He calmly knows that what came from earth goes back to earth.[240] He had developed an interest in Socinianism precisely because it dealt with a lack of immortality of the soul. Soul and body are from earth and go back to Mother Earth. Hamann is like Luther in concentrating on faith now, salvation now, creative living now. Like Luther, Hamann held that if there is a life after natural death it will be a very new life in which 'Deus semper facit nova'. But Hamann is primarily interested in the reality that he and God always make new things out of old things now.

Spinoza may proclaim that 'the human mind cannot be absolutely destroyed with the body; something of it remains . . . '[241] Hamann was not excessively concerned over this supposed immortality of a part of mind. When Locke supposed that matter could think,[242] he frightened his friend Stillingfleet, who thought that this could weaken the proofs of the immortality of the soul.[243] Stillingfleet was perceptive. Locke replied that it could not be proved that matter did not think.[244] Hamann would have frightened Stillingfleet to death, which would have allowed him to certify his belief concerning the immortality of the soul.

Hamann liked Pompanazzi who could state clearly that the soul is mortal, in language almost as blunt as much of Locke's. Hamann can refer ironically to the 'immortal worms . . . '[245] of Augustine and Anselm. Man is simply fooled by thinking that his soul is immortal.[246] Immortality appears to be impossible in Hamann's writings,[247] although a passage will occasionally refer to a form of immortality.[248] Hamann lived his life with intensity. He received a form of this worldly immortality when Herder said of him 'He remains a phenomenon for ever.'[249] When Hamann died, he would have wished people to live their own lives intensely in memory of him, as he had written about his mother when she died, 'He mourns the Dead, who live as they desire.'[250]

---

[237] Ziesemer-Henkel, I, p. 309.
[238] Nadler, III, p. 52.
[239] Nadler, III, p. 299.
[240] Ziesemer-Henkel, II, p. 276.
[241] Spinoza, *Ethics*, prop. XXIII.
[242] John Locke, *Essay concerning Human Understanding*, p. 267.
[243] Stillingfleet would have perhaps preferred Berkeley on this point.
[244] Locke's views concerning the meaning of proof were a little unclear.
[245] *Konxompax*, Nadler, III, p. 223.
[246] Ibid., II, p. 365.
[247] Ibid., III, p. 217, Nadler, IV, p. 387, and Roth, VI, p. 261.
[248] Ibid., I, p. 72.
[249] Herder, *Ausgabe*, V, p. 226.
[250] Mann, Otto, *Hamann: Magus des Nordens*, p. 186.

IV

HAMANN'S FASCINATION WITH TIME IN THIS WORLD

The reader of Hamann must be ready to face his paradoxes. The many facets of time as an element of human creativity is one of his paradoxes: his immersion in time, a time which is changing not only itself, but also Hamann. In time, he found that the cryptic passages in his writings not only confused his readers but also himself, as he laments to his close friend Jacobi 'If it so happens that I cease to be clear to myself as soon as I have cooled off, how little should I be surprised that I am not sufficiently clear to others.'[1] The words 'as soon as' show that he recognized that time played a part in this form of confusion. At the precise moment when he was writing he knew creatively what he was doing, but with the passage of time, with the cooling of emotions, the ability to grasp all the intended meanings in a particular passage was lost, even to himself, because he too, as an individual was permeated by time, which changes in itself and changes persons.

He once wrote to F. Bucholtz 'The reviews of many of these abortions have been distasteful to me. No one can imagine how much. Most of them were grounded on accidental occurrences which I no longer remember from my present standpoint.'[2] Life for human beings is composed to a large extent of accidental occurrences which cannot be planned rationally and do not follow set rules. Man therefore jumps into experience knowing that if he is faithful to the accidental character of experience he will not always be rational enough to remember all his experiences. A man's present standpoint is always the most powerful influence upon his experience, so that present standpoints can change or obliterate past standpoints in regard to accidental happenings. Many think of Kant's *Critique of Pure Reason* in contradiction to Hamann as having been meticulously written over a long period of time, but, actually, it was written within four to five months, almost in flight. It is not obvious whether it was clear to Kant even while he was in the process of writing it. Hegel prided himself on the fact that his *Phenomenology* was written in the same way as Kant's *Critique* in

---

[1] Ziesemer-Henkel, VI, p. 276. [2] Ibid., p. 388.

contradistinction to the dry writing methods of the most serious philosophers, but Walter Kaufmann pushes the point when he writes 'The *Phenomenology*, like the *Critique*, was written about as fast as it would take anyone to copy the text; that is, without time enough for the author to reread the text.'[3] As Hamann grew older he did try to review all that he had written since the 'early days', and he remarked to Scheffner 'It has really been a Herculean task to run through what I wrote from 1759 to 1783 ... Often I no longer understand it myself.'[4]

In these passages Hamann is first of all honest about the difficulties he faced in interpreting his own writings, but he has also found a partial justification of these difficulties, because in his effort to be concretely faithful to the events which happen in time, in one particular area affecting the human emotions, he narrows in a special way the ability to step outside time. Gadamer claims that the meaning of a sentence is always related to a question being asked by the writer himself at a given point in time which is then seen in a different light by any reader of the writer's work.[5] He does not create a work that, because of its abstraction from a particular point in time, can be retained in its clarity through the years. Hamann must be faithful to the emotional experiences grounded in time which must be expressed in words embracing materiality and emotion in union with a spiritual creativity. Abstraction for the sake of structural clarity is always to be avoided. Words are at all times modifying the expression of an experience through the accidental creativity in time of a particular genius.[6] Language is always changing in time; the genius is always creating new words in order to express new experiences.

However, people still usually look for an orderly meaning in writings. Hamann sees order in his writings as being dependent upon time because he knows the true power of words and creativity, for words are creatures of which it can be said 'like numbers, words derive their value from the place which they occupy, and their concepts are mutable in their definitions and relations according to time and place just like coins.'[7] Josef Simon describes the relativity of language with precision.[8] People cannot demand of words that they fit the best order conceived by other persons in their own minds, because words

---

[3] Walter Kaufmann, *The Times Literary Supplement*, 2 Jan. 1976, p. 13.
[4] Ziesemer-Henkel, V, p. 359.
[5] F. Blanke, *Die Hamman Forschung*, Gütersloh, 1956, p. 15.
[6] Nadler, II, p. 261.   [7] Nadler, II, p. 71.
[8] Josef Simon, *J. G. Hamann: Schriften zur Sprache*, Frankfurt am Main, 1967, pp. 68–74.

have an inherent order of their own which is dependent upon their arrangement within sentences; this order is also dependent upon the times at which they are used and the places in which they are used.

Man must humbly seek to unlock the messages that words convey according to the good intentions of the words themselves and the genius who has arranged them. Even the genius who writes words only within special sequences of his own life cannot be expected to retain totally what he had previously thought and written, although at the time when his thoughts and creative desires are written he writes them in an intricate pattern of values which are mutable in their meaning precisely because their value comes from time and place. Thus, when Hamann was quite old in 1786, he did not need and could not expect to remember exactly what he meant in one of his writings of 1759, for the meaning of language, the meaning of relational symbols, is fleeting in the orders of time and place, and this demands a constant renewal in the present of what one was seeking to symbolize in language forms during a previous period of one's life in a particular place. Language is inevitably circumscribed and intermingled with various realities of time and place.

Although Hamann is confident of his own writing ability with its carefully designed guiding logic,[9] he is constantly bothered by the fact that words, not of necessity, but on occasion, can be misintepreted, not by the writer at the time of the writing, but by the reader. He sees that 'every sentence, even if it comes from the same mouth and heart, is subject to a vast number of secondary notions which are given to it by those to whom it is addressed . . . '[10] When one speaks and writes from the heart can one be certain that one's knowledge flowing from the self will be understood by others in the same fashion as the self understands it at the time? Hamann is here realizing the difficulty of communication in time which Wittgenstein realized in the *Philosophical Investigations*, a difficulty which at times caused him to compress his thought into what some readers saw as apparently unconnected paradoxical reflections, just as Hamann sought to compress all his thought into the fewest of words, into a nutshell, a microscopic forest of symbols which meant something to him but which possibly did not mean very much to other people, to other minds at other times.

It is not surprising that Hamann and Wittgenstein are so closely allied in their experience that people not only find difficulty in communicating with other people but also that the speaker himself may

---

[9] Ziesemer-Henkel, I, p. 373.   [10] Nadler, II, p. 72.

have trouble in understanding his own words, because of the variables of space and time. There is a limit to the level of confusion. For example, the play *L'Hypothèse* by Robert Pinget, the disciple who shared Samuel Beckett's absurd view of reality, presents a confusion in a creative mind in which many voices are consistently destroying each other so that very little real aesthetic creativity can be communicated. It is one of those happy progressions in time that makes one realize that Wittgenstein's *Philosophical Investigations* is heavily dependent upon Kierkegaard's *Stages on Life's Way*, which defends a good deal in its methodology upon the writings of Hamann.

Hamann sees that the true writer must be a kind of genius: a poetic genius in his heart of hearts. The poetic genius must explore hidden meanings of language in order to create new linguistic forms from them, because he knows that 'the spirit of observation and the spirit of prophecy contain human genius. Everything present belongs to the sphere of the former. Everything absent, both past and future, belongs to the sphere of the latter . . . the poetic genius expresses his power inasmuch as he transforms the visions of the ancient past and future by means of fictions and represents them in the present.'[11] Hamann's spirit of observation and spirit of prophecy, his poetic genius, must be used to allow him creative materials for his message. He aims to put God-language in human form, to address the question, who is ultimately God. God is found in the God-language of the past, the visions of fictions given to other men at other times, and God can be envisioned in the present as man forms new images which are related to but are not totally like the images used by the geniuses of the past. God is met in God-language verging upon and becoming human language. Hamann senses that images, notions, rules of expressing human experience can change and become outmoded in time. New geniuses will transform the expressed experiences of older geniuses from ages past with different fictions.

He asks 'What replaces for a Homer ignorance of art's rules which an Aristotle worked out after him, and what replaces for a Shakespeare the ignorance or transgression of those critical laws? Genius is the universal answer.'[12] Homer appeared to have no rules of art which he expressed to others as having been the keys to his power of writing; he may have mentioned them, however, to his admirers, but if he had done so they were neither written down nor retained in the oral tradition. Hamann mentions that Aristotle worked out a series of rules of art.

---

[11] Nadler, III, p. 383.   [12] Nadler, II, p. 75.

Hamann did not care for Aristotle and perhaps thought his rules of art were too rationalistic, too much lacking in a sense of history. He supposes that Shakespeare may not have known Aristotle's rules of art even though it is objectively doubtful whether he was in fact not aware of them. If he had been aware of them he quite deftly transgressed them. The creative act of genius in time has more power than time-honoured rules of creating.

The genius is the lover of words when he wishes to create with words; a particular type of genius is the philologian who has a special taste for words. 'What can we say about the taste of the philologian? His name symbolizes a lover of the living, energetic, two-edged, penetrating, marrow-piercing, and critical Word.'[13] The word is always alive, changing, and on the move. Thinking and its expression in words are always changing. 'Every manner of thinking that enjoys brief fashion, every imperceptible change of emotion colours the expression of our concepts. The style of the Christian . . . must in the same fashion receive a new tongue and a holy style to distinguish it.'[14] Since emotion always colours the expression of our concepts one must see that concepts arise from emotions which are partially concrete, the throbbing feelings of men of flesh and blood.

Hamann finds the roots of all language as expressed in words closely interwoven within deeper human experiences. 'The oldest language, clearly conceptual in nature, was music caused by the perceptible rhythm of the beat of the pulse and breathing in the nose . . . it is the physical prototype of all measurement of time and its mathematical proportion. The oldest writing was painting and drawing which was concerned with economy of space . . . the concepts of time and space through the great and continuous influence of the best two senses (sight and hearing) have made themselves quite "necessary" and universal throughout the process of understanding . . . thus time and space appear to be no *ideae innatae* but instead matrices of all intuitional knowledge (its mother) . . .'[15] This quotation is a profound explanation of the origin of language. In it are found also the seeds of Hamann's dislike for Kant's view of the power of time and space, for the words which Kant uses to put forward his explanations concerning time and space, which are supposed to be exterior to time and space, are rooted also in spatial and temporal experience. How can one find words to really get behind the temporal, physical experiences which give rise

---

[13] Nadler, II, p. 263. [14] Ibid., pp. 170–1. [15] Ibid., III, p. 286.

to the notions of time and space? It is impossible. Time will always be a descriptive notion of an ultimately indefinable experience, and so will space. In reference to time alone a person cannot actually improve upon Augustine's comment in the *Confessions* that he 'knew' what time was just as long as no one asked him to define it. There is physical time, psychological time, mathematical time, cosmological time, aesthetic time, etc.[16] One can begin to describe time but one cannot ultimately define it. Astronomical speculations deal quite often with departures from and aberrations of constant ratios for cycles of events and happenings. No universal definition of time can be put forward in words because words are engulfed in temporal experience. Time has different descriptive meanings as cycles of events are grasped; variegated uses of the word 'time' cannot be reduced to a simple formula. If one could define time totally one could replace the word 'time' with its definition, but this has never happened correctly and never will happen correctly. For this reason 'time' is a word which demands metaphor because it is rooted in enfleshed experiences. The experience of time is rooted in music which is rooted in physicality. All measurement has a physical prototype. The written word is also concerned with economy of space. The process of understanding, expressed either through sound or words, is rooted in and pervaded by the physical flow of temporality. Time and space are the mother of all intuitional knowledge, which is the beginning of more clearly defined conceptual knowledge.

Let us now look more closely at Hamann's attack on Kant concerning time, since it is directly related to his experience of genius, a word which Kant also agonized over. Only a concrete/spiritual metaphor can express either the experience of time or the experience of genius, for both experiences are concrete/spiritual experiences. The quotation on p. 98, which is part of Hamann's central attack against Kant's notions of time and space, was from the *Metacritique of the Purism of Reason*.[17] Hamann wrote this in the early 1780s but he did not allow it to be published until after his death, because of his friendship with Kant, in spite of the fact that he disliked *The Critique of Pure Reason*. He attacks Kant's notions concerning time and space, as has already been shown, and he also presents the problem of the use of words in Kant's writings, for words are always partially rooted in concrete experience which means that even the genius who creates new words—much less a person like Kant, who merely rearranges words —cannot use words to work out questions concerning pure reason,

---

[16] See Richard Gale, *The Languages of Time*, New York, 1968.
[17] Nadler, III, p. 286.

for if he knew words correctly he would know that the notion of pure reason in actuality is an impossibility. Hamann not only criticized Kant after his *Critique* had been written, he also corresponded with him during the 1780s, hinting at these problems on several occasions. Kant simply chose to ignore Hamann on this point.

In Hamann's view in the *Metacritique*, Kant's *Critique*, however admirable, was merely one possible critique of many possible critiques. He even says Kant's *Critique* may not be so bad, but his major objection lies in the question why Kant will not let other people also write critiques, critiques which might be just as good as his and actually in the end help man to discover more clearly the many mysterious avenues open to human experience. This would exhibit a more honest searching for truth. In the defence of his *Critique* in a later work, *On a Discovery because of which any new Critique of Pure Reason has been made useless by an earlier one*, Kant explains that his is the only possible critique. This shows how much he feared Hamann's contention, among others, that there could be other critiques. Hamann derides the criticality of 'pure reason'[18] and, in contradiction to Kant, says that Holy Scripture is the basis of critical method[19] because it expresses the variety of human experience more clearly than just one critique. Hamann had begun to criticize Kant's *Critique* in depth three weeks before it was published because Kant had given him a manuscript copy.[20] He always held that there will be 'new translations and new dogmas, and new homilies'.[21] There is never any final definitive critique; there will always be a need for new critiques. Critiques involve creativity and 'there is no absolute creation'[22] which demands that there be no absolute critique. No man can create the final, definitive critique of any human experience. 'To a history of creation belongs a restless manifestation.'[23] Danzel points out that Hamann is more complex 'than an oracle which is very difficult to understand'.[24] Various oracles will be the heart of various critiques.

Kant, however, wrote only one critique for his *'Pure Reason'*. In the *Critique of Pure Reason* he decided to see if one could 'have more success in the tasks of metaphysics, if we suppose that objects must

---

[18] Schmitz-Kallenberg, p. 95.
[19] Ziesemer-Henkel, I, p. 293. See also Nadler, II, p. 253, Roth, V, p. 71, and VI, p. 58. Scripture is closer to the roots than words which are the basis for criticism.
[20] Nadler, III, p. 275.   [21] Ibid., p. 150.
[22] Gildemeister, VI, p. 515.   [23] Roth, III, p. 381.
[24] Theodor Wilhelm Danzel, *Zur Literatur und Philosophie der Goethezeit*, ed. by Hans Meyer, Stuttgart, 1962, p. 49.

conform to our knowledge.'[25] Somehow the mind had great power in arranging concepts; the key to knowledge was not to be found so much in the objects as in the power of the mind itself. Kant does finally arrive at a notion of a thing in itself, outside the knower in a sense, but the earlier quotation from Hamann still points to the fact that we learn from experience that we cannot know any one thing with absolute certainty because its roots, the ground of its being, escape the power of knowing. He insists 'that the entire ability to think rests upon language.'[26] We have seen that language is involved with and is part of the physical human experiences of space and time. No words can be so removed from time and space as to be able to define them. Hamann objected to Kant's 'thing in itself' in 1787. Between 1784 and 1787 Hamann and his friend Jacobi wrote letters concerning Kant's *Critique* including the problem of the 'thing in itself' and other problems of mutual interest. Hamann helped to form Jacobi's disagreements with Kant which were more acerbic than his own disagreement with him. Jacobi writes in 1787 'this objection [to the thing itself] has stopped me quite a bit in my study of Kantian philosophy so that for several years I continually had to begin the *Critique of Pure Reason* from its first sections again, because I was consistently irritated by being unable to find my way into the system without this presupposition.'[27] Jacobi also complained that 'without the thing in itself one cannot enter into the critical system [in reference to Kant's *Critique*]: with it, one cannot *stay* inside it.'[28] In a sense, Jacobi is correct in a kind of phenomenalist way, but he never carried his thought processes far enough in his attempts to invalidate Kant. It was during these years, while Jacobi was puzzling over the *Critique* and corresponding with Hamann, that Hamann definitely came to think that Kant's insistence upon a thing in itself leads to a form of rational knowledge which, although partially abstract, is still symbolic of something other than itself, a form of concrete knowing which is partially intuitive, partially representative, which is not conducive to a strict Kantian view of knowing. Language,

---

[25] *Critique of Pure Reason*, second edition, translated by Norman Kemp Smith, London, 1973, B xvi, p. 22. He tended to fear an object which could not be thoroughly known. Kant was disturbed by the confusion existing in his time concerning the direction of metaphysics.
[26] *Metacritik*, Nadler, III, p. 284. He accepted the fact that one would never know the object thoroughly.
[27] F. H. Jacobi, *Werke*, Leipzig, 1818-25, 6 Bde., II, p. 304.
[28] F. H. Jacobi, *Werke*, II, p. 305. See also J. de Nees Herman, *The Development of Kantian Thought: The History of a Doctrine*, translated by A. R. C. Duncan, London, 1962, p. 167.

as Hamann said, gives rise to all knowing, and language is rooted in the earth temporally for 'it takes no deduction to prove the genealogical priority which language and its heraldic forms has over the seven holy activities of logical propositions and inferences.'[29] Hamann writes to Jacobi that 'For me the question does not revolve upon "what is reason?" so much as "what is language?" . . . ',[30] because 'A general word is an empty skin that changes each minute.'[31] Concrete language is always the root of abstract thinking.

Kant may claim that he really can find one word uninfluenced by temporal duration: substance.[32] He claims that substance is an unschematized category in one's mind and therefore signifies only subject rather than predicate. But the word 'schema' is such an ambiguous one in Kant's writings, because of its parallel ambiguity in usage during Kant's lifetime in European philosophical history, that one cannot really know definitely what 'unschematized' could mean.[33] Hamann's schema is the mystery of the Incarnation. He explained: 'the wicked snake in the bosom of ordinary popular language gives us the best parable of the hypostatic union of the two natures of sense and of understanding . . . the synthesized mysteries of the two corresponding and contradicting forms of *a priori* and *a posteriori*, together with the transubstantiation of subjective conditions and underlying assumptions into objective predicates of power are a curse to stop boredom short and to fill out the void of space in periodic galimatias [confused language] by thesis and antithesis . . . '[34]

We play as if we know things definitively. Hamann is amazed how the mind is always creatively transposing and representing experiences on various levels temporally. But the mind alone is not doing the transposing and representing definitively. Man as a unified, fully alive, existent being is doing the transposing and representing, which means that these activities transcend the power of the mind alone; when a person thinks the mind does everything alone, he has become one of the 'bored' members of the Enlightenment derided in *Socratic Memoirs*. In the *Critique* Kant is also concerned about the meaning of the word 'representation', and he concludes 'the genus is representation in general (*repraesentatio*). Subordinate to it stands representation with

---

[29] Nadler, *Metacritik*, III, p. 286.
[30] Gildemeister, V, p. 267.
[31] Ibid., V, p. 267.
[32] *Critique*, B228, p. 215.
[33] Karl Rosenkranz, *Geschichte der Kantischen Philosophie*, Leipzig, 1849, pp. 93 and 103. See also Ernst Robert Curtius, 'Das Schematismuskapitel in der Kritik der reinen Vernunft', in *Kant-Studien*, Bd. 19, Berlin, 1914.
[34] Nadler, *Metacritik*, III, p. 287.

consciousness (*perceptio*). A *perception* which relates solely to the subject as the modification of its state is *sensation* (*sensatio*), an objective perception is *knowledge* (*cognitio*). This is either *intuition* or *concept* (*intuitus vel conceptus*). The former relates immediately to the object and is single, the latter refers to it mediately by means of a feature (*Merkmal*) which several things may have in common.'[35] Sad to say, reading the *Critique* in German is much more difficult than in English, as Jacobi discovered. Kant actually apologizes for the fact that the first edition of the *Critique of Pure Reason* is so poorly written. He had thought up most of the *Critique* in Latin, but had decided to attempt writing it as his first work in the German vernacular. This transposition of the thought from Latin into the written word in German inevitably led to difficulties in the order of understanding. One of Kant's admirers, who could not understand this particular work very well in the original, translated it into Latin and gave a copy to Kant; Kant had difficulty in understanding this Latin translation of a book written in German but thought up in Latin. The problems of various levels of translation are difficult indeed. Kant thought a great deal in Latin rather than German so that Latin terminology at times helps one to grasp Kant's idea. The English translation of the *Critique* by Kemp-Smith may be more faithful to Kant's original Latin 'thoughts' than the German 'translation' of those thoughts. Kant also when writing not only had difficulty thinking and writing in German but in reading English. The basic influence of Hume upon him came through a translation of James Beattie's *Essay on the Nature and Immutability of Truth*, 1770, which investigated Hume's thoughts[36] with the result that his Humean thinking was already influenced by a translation. Kant was awakened from his dogmatic slumbers by Hume two years later in 1772. He worried that Hume left man with only a 'bastard of imagination',[37] so he must find a synthetic *a priori* for experience.

In this instance, Hamann thought that the process of thinking is a bit more complex than Kant is willing to see in his various categories of operation. Hamann explains 'The possibility of human grasping through mind of objects of experience coming from outside and *somewhat preceding* all experience (which is human in an internal sense) and coursing after and in conjunction with this, the possibility of sense

---

[35] Kant, *Critique*, B 376-7, p. 314.
[36] Robert Paul Wolff, *Kant's Theory of Mental Activity*, Cambridge, Mass. 1963, pp. 24 and 25. He also had become interested in Hume as early as 1769 through a reading of Leibnitz's *Nouveau Essais*.
[37] Kant, *Gesammelte Werke*, IV, p. 258.

intuition preceding all experience of an object belongs to secret mysteries whose exploring and ferreting out much less their descriptive definition and verification has not come into any philosopher's heart to dare to accomplish . . . for [its complete analysis] is a two-fold impossibility . . .'[38] He then proceeds to explain that 'receptivity of language and creatively acting present ideas! These two sources are the ambiguous ground from which pure reason draws all the levels of its representation.'[39] Man simply cannot find the set of categories or concepts which will allow him to define with infallible accuracy the manner in which representation takes place within a temporal context. Kant works very hard to define the question of representing and conceptualizing but he is doomed to failure in seeking absolute definition because he must use representative words to define what it means to be representative.

Kant does talk about texts in an intriguing fashion even in the *First Critique* when he says that the text is a cipher. Nature through its beautiful forms speaks to us in figures,[40] but it is doubtful that the words 'text', 'cipher', 'Nature', 'speaks', and 'figures' meant the same experiences to Kant as they did to Hamann, and Hamann definitely would have disliked the word *forms*.

Hamann simply cannot accept that Kant's time and space are the underpinning combined matrices of all knowledge: 'The concepts of time and space influence in a constant and large sense the two most kingly senses: sight and hearing, and have caused themselves to be as universal and indispensable in the entire realm of understanding as light and air are for the eye, ear, and voice. Therefore time and space are not *ideae innatae*, but are apparently at least the matrices of all knowledge which comes through intuition.'[41] Time and space are never totally separate from each other and never totally separate from the intuitions of sensibility. Kant seems to claim that outer sensations demand a representation of space and that successive sensations demand a representation of time, but that does not mean that time and space have a kind of priority over the sensations as Kant claims, for as Hamann sees, both have 'influence' in a constant and large sense[42] on the two kingly senses, but they are still not *ideae innatae* for there are always interactions with human experience between the concepts of time and space and the material sensible experience from which they flow.

[38] *Metacritik*, Nadler, III, pp. 283–4.   [39] Ibid., p. 284.
[40] Most of Kant's great insights concerning language are in the Third Critique.
[41] *Metacritik*, Nadler, III, p. 286.   [42] Ibid., p. 286.

Fascination With Time In This World

In contradiction to Kant, Hamann found that he must work out metaschematisms in his writings. He thought that most particular schemata were incorrect and that various schemata ought to be played off against each other in order to obtain new points of view in time. The word 'schema' was a very ambiguous word at that point in history and yet Kant deals with the question of time and space within the framework of it. The chapter in the *Critique* entitled 'On the Schematism of the Pure Concepts of the Understanding' is very obscure. Kant says 'there must be some third thing, which is homogeneous on the one hand with the category, and on the other hand with the appearance, and which thus makes the application of the former to the latter possible. This mediating representation must be pure, that is, void of all empirical content, and yet at the same time, while it must in one respect be *intellectual*, it must in another be *sensible*. Such a representation is the *transcendental schema*.'[43] Kant has rather too many 'musts' in the explanation of the transcendental schema. 'There must be a homogeneous something.' But is this 'must' merely a wish? Is this 'must' not just another projection of a god as Feuerbach demonstrated was true of human beings in relation to their 'need' for a god? Is this 'must' an incorrect use of the will as representation?

Kant wants a schema which is capable of attacking and grasping knowledge, which is quite imaginative, but the distinction between the words 'schema' and 'image' in Kant is unclear, so that the possibility of incorrect acts of knowing through the schema is still possible. Schema implies knowing how to apply a concept but one could know a concept without knowing how to apply it.

Kant's best definition of the schema of a concept is 'the representation of a universal procedure of imagination in providing an image for a concept.'[44] This definition however, remains descriptive because the words 'representation', 'procedure', and 'imagination' are not defined adequately and even the word 'concept' lacks a universal definition. Kant himself is still left with the problem that the 'conditions of sensibility constitute the universal condition under which alone the category can be applied to any object. This formal and pure condition of sensibility to which the employment of the concept of understanding is restricted' can be entitled 'the *schema* of the concept. The procedure of understanding in these schemata' can be entitled 'the *schematism* of pure understanding.'[45] The schematism of pure understanding is

---

[43] Kant, *Critique*, B 177, p. 181. [44] Kant, *Critique*, B 179–180, p. 182.
[45] Ibid., B 79, p. 182.

unclear. Kant's union of time and space is dependent upon a synthetic activity of a transcendent synthesis in which a determinant 'something' of consciousness acts.[46] This sounds more like Hamann's recognition that time and space are mysterious matrices of knowledge.[47]

Hamann himself glories in his view that reality should be experienced rather than excessively rationalized. 'The first clothing of all men was a rhapsody of fig leaves.'[48] The word 'rhapsody' for Hamann refers first to the temporal experience of music and the rhapsody of the written word flows from the rhapsody of fig leaves referring to the creativity of the human person as enfleshed.[49] In a slightly more intellectualist sense he explains: 'What type of warehouse makes up the history of learning? What is it all based upon? Five barley loaves, five senses which we have just like the non-rational animals . . . the treasury of faith *per se*, rests upon this material . . . '[50] The five barley loaves refer to a religious miracle which is related to the five senses which are a natural miracle. These five senses are the basis for Reason which is also a miracle.[51] The five senses upon which Reason is based are held also by the non-rational animals. Man is first flesh, part-animal.

Even when dealing with rational thought one ought to do as Hamann always does himself: 'I hold myself to the letter, to the visible, to the material.'[52] Since rationality flows from materiality, one must always keep one's feet on the ground; one must retain the intermingling of materiality and spirituality if one is to be true to human experience. Hamann's experience is based upon the enfleshed experiences of presence: 'The first shout of creation; the first giving life of its historian; the first revealing and gratification of nature are all joined together in the words: Let there be light. For it is in this that the experience of the presence of things is given birth.'[53] Presence and the present in which it takes place are the heart of creation. Creation shouts presence and that presence is enfleshed.

This presence is ultimately experienced as God in the present. Once one begins to experience this presence one must exclaim 'one does not know where to turn in order to avoid the intensity of His most amazing workings directed towards us.'[54] It is a paradox that for various reasons

---

[46] Ibid., B 143, p. 160.
[47] *Metacritik*, Nadler, III, p. 286.
[48] Nadler, II, p. 198.
[49] Nadler, II, P. 198. The notion of Rhapsodie in the *Aesthetica in Nuce* is present in this passage.
[50] Ibid., I, p. 298.
[51] Ibid., III, p. 102.
[52] Ziesemer-Henkel, III, pp. 416-7.
[53] *Aesthetica in Nuce*, Nadler, II, p. 197.
[54] Nadler, II, p. 204.

some people do not experience this presence at all, but when one does begin to experience the presence of God one's life is engulfed by it. This type of person seeks to re-express the experience through poetic genius, for 'the poetic genius brings the future and past into the present through images.'[55] Since God has been experienced in the past and will be experienced in the future, the poetic genius deals with these two sectors of time as experienced, but he seeks to bring those experiences into the present because God's presence is felt primarily by enfleshed persons. The poetic genius can change past expressions of God into new expressions of God in order to make God visible to man now. There will be 'new translations, new dogmas, new homilies . . .'[56]

Translations, dogmas, and homilies must change to meet experience through existing because 'Our existence is older than our reason.'[57] Reason helps translate; reason can be very dogmatic, but translation and dogmas must be rooted in existential experience rather than mere reasoning. No translation or dogma can exhaust the temporal depth of existence. Creation itself which makes up existence has unlimited depths because 'there is no absolute creation.'[58] Hamann exclaims that 'To a history of creation belongs a restless manifestation.'[59] Creation, history, and poetic genius are always seeking to make the presence of God more clearly present. There is a peculiar form of genius which seeks to do the direct opposite, for 'philosophical genius expresses its power in an effort through the use of abstraction, in making the present absent by a process of unclothing real objects and making them naked concepts.'[60] Philosophy sees reason overtaking other areas of human experience. This imbalance leads man away from the experience which could lead to his integration as a being of flesh, blood, and spirit. Man stupidly seeks for what he thinks is a wider form of knowledge through philosophical manipulations which make the present actually absent. This is an injustice to mankind.

Hamann does not totally dislike absence from the present, for it supplies time for fictions in the present, which can explain the present better to both the past and the future. As long as the quality of absence arises from the fact that it allows the present to be part of the past and future, rather than the present surreptitiously removed, Hamann will accept that form of absence. He also rejoices in the fact that 'Poetic genius unveils its power by transfiguring the visions of the absent past

---

[55] Ibid., II, p. 381.
[56] Ibid., III, p. 150.
[57] Ibid., p. 191.
[58] Gildemeister, VI, p. 515.
[59] Roth, III, p. 381.
[60] Nadler, III, p. 382.

through the means of fictions into present representations.'⁶¹ It is always the present which man must ultimately seek, for 'the present is an indivisible and simple point in which the spirit of observing is built up . . . The absent has a double dimension which is divisible into the past and the future which corresponds very much to the ambiguous spirit of prophecy.'⁶² The absent is good in so far as it has power to enrich the present, but when the absent is used to disinherit the present, and to abuse the present, the absent is a monster used by philosophy to destroy man.

The great men know how to make all times meaningful to the present. The major effect of philosophy is that the deceptive experience of reality forced upon man in his everyday life becomes unbearable and leads to a depression in relation to what is real life, and adherence to what is thought to be life, but which is, in effect, a living death. 'The heroic times are for giants and the philosophical times are fruitful for deceivers.'⁶³ Hamann laments the fact that so many persons in his time are philosophical deceivers. He himself wants to be a man fully alive, and this demands escaping the deception of the philosophers. He wants to write because 'One can certainly be a man of sorts, but one also has a need to become an author.'⁶⁴ He does not want to write philosophically however, because he heroically wishes to present enfleshed truth to man.

He has seen through the temporal changes of any philosophical system and knows that 'the system which this year allows you yet to prove definitely your presuppositions is going to be next year's mythical story.'⁶⁵ Hamann sees so well that philosophy is based on a changing language that he can call his philosophy 'Verbalismus'.⁶⁶ One may say verbalism is a kind of superstition but Hamann knows that respected philosophy is both a 'cancer'⁶⁷ and a superstition.⁶⁸ Philosophy pretends to control time but it cannot encapsulate time within its system and set of presuppositions, for as time marches on these presuppositions become the ground for new mythical stories which are quite unphilosophical in the eyes of the philosophers, whereas all philosophy is actually grounded in various mythical forms. If a man should happen to discover that he has been tricked by philosophy into living a deceptively abstract life, supposedly unbothered by the vagaries of time, he must awaken to the use of the perception that 'the natural

---

⁶¹ Ibid., III, p. 384.
⁶³ Ibid., II, p. 332.
⁶⁵ Ibid., p. 140.
⁶⁷ Nadler, III, p. 193.
⁶² Nadler, III, p. 384.
⁶⁴ Ibid., p. 201.
⁶⁶ Gildemeister, V, p. 493.
⁶⁸ Ibid., p. 224.

use of the senses must be purified from the unnatural use of abstractions.'[69] Hamann is saddened that some people are so deceived by a philosophy which links up the whole of reality without being influenced by a time which is mysterious at its core.

Time is the key to life precisely because it is mystery. Time is a mystery which is always there. Philosophers divide everything into cause and effect without giving the mystery of time its due respect because they claim to link cause and effect in various unmysterious fashions. Hamann almost pleads 'Can you not learn finally, you philosophers, that there is no physical link between cause and effect, means and ends? There is a spiritual and ideal one which is seen by you as a vulgar belief, as the greatest earthly historian of his motherland and of natural religion has declared.'[70] This passage is exceptionally difficult because the words physical, spiritual, vulgar belief, earthly historian, and natural religion seem juxtaposed in a strange fashion. Hamann uses the world 'physical' to denote a philosophical process which leaves no room for spiritual or transcending experience. Hamann loves matter but here he is referring to an incorrect use of the notion of the physical by philosophers who hope to analyse and dissect matter in such a way that matter can be totally known in all its forms and powers. Matter for Hamann has a spark of the spiritual, the ideal, the transcendent which for him differs from rationalistic reasoning. He is saying that philosophers misuse both the physical and the spiritual by not giving each of them their proper place in human experience.

Paradoxically, Hume, who was considered to be a great philosopher by many philosophers, never claimed to know the complete meaning of cause and effect, which made him in Hamann's eyes a respecter of earth and of history, for history gives a human mysterious temporal flavour to the meaning of cause and effect. Hume grasped somehow that earth was his motherland whereas many philosophers seek to build ivory towers dissociated from the earth. Hume also saw that there was such a thing as natural religion, or at least he grasped the fact that man by nature appeared to have a religious drive, passion, or appetite, although he (Hume) was quite uninterested in developing a personal religion for himself.

Although Hume is seen by many to be a destroyer of religion because of his scepticism, Hamann paradoxically admired his scepticism precisely because it could be used to destroy the rationalistic certainties of the 'Enlightened' ones who used their rationalism to destroy any

[69] Ibid., II, pp. 283–4.   [70] Nadler, IV, p. 27.

need on their part for belief in a living God. Hume's biographer, E. C. Mossner, relates Hume to the Enlightenment by saying that for Hume 'the whole [of life] is a riddle, an enigma, an inexplicable mystery.'[71] Hume was filled with doubt and paradoxically founded his views concerning miracles upon the works of Pillotson[72] who tended to be quite rationalistic.

Yet Hamann can write 'I studied Hume just before I wrote my *Socratic Memoirs* and this is the source to which I am indebted for my doctrine of faith',[73] because Hamann sees in Hume's 'doubt' a kind of faith against the Enlightenment.[74] Hamann sees through Hume that 'doubt', in contradistinction to the rational certitude of the Enlightenment, is not a lack of faith,[75] but rather can be interpreted as a true sign of faith, recognized as a partial mystery, which can at times cause doubt. He can thus exclaim that doubt is the '*summum bonum* of our reason'.[76] In this correct use of reason as including doubt of a Humean variety, Hamann can write 'Faith has need of reason.'[77] Once 'one grasps what reason really is about, all divergence with revelation stops.'[78] When man treats the reason and the understanding correctly, one can say 'The understanding is holy, right, and good . . .'[79] In union with belief dependent upon an element of doubt there is a 'health of the understanding . . .'[80] Then reason and understanding can help man to see that 'Being is realism which must be believed . . . .'[81] Then faith can reveal the 'majesty of existence.'[82] Hume can err,[83] but Hume is believable as a philosopher because he admits the possibility of error. This is a type of real religious appetite. Hamann therefore derides most philosophers because they claim to know everything, even the meanings and relations between cause and effect, whereas Hamann knows that man's motherland is the earth which is vulgar and mysterious in some respects, a motherland which naturally builds in man a form of religion. The philosophers simplify everything and lose the experience of being human. Human experience is processional mystery and is a faith, for

---

[71] E. C. Mossner, *Bishop Butler and the Age of Reason*, New York, 1936, p. 155.
[72] Sir Leslie Stephen, *History of English Thought in the Eighteenth Century*, London, 1962, p. 65.
[73] Gildemeister, V, p. 492.
[74] Ziesemer-Henkel, I, p. 355.
[75] Roth, VI, p. 200.
[76] Ziesemer-Henkel, III, p. 34.
[77] Gildemeister, V, p. 502.
[78] Ibid., V, p. 401.
[79] Nadler, II, p. 108.
[80] Ibid., III, p. 189.
[81] Gildemeister, V, p. 507.
[82] Nadler, IV, p. 282. See Nadler, III, p. 247, concerning Hamann's views on Hume's *Dialogues of Natural Religion*.
[83] Roth, VI, p. 187.

Hamann is involved in man's temporal experience. 'These temporal and eternal historical truths from the king of the Jews ... are the Alpha and Omega, the ground and peak of our faith.'[84] The key to human experience in time is for Hamann, not merely as a Christian, a belief in a man named Jesus, a Jew, who is also God. Hamann shows people that 'without abandoning one's self to principles which in part rest upon misjudgments of our age, nor scorning the same since they belong to the elements of the present age and to our connection with it, still the surest and most unshakable base of all peace is to be found with the pure milk of the Bible in childlike simplicity. One must fix upon the light given by God, not by man, a light which shines for us in a dark place until the day breaks in and the Morning Star appears to cast all our cares upon Him from whom we have the promise that He will care for the future of ourselves and ours; to abandon ourselves to the only Mediator and Advocate who speaks things better than that of the first saint and martyr, Abel, and has redeemed us from the idle ways of our fathers. Herein is found the Alpha and Omega of my entire philosophy. More I know not and do not wish to know.'[85] The first section of the quotation may appear to be scornful of the present, which would be unlike Hamann who sees so much within the present. Actually Hamann is speaking of the misuse of the present. The prejudices are caused by misinterpretations of the enlightened ones of the present age. If one wants true peace one should read the Bible, because the light from God, which is His Presence in the present, comes to a large extent through the reading of His Bible.

Man may live on this earth, but without God he is living in the dark on this earth. When he reads the Bible, the light of God, the Morning Star, comes to light up his entire day. Jesus Christ has come and is here as our Mediator and Advocate who will make our present days more enjoyable for us if we will only cast our cares on His shoulders. Abel, who was the first saint and martyr, spoke many beautiful things, but Christ, our Advocate, speaks even better things to us in our present day. Our fathers were often idle, but we are alive in the present through Christ. Hamann lived a life of intensity grounded in time.

Hamann appears to be a man grasped by the intensity of present time showing ever more clearly that time was at the heart of his lived and written experiences, which he always sought to intermingle. This became clear in the section on Hamann's style of writing. He remarks

---

[84] Nadler, III, p. 311.
[85] Walter Lowrie, *Johann Georg Hamann: An Existentialist*, Princeton, New Jersey, 1950, p. 20.

in his analysis of Moses Mendelssohn's work on the Jews 'I also know of no eternal truths but rather incessant temporality.'[86] God experiences eternity and time together in Himself.[87] Ronald Gregor Smith held that for Hamann, God is present to man only in the 'present' temporal moment.[88] Horst Stephan sees the experience of God in the moment as crucial in Hamann's experience.[89] Indeed Hamann claimed that God works in 'moments'.[90] Moses Mendelssohn's attempt to keep God from the world was like Golgotha, which was the last triumph against divine power.[91] The interest at this point is not only 'what is truth' but the relationship of truth to both eternity and time, and also the experience Hamann has of incessant temporality, for he grasps temporality, the changing of the present, as a constant change. Man must learn to live in a reality which is moving. Man ought not to seek security in restfulness or complacency for he would then be seeking to escape incessant temporality. As Heraclitus had seen so perceptively, 'It rests by changing.' True reality is change which is temporal.

The truth is not eternal; Hamann does not state that the temporal is truth but he does imply that reality, or his experience of reality which would approximate to some form of truth for him, is incessant temporality. The rational mind may flee from the fears inherent in some human beings if they accept the responsibility of living in incessant temporality, but the imagination glories in that very spontaneity of temporality. Hamann perceives that 'In most instances the dregs remaining after the spontaneous abundance of the imagination are bedecked with the name "philosophy".'[92] The imagination enjoys an abundance of experience of reality in the spontaneity of the moment, whereas philosophy gets the dregs or the little that is left after the abundance of spontaneity is ignored or cast aside out of fear of temporality. If language is to be true to its source it must continue to be faithful to the spontaneous abundance of the imagination rather than to the dregs of philosophy, for it is in immediacy that language has its source. 'The origin of language was as natural and immediate and easy as child's play.'[93] Abstract language may be difficult, which could be

---

[86] Nadler, III, p. 303. [87] Ibid., III, p. 191.
[88] R. G. Smith, *J. G. Hamann*, London, 1960, p. 19. Eberhardt Mannack holds that Hamann grasps the eternal God in the moment by hearing Him. See *Mystik und Luthertum bei Johann Georg Hamann*, Berlin. 1954.
[89] Horst Stephan, *Hamanns Christentum und Theologie*, Berlin, 1952, pp. 76-9.
[90] Nadler, I, p. 248 See also *Golgotha und Scheblimini*.
[91] Nadler, III, p. 403.
[92] Ibid., II, p. 394. [93] Nadler, III, p. 32.

a sign of truth, but the concrete experiences simply are not used and are rejected as foundations for truth because the philosophers demand a necessary truth which can be proved. Hamann knows that truth cannot be totally proved in a rational sense and that the necessities of truth are partially hidden in the mystery of the Spirit. If there are necessary truths, human beings in this world will never know them fully in the order of rational proof nor would their necessity be a rational necessity.

The people who cling to Holy Reason are not human. They live nonsense but do not realize that they are living nonsense. Paradoxically, they consider themselves to be the most human of the human beings. But the human being must accept a 'this is my body'. The human being must somehow accept that facticity of the mystery of his physicality in time, a physicality in time which even God assumes as an experience of beauty. One can become interested in God and this interest in God is a present interest, which can cause one to exclaim at times 'I was overcome by consolation . . . in the blinking of the eye I was overcome by consolation.'[94]

As a God-centred person Hamann can examine the question from the Christian viewpoint: 'Christianity . . . does not believe in Pythagorean-Platonic numbers or in any shadows of actions . . . Christianity grasps no other shackles of faith except the firm prophetic word . . .'[95] This is a firmness or stability with the prophetic word which is a temporal happening. Hamann knows that people want security and stability; they usually seek these qualities in a form of eternity and rationality whereas they ought to seek for them in time and prophetic faith. The stability which comes from both eternity and reason is illusory, whereas the apparent beginnings of language in the concrete are as easy for a child as his various games.

Hamann has seen too many persons forget the origin of their language experience which arises in temporality. He complains, 'Should an arrogant philosophy and hypocritical philosophy crucify the flesh and destroy the book because the letter and a form of "historical faith" are not able either to be the seal or the key of the Spirit?'[96] Persons get reality mixed up through too much abstract thought. They crucify the source of their experience and dwell upon one of the effects: the enemy, arrogant philosophy, hypocritical philosophy. They pretend because of their dwelling upon the effects of their lived experience that these effects control and in a sense give rise to the experience itself. But these effects can neither be the key to the Spirit who is alive now,

---

[94] Ibid., II, p. 41.   [95] Ibid., III, p. 306.   [96] Nadler, III, p. 227.

nor can the effects be the end, the seal of the Spirit, because the Spirit is always seeking to cause new effects, searching for new ends and goals in human experience.

But the powers of the philosophers are massive and Hamann laments of persons such as Lessing: ' "Holy Reason" for them steps into the place of revelation and orders us to genuflect in worship before "rational consciousness" . . . because neither "accidental truths of history" nor physical facts, nor political appearances can ever be valid proof of necessary truths of reason—such nonsense is a set of paradoxes which are unendurable . . . who do not allow themselves to be content with a *hoc est corpus meum* . . . or communion in flesh and blood.'[97] Devotion to the true Spirit, the source of living dynamic human experience, is lost, and men foolishly genuflect to 'Holy Reason' as their new God, their beginning and their end. Accidental or spontaneous truths, which happen in time and are historical, physical facts which demand the mystery of cause and effect, political appearances which express the changing strivings and desires of human beings, must be accepted.

The constant flow of time has a form of firmness if it is a time of prophetic faith. Hamann perceives that 'through long years the old community has understood eternity or another life to be the greatest form of security. Both concepts together mean a happy eternity, but a man can also take the first to mean a long temporal life.'[98] Hamann is struggling with the relationship of eternity to time in this passage. Eternity gives a notion to people which implies a stability or firmness People usually have insisted that the form of stability or firmness they want will have to be in another life because they find this life to be so unstable. But Hamann is moving in the direction of feeling that temporality must include some form of stability in itself. It has a length which is a consolation in itself to most people. Ultimately, Hamann is moving in the direction of seeing a form of stability in the very presentness of the present. His life is always intrigued by the present happening.

Mankind can search for a security so that he can 'rest each evening in a feast . . . that you, as Jeremiah said, sleep an eternal sleep.'[99]

Eternity must be for people a pleasant sleep. But Hamann wonders if mankind is not playing with these notions so that security can be built up 'through such word games of physiognomical and hypocritical nonsense.'[100] Perhaps man would be far better off if he explored the limits of temporality now. 'Rest and security (as people wish to know

[97] Ibid., p. 218.
[99] Ibid., III, p. 303.
[98] Nadler, I, p. 154.
[100] Nadler, III, p. 303.

them) are as sharply cut off (for man) as the temporal from the eternal.'[101] Hamann is wary of the meaning of the eternal. He is aware of the fact that he is alive now. Living is a great gift in and of itself and man should not throw it away in a vain effort to build up a system of security which rests primarily upon an eternity which is part of another life.

In speaking of God's action Hamann exclaims 'Let us now hear all of the matter of his new aesthetic which is the oldest; the time of his judgment is come.'[102] God acts now as he acted in the past and as he will act in the future. All of his acts are aesthetic because they are creative. God acts now and man should find his greatest strength in God's present acts. There is always a time which is an opportunity for God and man to experience pulsing life together.[103] Even ideas can be immediate or present. Reason need not be an abstract nontemporal experience. Hamann admired Socrates because he spoke 'immediate ideas'.[104] Socrates in a sense 'did not understand dialectics'.[105] Hamann is implying that if Socrates had become exceptionally dialectical he would have perhaps forgotten the immediacy and temporality of thought. Hamann does not admire Socrates because he talks off the top of his head without thinking, although his thoughts are swift[106] and immediate. Like Socrates, Hamann has swiftness of thinking, especially with a creative imagination. 'One instant I am a Leviathan ... the next instant a whale.'[107]

Hamann wants to be creatively free in time. He is obsessed with the intensity of the present, just as a Meister Eckhart could speak of the *nunc* of God as a taste of time.[108] Hamann is no mystic in the Eckhartian sense since Eckhart was too deeply influenced by Proclus and tended to have a mystical view which was too intellectualistic, but he does grasp that the end of time is a special intensity of time in time. Hamann accepts his finitude in relation to God in dealing with the blessings of the present. Although Nietzsche's view of human relationships with God is unlike Hamann's, his view on the finitude of man approaches Hamann's view quite eloquently. Nietzsche states that a person who believes in his own finitude 'accepts the future and redeems the past because he wants to perish through the present.'[109] Hamann wants

---

[101] Ibid., p. 302.
[102] Ibid., II, p. 217.
[103] Ibid., p. 215.
[104] Ibid., p. 76.
[105] Nadler, II, p. 76.
[106] Ibid., p. 75.
[107] Ziesemer-Henkel, p. 182.
[108] The *nunc* of God meant Eternity alone for most people.
[109] Preface to *Zarathustra*.

the future and the past to be related to the glory of the original present. Hamann lives in the present and ultimately knows he will die or perish in the present.

Nietzsche disliked Spinoza's view on time and thought Descartes and his writings were too rationalistic, just as Hamann disliked their views on the subject of time. Hamann could not have written more incisively than Nietzsche when he writes 'Against the value of that which eternally remains the same [Spinoza's naïvety and also Descartes'] there must be set the value of the shortest and the most transitory, the seductive flash of gold on the stomach of the serpent *vita*.'[110] The value of the shortest and the most transitory is the heart of Hamann's thought, the value of man as he experiences God in the transitoriness of the present. Hamann would not see the flash of gold, the creative moment, as a seductive serpent. He sees God working in time. God works with man now through the creative powers of music, painting, and words which are partially concrete. With Nietzsche he could exclaim 'the inventive force which devised categories worked in the service of the need for security, for quick intelligibility in the form of signs, sounds, and abbreviations:—substance . . .'[111] Away with quick, superficial intelligibility! Away with the word 'substance'! This word Hamann saw as destructive in Kant's view of reality.[112] Where is one's security? It is with God in the transitory present. It is not found in systems of intricate intellectuality.

Hamann knows that 'I overcome myself and my fate in the complete providence of God.'[113] He is dedicated to the belief that 'I will do what God writes for me to do everyday.'[114]

God knows best how He will inspire Hamann in the present so that Hamann can create in the present, and by creating in the present experience, relate to God, other humans, and himself. Hamann has faith in the present. 'We must through faith in the instinct of His Presence feel all.'[115] He lives in time with joy and thus can rejoice 'God, my

---

[110] Nietzsche, *The Will to Power*, translated by A. M. Ludovici, New York, 1924, p. 853.

[111] Ibid, p. 854.

[112] Although Kant believed in a thing in itself, he held that man had no immediate intellectual access to it, whereas Hamann claims that the creative person communicates immediately with objects which are changing outside oneself. Kant saw substance or *noumenon* in such a way that it was freed from the transitoriness of time. Hamann thought that Kant's view was a dangerous rationalistic form of escape.

[113] Roth, I, p. 96.

[114] Ibid., p. 36.   [115] Ziesemer-Henkel, I, p. 69.

day'.[116] God can be a man's day. If man lives correctly in time, God will come to him in time, in his day.

He sees the glory of experiencing God in the present. 'What one sees in each revelation—things which one can say nothing about afterwards.'[117] God has said through Jesus Christ 'See, I am with you always until the end of the world'.[118] God in the temporal world can be seen by Hamann whereas many persons do not have the same set of eyes, and so are led to seek their God in the security of eternity.

Hamann knows that the height of human experience consists in grasping that 'our whole life . . . is prophetic.'[119] Our lives are prophetically rooted in time united paradoxically, if we have but the eyes to see, with the God who gives the prophecy.[120] We do not so much have to strain our eyes or seek to lift ourselves up to a God who is totally transcendent and non-temporal because God deals with us according to our own human nature which partially transcends time but which is always immersed in time. Hamann ponders 'Why did it please Him to make in six days, what according to His will He could have really made in a moment of Time?'[121] God works according to our ways and He envisaged us to be a temporal reality moving from one temporal experience to another. Thus, the great act of initial creation was a series of acts in time.[122] It is true that God could have made everything in a moment of time, which would be considered by many philosophers to be a great sign of perfection as they grasp the meaning of perfection to be non-temporal, but the initial creation serves as a type of man's life in the world now which consists of a series of happenings in time.[123]

God is always with us in time. 'He repeats Himself in nature, in writing, in the kingdoms of the world, in the building of His Church,

---

[116] Nadler, I, p. 237.

[117] Ibid., II, p. 337. Hamann's statement that one cannot say anything about the revelation is the Wittgensteinian sense in the *Tractatus* that one must remain silent. Hamann will seek to begin to re-express his revelations in words in so far as they can be expressed in words.

[119] Ibid., I, p. 128.   [118] Ibid., III, p. 403.

[120] The prophecy concerns the present much more than one special form of prophecy which seeks to describe the future.

[121] Nadler, I, p. 10.

[122] The temporal series of this act may not necessarily be taken in a literal sense, but it definitely cannot be taken as a mere symbol designed only as an aid in the order of human imagination to meet man's epistemological needs. Concrete reality always ultimately precedes epistemology.

[123] This process will always remain a partial mystery. Whitehead's *Process and Reality* is one of the noblest efforts to understand the process philosophically, although the effort to do so is still a partial failure.

in the change of times.'[124] Hamann sees no vast distinction between what could be called the religious and the secular. God works in nature; all writings, which for Hamann can mean all of the arts, and all kingdoms, which includes political/sociological/economic/military aspects of human experience, are related to God. God also works in the Church which is one of the more explicit manifestations of His power in the world, which participates in the changing times. By including God as being present in the changing times, Hamann means that God is always present, because time changes everything including nature, kingdoms, cultures, and the Church.[125]

Hamann rejoices in reflecting 'How consoling it must be for us to have a God who has a concern which comes along with all our steps and abandons us no more than do our shadows.'[126] If man had always the eyes to see the phenomenon/noumenon[127] of God accompanying us as we course through various events in time in our lives, how secure we would feel, how consoling the experiences of our lives in time would be to us. Most men are blind and cannot grasp this form of security; they build up the security of intellectualist systems in a vain effort to assuage their fears and tremblings. But everything man experiences in the order of time has an aspect of God's presence embedded in its heart, for 'God made the changes of day and night . . . signs of His consolation and true signs of faith.'[128] Man does not know that 'God is the best method and the best time.'[129]

If only man could see that he exhausts himself uselessly in setting up systems which he hopes will become his final end and security. He will never find a perfect system. God Himself is the best method which is better than a system; He is a method which works in time because man is created in time. A method of security which seeks to escape time cannot be the correct method for man. 'Time is in His hand and not in ours.'[130] Man cannot escape time as part of his necessary method or mode of living because God, not man, has placed it in man's mode of living as a necessary aspect of that mode of living. If man takes time

---

[124] Nadler, I, p. 238.
[125] The effort to find clear distinctions between the secular and the sacred which is epitomized by a book such as Harvey Cox's *The Secular City* has thankfully failed.
[126] Nadler, I, p. 253.
[127] Hamann insists that all mental experiences are partially sensible so that phenomenon and noumenon are consistently linked in human experience. We think partially with our feet. Kant's Platonic leanings in relation to the concept noumenon will not allow man the ability of relating directly to noumenon.
[128] Nadler, I, p. 227.
[129] Roth, VI, p. 248.
[130] Ibid., VII, p. 393.

into his own hand he very often throws it away in desperation because he cannot control it totally. Man is wisest when he allows God to lead him in the order of time, with man participating in the process, because God knows the best method which will be useful in an unsystematic world.

God plans our lives in a mysterious fashion. Once we become explicitly Christian then 'the entire course of life of a Christian is the masterpiece of the ungrasped genius.'[131] Man can never totally grasp the unending genius of God, but he will be happiest in his temporal existence if, as a Christian, he allows this genius to plan the ultimate course of his life. This genius is the truth, Jesus Christ, who is also the way and the life.[132] God is an 'ever-present God.'[133] He is always seeking to exercise a good providence towards us.[134]

Man must always seek to use time correctly; he must not be greedy towards time by forcing it to give him more than he deserves.[135] The man who sees God in faith can always say 'Wake me in the morning when it is your gracious will. Wake me at the correct time to your command and to your service.'[136] God always knows the correct time when man can most perfectly be of service to Him, which also means being of service to his fellow men out of love. God's ultimate command is that man should love both God and his own neighbour. Hamann knows with his special sense of time that by loving both God and his own neighbour, man seizes the heart of being in the moment.[137] Nature is a vast part of being and 'the whole of visible nature is nothing but the fact and hands of the clock.'[138] God's hands, His face, with all of its manifold expressions, appears in all of the visible aspects of nature. 'Everything lives and is full of hints of our calling, of the grace of God.'[139] Everything that lives is vibrantly filled with the grace of God which is His life, His very own communication of self. Hamann says 'One must with wonderment see how God inserts Himself into the smallest circumstances and the revelation of His kingdom in the common happenings of human living.'[140] God does not force man to become like Him so much as God communicates Himself in the common

---

[131] Nadler, II, p. 140, and I, p. 251.   [132] Roth, VII, p. 147.
[133] Ziesemer-Henkel, I, p. 369.   [134] Nadler, I, p. 7.
[135] Ibid., II, p. 363.   [136] Ibid., I, p. 310.
[137] Ibid., II, p. 261.
[138] Ziesemer-Henkel, IV, p. 151. Hamann wrote this letter on New Year's Day, which may have caused him to think of the metaphor of a clock to represent the newness of God's presence in all of nature.
[139] Nadler, I, p. 303.   [140] Ibid., p. 36.

experiences of everyday human living, inviting man to be in communication with Him.

Man's mind has the power to begin to anticipate what may happen in the future, but man must not force the future by seeking to drag the present more swiftly towards it, for the future in actuality comes more towards the present than the present towards the future. Man, although he has the power of anticipation, must be patient and say with Christ 'My hour has not yet come.'[141] The theme of patience is central in Hamann's view of the experience of time in the present. There is always the 'fruitful' moment.[142] God always 'alone knows the time which is the best time in which He will manifest the beginning of His help.'[143] God's presence must be the ground of man's faith as he seeks to act correctly, always patiently waiting for the appropriate moment to act in union with God.[144]

If man is unwilling to wait for the correct time which is the 'living God',[145] he will act not according to the truth but according to a 'lie'.[146] Whenever man acts outside the correct time he helps to create lies. The partial insertion of evil into the world often consists in an incorrect use of time. Lies are immoral, although what is moral changes in time, for Hamann agreed with his favourite English author, Young, who says:

> Thou maker of *new* morals to
>   mankind.
> The *grand morality* is love of
>   THEE.
> 'As wise as *Socrates*' if such
>   they were
> 'As wise as *Socrates*' might
>   justly stand
> The *definition* of a *modern*
>   Foot.
>
>   'The Christian Triumph'[147]

Morals change with time; there are new morals to fit new times. The height of morality is a love of God. God allows man to love him according to his level of loving, for God always humbly condescends towards man.

Thus, as man changes in time, man loves God differently and man

---

[141] Ibid., III, p. 70.   [142] Roth, III, p. 88.
[143] Nadler, II, p. 38.
[144] Nadler, II, pp. 28 and 218, and Gildemeister, V, pp. 87 and 370.
[145] Gildemeister, V, p. 228.   [146] Ibid., p. 228.
[147] *Beylage zu Denkwürdigkeiten*, Nadler, III, p. 121.

loves his fellow men differently. The wisest lover was Socrates, because he was a lover of both God and mankind. If a man grasps this form of loving, then he participates in the Christian triumph. Christian love can triumph; one must have hope. Everything human, including morality and love, is grounded both in time and in a God who works with man in time. Life is a constant creation, for although there was a first creation, the world is always on the move in time and there is a series of creations, of changes, day by day.[148] Every moment is important for it is in the moment that man changes and is changed.[149] The Christian who triumphs knows that his moments are in Christ because the moments of his life are moments of a new life.[150] The Christian, in so far as he is with and in Christ, is older than the heathen or Jew, because in Christ the Christian participates in all the great moments of the past in the present moment.[151] The power of Christ is so great that 'Christ wants us through the Spirit to be made into such a man as He is—God.'[152]

Man as a Christian remains man, but he also becomes God now, in so far as God empties Himself in and through Christ into the world of time. Christ is the grandest Word in the world and He is 'a living speech directed to man in each moment'.[153] The providence of God enters into the world of man in all possible ways. Writing, which can be a deadening letter, in God's providence is vibrantly alive for 'Should not His providence include writings?'[154] Fire will some day utterly destroy the world,[155] but the world is now impregnated with the presence of God in a temporal flow. The Christian must always be aware of this incessant temporality, for Hamann knows first and foremost that 'This life is not a holiness, but a holy *becoming*, not a state of health, but a *becoming* healthy, not a Nature, but a *becoming*. We are not yet, we are *becoming* . . . It is not the end, it is however, the way . . .'[156] Everything is a becoming in this life. There is not health; there is a becoming healthy. There is no holiness; there is a becoming holy. There is no nature in a pure essentialist sense; there is a becoming. Man is not a stable, secure, established entity; man is a becoming. The world is not an end in the sense of a perfection which man should seek to know in such a fashion that it gives him security; the world is a process. Hamann is immersed in change. He is almost like Heraclitus who says 'It rests by changing'.

[148] Nadler, I, p. 87.   [149] Ibid., p. 31.
[150] Ibid., p. 212.   [151] Ibid., III, p. 149.   [152] Ibid., I, p. 22.
[153] T. Schack, *J. G. Hamann*, Copenhagen, 1948, p. 192.
[154] Nadler, II, p. 63.   [155] Ibid., III, p. 106.
[156] Roth, VI, p. 127.

Since Hamann is so rooted in the presentness of temporality he can muse upon the relationships of the future and the past to the present. Hamann views the relationship of past and future to the present first through what he sees to be experience for God. 'What is past is present for God and what shall be is as the past for Him.'[157] Hamann wants to show that God is first and foremost a God of the present. He feels that the past is more easily believed to be subsumable into the present than is the future, for he is so eager to show that the future is relatable to the present rather than the present being at the mercy of the future in God, that he claims the future for God will be like the past, which is more readily subsumable into the present. In God the present reigns supreme.

Information about the past is useful for man if it teaches him to seize the present more fully. Prophetic insights concerning the future are of the greatest use for man if he learns to live the present more fully through an understanding of prophecy. The present is the heart of man's life but the past and future are very helpful to the present for 'What would the most precise and diligent knowledge of the present be without the initial grasp of the future in the manner for which Socrates had to thank his daimon?'[158] God renews the powers of the past in the present and the spirits give insights into the future for man so that he can live more fully in the present.

Hamann jokingly presents a situation in which a false god is reigning over part of the earth, and one of his followers, 'the hungry prophet',[159] must try to get the god's attention so 'that he will awaken'[160] because he may be asleep. The true God could never sleep because he is always awake in the present. A 'hungry prophet' perhaps is merely showing that He, God, is not able to give him enough insights to make his prophecies worthwhile, whereas 'the spirit of prophecy is the witness of Jesus'.[161] Jesus is present in both the past and the future, and leads His prophets in the direction of perceiving past and future in relation to the living present. 'Each Christian is his own prophet.[162] This is a reality because every Christian instructed by Christ learns to perceive the relationships between the past and the present and the future and the present. Each time has a heart or middle point in the present which a prophet must perceive. 'The plan of each time has a middle point on which all lines, all figures, come together and are united . . . the present

---

[157] Nadler, I, p. 170.
[159] Ibid., p. 159.
[161] Nadler, I, p. 39.
[158] Ibid., III, p. 385.
[160] Ibid., p. 159.
[162] Ibid., p. 308.

is the front . . . the past and the future are different just as each movement of the eyes gives us another direction or the same picture from another direction.'[163] All lines of time converge upon aspects of various present points. The present is always the front or the face of experience, but the past and the future are always aiding the present. The past and the future in their own ways are different from the present, but they are always aiding the present.

In the *Hellenic Letters* Hamann makes the intriguing statement 'one needs almost as much cunning and *vis divinandi* in order to read the past as the future.'[164] Many scientific historians seem to think they can decipher the past quite easily and adapt it to the experience of the present age, whereas they will not begin to try to grasp the future because they realize it is not predictable as they suppose the past to be, and they most certainly would not accept any inspirations from an exterior source which might make the future partially understandable to men living in the present. Hamann is of the opinion that one needs both cunning and a form of divine power in order to begin to read the future, but he also insists that one needs almost as much cunning and divine inspiration to read the past because, once the present becomes past, its many facets and levels of reality are very difficult to grasp. Reading either the past or the future in relation to the present is difficult work and demands a combination of human mental cunning with a certain openness to the inspiration of divine power.

The divine power Himself encompasses past, present, and future. His power is different from our human cunning because 'According to our conceptions the past comes before the present; in God the present is the ground of the past and the future. He is—I will be with you always . . .—he was—the Word became flesh and dwelt among us full of grace and truth—He will be—See, I come.'[165] To us the past really does come before the present, but to God, who is presence, His present came before what we in our present see as past. He is, was, and will be. Primarily, He is because His presence expressed in the present is always the heart of His existing. Man seeks to have correct ideas concerning the past, present, and future, but Hamann wonders 'Who can have succinct ideas of the present without grasping the future, for the future determines the present and the present determines the past?'[166]

There is a sense in which for man the present is coming forth from the future into the past. It is always ultimately the presence of God

---

[163] Ibid., p. 124.
[165] Ibid., I, p. 248.
[164] Nadler, II, p. 175.
[166] Nadler, II, p. 175.

who is, was, and will be present in all three. To us the future seems somehow to determine the future-present, and the present determines the way in which we will view the past. If we view the past incorrectly as an idyllic age, we can be led to moan 'The days of yesterday, the lost yesterdays, make the present day unsettled and unuseful . . .'[167] It is very important to interpret the past well because that interpretation influences the present, which is the heart of human experience. Some form of faith or belief is necessary to interpret both the past and future correctly because 'This characteristic difference between the Jewish faith and Christianity deals with historical truths of both the past and of the future times which are trumpeted ahead of time and prophesied by the Spirit of both a universal and a particular providence. This reality can be accepted in essence only through means of faith.'[168] Providence always aids the interest of the present.[169] God's truth, which is partially temporal, comes to man through his providence.[170] His providence comes through both revelation and nature.

Hamann recognizes that some people see a temporal difference between the two forms of providence, but he is not too interested in becoming involved in the possible difference between the two forms. He states 'It is not necessary for me to remain a long time upon the difference between direct revelation through the channels of Word and Scripture which is graspable merely here and now, and indirect revelation by means of the thing which is nature and the concept which, because of their inscription in or upon the soul, are thought to be readable and graspable at all times and in all places.'[171] Hamann need not linger over that particular distinction because he already knows that the truth is 'teach me, Lord, to count my days'.[172] This is a godlike wisdom. As Heraclitus once observed 'Most godlike things escape knowledge because of incredulity.' Hamann counts his days in the presence of God and receives a form of security which is grounded in the changeability of temporality. He tries to awaken Kant from his brand of nonsense by writing 'Thus know that I am a prophet'.[173] There are many dead prophets in this enlightened world. In an uncanny

---

[167] Ibid., I, p. 180.
[168] *Golgotha and Scheblimini*, Ibid., III, p. 305.
[169] Ibid., I, p. 239.
[170] See *Golgotha and Scheblimini*.
[171] *Golgotha and Scheblimini*, Nadler, III, p. 304.
[172] Ibid., I, p. 70.
[173] Ziesemer-Henkel, I, p. 379. This view of Hamann concerning Kant's view of time precedes Kant's *First Critique*, but it follows the thought in Hamann's *Metakritik* which he wrote after reading the manuscript of Kant's *First Critique* given to Hamann because of their friendship in Königsberg.

sense Nietzsche explains Hamann's experience with the moment: 'Can we remove the idea of purpose from the process and still affirm the process?—That would be the case if something within that process were attained in every moment . . . Every fundamental characteristic which underlies every event, which expresses itself in every event, would have to drive the individual to affirm triumphantly every moment of existence in general, if the individual experienced it as his fundamental characteristic.'[174] Purpose is not necessarily a teleological event which makes the present moment merely a servant in the hands of an Omega point.

The moment is the greatest human characteristic for Hamann. In the moment when God is present to him he is most human. God in a sense is the 'moment of culmination'.[175] Hamann is like Abraham who rejoices in seeing His God who can be called the Eternal, in the present day.[176] When Hamann refers to God as the Eternal he is thinking of eternal in a Jewish sense. One can only seek humbly to begin to try to see where Hamann receives his view of temporality other than from the Bible, and the observations which he makes concerning the views of time, which someone like Kant of his contemporary age held.

The threads of historical philosophizing and theologizing which existed before Hamann's time and which influenced him in a positive sense concerning his views on time were Jewish writers, some Arabic writers, Leibnitz, and Hume. Certain writers who were unpalatable to him were Plato, in certain respects, but more particularly Aristotle, some of the medievalists, Descartes, Spinoza, and Berkeley. Hamann also fought with Kant because of his view concerning time. Hamann's time flows through the heart of human living in the present in which the presence of God is present.

Since the heart of Hamann's view of time is linked to his desire to be a person living in the presence of God it is important to see which passages reflect and describe Hamann's life with the God who is present. It is the power of the presence of God which really causes man to 'live in this world'.[177] Hamann has a new heart when he grasps how he lives in God's presence and he can reflect back upon the old heart which he had when he lived in this world without having been aware of the presence of God in his old life.[178] Without God he was locked in the old ways of a living death, but through God the old ways have been brought to an end.[179] Man's soul is definitely changed.[180] Everything

---

[174] Nietzsche, *The Will to Power*, p. 855.   [175] Ibid., p. 855.
[176] *Golgotha and Scheblimini*, Nadler, III, p. 293.
[177] Roth, I, pp. 213 and 225.
[178] Ibid., p. 217.   [179] Ibid., p. 213.   [180] Ibid., p. 224.

in Hamann's experience of reality takes on a new aspect. He can describe it in one way by saying 'I have tasted the honey and the sting of earthly friendship . . . How wise He is [Christ] for one cannot find His like . . .—an entire world of friendship is a waste and a detriment—in this one friend all timely compensation and preparation are given.'[181] Hamann had been living in a world of constant 'friendship-seeking', moving through Germany, Holland, England, and back to Germany, seeing how many friends he could amass. In many ways it proved to be a rather worthless use of his time.

Christ gives him faith and faith is ultimately a gift of God, given as timely recompense for living in the world of the living dead.[182] The work of God in Christ is the new ground of Hamann's life.[183] Hamann is convinced that he is living a new life on this earth. He will always wait now for 'the world of the Saviour'[184] to guide his new life. Christ has a 'godlike presence'[185] which is 'in all places and all days'.[186] God has become the Spirit in Hamann.[187]

God is always in time helping man.[188] Christ is living truth and truth metaphorically is the daughter of time.[189] The truth, which is the daughter of time, is not totally viewed as the living truth who is Christ, for it is from one aspect a conceptual truth that arises out of concrete temporal human experience, in which Christ has humbly condescended to participate with joy. The Spirit teaches 'man in time'.[190] The Spirit is the first of Hamann's great helpers and Hamann perceives 'what a maze the present would be without the Spirit of prophecy as it gives hints from the past and the future.'[191] Through the Spirit 'Every moment of time is perfectly formed'.[192] This form of perfection is not the perfection which arises from absolute knowledge or from a form of immutable security. The perfection consists in a communication between God and man in the moment of temporality.[193] If a man is in communication with God he can, as a Christian, claim that 'the Christian alone is lord of his days.'[194]

Man is not always Christian because his own imperfections and faults get control of his person, which Christ also seeks to control

---

[181] Nadler, I, p. 266.
[182] Roth, I, p. 512.
[183] Ibid., p. 379.
[184] Nadler, I, p. 275.
[185] Ibid., p. 273.
[186] Ibid., p. 273.
[187] Ibid., p. 45. Hamann refers in different passages to God, to Christ, and to the Spirit. Sometimes Christ and the Spirit appear to be interchangeable, and sometimes Christ and the Father appear to be interchangeable.
[188] Roth, VI, pp. 96 and 100.
[189] Gildemeister, VI, p. 153.
[190] Ibid., p. 74.
[191] Nadler, III, p. 398.
[192] Ibid., I, p. 125.
[193] Ibid., p. 125.
[194] Ibid., p. 71.

with kindness. Hamann therefore humbly says 'No hero or poet . . . lacks stretches of his life when he has many reasons to confess with David, "I am a worm and no man".'[195] There are suggestions that Hamann considers the true poet to be a Christian in so far as a Christian leads a good life. But there are times when a person who is a poet lacks the qualities which would cause him always to be a poet of the first calibre. During these times a man who has the quality of being a poet becomes a worm at best, and, at worst, no real man or real poet. During these times when a man is actually a worm, he lacks the 'Spirit of love'.[196] Once a man lacks the spirit of love he neither loves God nor his fellow men in 'temporal ways'.[197] Lack of love makes man a worm. Because of this, Hamann always wants God in the Spirit of love to be the 'government of my whole life'.[198]

It is interesting that Hamann's life included the enjoyment of eating and drinking with friends. Could it be that at times he allows himself to enjoy things a little too much by subtly supposing the enjoyments to be part of the presence of God in his life? He glories in eating and drinking in the moment.[199] He tells others to 'Eat your bread with joy, drink your wine with good spirit because then your work pleases God.'[200] The impression received is that he had a great capacity for enjoying food and drink but not to excess, and that he was sincere in feeling that his liking for food and drink flowed from a union with God who had a taste for life of His own. Hamann is interested in food and drink because they are part of the tree of life for a man who is enfleshed. 'The tree of knowledge has deprived us of the tree of life—ought not the tree of life to be a little more dear to us than the tree of knowledge . . . All the terminology of metaphysics comes finally to this historical fact, and (we can be new children of Adam if we escape it) . . . *sensus* is the principle of all *intellectus*.'[201] Eating and drinking help him to be aware during the day that he is physical. Man is from the earth.[202] God comes into the present and is with man on this earth.[203] Man must, through Christ, always be interested in the present on earth.[204] God always works in 'a moment of time'[205] in this world.

Time is good for man in communication with God. 'All temporal unhappiness is a sin or flows therefrom.'[206] Sin causes man to be

[195] Ibid., III, p. 38.
[196] Ibid., II, p. 41.
[197] Ibid., p. 41.
[198] Nadler, II, p. 41.
[199] Roth, VII, p. 400.
[200] Ibid., V, p. 276.
[201] Ziesemer-Henkel, V, p. 266.
[202] Nadler, I, p. 72.
[203] Gildemeister, VI, pp. 351 and 352.
[204] Nadler, III, p. 25.
[205] Ibid., I, p. 248.
[206] Ibid., p. 252.

unhappy in time. Hamann believes that sin is real and that its effects are real in this temporal world when man is cut off from the presence of God. He can see that 'God allowed the human community to fall into a grave for a long time.'[207] Man freely chose to sin; God allows man the freedom to sin. Sin for man is a form of death. In this sense Hamann can say 'all those things which make a day terrifying and a night fearful are joined together in man's life.'[208] Without the presence of God, time, temporal life on this earth, is a frightening experience. The 'enemy'[209] lurks everywhere. But when man is grasped by the presence of God he is happy, and he knows that the fear of the Lord is the beginning of wisdom and his evangelical love the end and the point of wisdom.

In contradiction to Descartes, who thought man's existence was best defined by saying 'I think therefore I am', Hamann can exclaim 'I believe, therefore I speak'. Belief is the foundation of all man's new life in God. When man believes, he is moved to communicate his belief; man is moved to speak of his new life in God to those who may still be in the grave on this earth. He must do battle especially with those who think that thinking is the final end of their living, for by thinking *ad nauseam* they are living a living death. They must be brought to see that religion and belief find their foundation 'in our whole experience, and our powers of knowledge taken all together, are the most *ephemeral* and abstract mode of our existence.'[210] Thinking man thinks he is fully alive but he is actually dead, for his thoughts by themselves are very ephemeral, whereas the believing man is truly alive because he has his life inserted into the heart of life who is God. Belief always underlies reason; belief in one's own living style, and also in one's own reasoning style, which is dependent upon one's living style, is of the utmost importance for man.

Hamann states 'He who believes in another's reason more than his own ceases to be a man.'[211] A man must always be true to his own life-style first, for it could be indirectly subverted through adopting the reasoned viewpoints of someone else. Hamann continues in a letter to Kant that 'Even the greatest human genius is not good enough for us to imitate.'[212] 1759 is a long time before Kant's *Critique of Pure Reason* was written, but Hamann already sensed through his friendly

---

[207] Ibid., p. 233.
[208] Ibid., p. 146.
[209] Ibid., p. 260.
[210] Nadler, III, p. 191.
[211] Ziesemer-Henkel, I, p. 92. Either natural or supernatural belief in this fashion would be harmful to man.
[212] Ibid., p. 93.

relationship with Kant in Königsberg that Kant was becoming enthralled by the notion of the greatness of a human mind which was a mind *sui generis* in its power. Hamann could see that a man must deal with his own reason in such a way that it is always subservient to his own belief as transcending mere reason. He also saw that a man should never become enthralled in the reasoning of another to the extent of subordinating his reasoning to the other man's reasoning, even if the other man doing the reasoning was a genius.

Instead of just depending either on one's own individual mind or on the mind of another human being, Hamann grasps how happy the man is who can visit daily the archives of Him who leads the hearts of all kings.[213] Man lives ultimately, day by day, through belief in the God of the present. 'Just as all kinds of unreason take for granted the existence of reason and its misuse, so all religions must accept the relation to the faith in an individual independent and living truth which like our existence must be older than our reason and is thus in a position that it cannot be known from the genesis of reason but by a direct revelation of the truth . . . the ground of religion lies in our whole existence.'[214] There is a touchstone for all religions which is a faith or belief in a living truth who is God, who is part of our existence through His loving communication.

He wants 'a new powerful prophecy concerning the present.'[215] The apocalypse should be and is being fulfilled in a sense in the present. Nietzsche came to see this desire for the prophecy and apocalypse of the present in somewhat the same way as Hamann although not for the same set of reasons. He states, 'to attain the superman[216] for one moment, for this I suffer everything.'[217] Hamann would suffer everything to enjoy the presence of God for one moment. Nietzsche exclaims that 'the moment is immortal'.[218] Hamann thinks man's immortality takes place now, in the moment when God's presence is manifested to him. Nietzsche feels that 'Light, peace, no exaggerated longing constitutes eternalized happiness in the eternalized moment correctly set forth.'[219] Hamann does not long for a false future of immortality. He lives in the present in faith. His light is the light who is Christ; his peace is the peace of Christ who appears now. The eternalized moment

---

[213] Nadler, III, p. 378. [214] Ibid., p. 191.
[215] Ziesemer-Henkel, IV, p. 236.
[216] Since the word 'superman' has an almost immediate effect upon Americans from comic books, a wiser translation of 'übermensch' is probably 'overman'.
[217] Nietzsche, *Nachlass*, in *Werke*, XIV, p. 306.
[218] Ibid., XIV, p. 371. [219] Ibid., XIV, p. 286.

is correctly applied when man seeks to create now while in communication with the creative power of God. Nietzsche can exult, 'If we affirm one single moment, we affirm not only ourselves but all existence.'[220] Hamann knows that, by affirming the moment, man is true to his own human temporal existence and the existence of other human beings, and also, that he is true to the God who manifests Himself to man in this worldly, temporal existence.

It will be helpful now to see how Hamann reacts to the notion of history as a view of time, because he uses a sense of history in order to help him be creative in the present. Hamann had begun to find interest in the historical through a set of conversations with his brother in the 1750s.[221] He saw sections of history as special, and could say that Egypt, Carthage, and Rome each had their special time.[222] There is always a 'present Fate'[223] as the present is related to past history and is in the process of becoming history itself. The art of history consists in an attempt to record in words the human experience(s) of a particular age in relationship to other ages.[224] Hamann recognizes, however, that words can never encapsulate or explain these human experiences adequately because the words used to explain the historical experiences arise out of the historical experiences themselves and are therefore partially subservient to them.

Hamann is related to Bolingbroke in the development of his view of history.[225] He realized that any history is seen through the particular eyes of the person who is writing it and who has a particular personal historical vantage point which inevitably colours his writing of history. Dilthey[226] also saw this fact at a later time in history and was possibly influenced by Hamann in regard to it. Gadamer is also similar to Hamann on this point.[227] Hamann knows that readers of an author 'must work hard as readers to put ourselves in the shoes of the particular

---

[220] Nietzsche, *The Will to Power*, p. 1032.
[221] Urs Strässle, *Geschichte, geschichtliches Verstehen und Geschichtsschreibung im Verständnis Johann Georg Hamann: Eine entwicklungsgeschichtliche Untersuchung der Werke zwischen 1756 und 1772*, Bern, 1970, p. 17.
[222] Roth, I, p. 303.   [223] Ziesemer-Henkel, III, p. 218.
[224] See J. Stolnitz, *Aesthetics and Philosophy of Art Criticism*, Boston, 1960. See also *Aesthetics and Language*, ed. by W. Elton, New York, 1954, and *Philosophies of Art and Beauty*, ed. by A. Hofstadter and R. Kuhns, New York, 1964.
[225] Unger, *Hamann und die Aufklärung*, p. 625.
[226] Dilthey, who received some of his ideas concerning history from Hamann via Schleiermacher, is one of the greatest German historians. His view of 'Verstehen' as a partial intuition is similar to Hamann's insistence that one must see historical figures in the context of their everyday experiences. See W. Kluback, *Wilhelm Dilthey's Philosophy of History*, London, 1952.
[227] Gadamer, *Wahrheit und Methode*, p. 502 ff.

author whom we are reading, feeling his feelings, and entering into his frame of mind in so far as that is possible through the aids of imagination, which is precisely the power which a poet or an historian has to a large degree.'[228] A good historian is like a good poet; he has great power of imagination which allows him to find the best words by which he can write his own works and also allows him to read the works of other writers with sympathetic insight. The reference to imagination implies that abstract reasoning cannot alone be the correct method of interpretation for a man who is seeking to do historical research. In so far as it is possible, the researcher must at least get into the shoes of the sources he is reading in order to be able to write a book of his own. If he could somehow feel with the feelings of the man he is seeking to read about, he could grasp what the moments of that man's temporal life were like in order to re-express them correctly in an historical document. The imagination is the greatest aid to that feat.[229]

Since 'the entire physical nature of man from his conception to his ceasing to be is a type of history, it is in itself a key to the notion of history.'[230] History is rooted in human physicality which helps to impart mystery to history in contrast to excessive abstract reasoning. Reason alone cannot be the correct historical guide because history is 'a cloaked witness, a riddle which cannot be solved until we plough with an ox other than reason alone'.[231] History is 'like nature, a sealed book, a hidden testimonial, a riddle'.[232] History is 'more secret acts and discovered wonder'.[233] History is rooted in the physicality of the earth. Even the words which we would use to explain history are rooted in physicality and therefore have a physical history of their own. Hamann marvels over 'the most powerful fresh-buried roots of a word or the unending root genealogy of a concept.'[234] One cannot even complete the genealogy of a word, much less claim to explain reasonably everything that exists genealogically in history.

Some people have attempted to rationalize history: 'the philosopher's God created the world in six days! But the philosophers have caused this world to be deformed into a chaos.'[235] The philosophers have accomplished turning the world into chaos through a misuse of reason. Hamann challenges those who would claim either to be philosophers

---

[228] Nadler, III, p. 8.
[229] Imagination in this section does not refer to a process of 'fancying' tales about reality.
[230] Nadler, I, p. 228.
[231] Ibid., II, p. 65.
[232] Roth, II, p. 19.
[233] Ibid., I, p. 139.
[234] Nadler, II, p. 126.
[235] Roth, VI, p. 258.

or who are philosophers: 'one cannot dare to be a philosopher unless he studies the history of the word philosophy in the abstract as well as in the concrete.'[236]

Much more wisely than any philosopher, Hamann, the philologian, knows that 'We find the history of each race in its speech',[237] not just in a philosophical investigation of words. Even mathematics, which is supposed to be the purest form of writing and of speech, is still, in a sense, made up of concrete speech and writing. 'All the wisdom of mathematics depends on the nature of its speech and its writings.'[238] The nature of mathematics is to be dependent upon speech and writings which well up from the histories of various peoples. Great mathematicians often see various mathematical problems as a kind of poetry.

Hamann marvels that 'the complication of speech is a history, a phenomenon, an unending wonder, and a likeness by which God always comes forth to speak with us.'[239] Speech is at the heart of human history and this speech is a revelation of God. Hamann can exclaim to his good friend Herder 'Your theme of language, experience, and tradition is my favourite idea, the egg I brood upon . . . my one and all . . . the idea of mankind and its history.'[240] Hamann broods over mankind and his history. Man is a combination of experience in the temporality of the present with the traditions built up through the historical ages of the past, and language, which is his best means of communication with God who is past, present, and future, the God who speaks to mankind. God speaks to us and wants to be understood by us, just as writers speak to readers and wish to be understood by readers. Hamann rejoices in 'The reader who will not only see into the things about which one writes but also sees what one wants to be understood, . . . '[241] just as God hopes to be listened to and understood by man historically, temporally, presently in the correct manner.

Hamann writes to his good friend, Herder, 'You need revelation for a history of creation. But a witty head can manage a history of society, as this mediocrity Ferguson shows.'[242] Revelation is man's greatest aid in his effort to begin to understand the historical realities of the creative power of God. Ferguson represents one of those worthy contemporary historians of Hamann's age who wrote up his little insights on human society with supposedly consummate skill. He may

---

[236] Nadler, II, p. 97.
[237] Ziesemer-Henkel, I, p. 393.
[238] Ziesemer-Henkel, V, p. 358.
[239] Nadler, I, p. 220.
[240] Ziesemer-Henkel, V, p. 501.
[241] Nadler, III, p. 133.
[242] J. G. Herder, *Werke*, Stuttgart, 1829, XVI, p. 214.

have a witty head but he does not know how to listen to Scripture in order to receive from Scripture insights concerning historical creation. Ferguson may be writing a history of society, but he is not writing a history of mankind informed by the presence of God, and this causes his history of society to be superficial.

Hamann especially despises so-called historians who idle away their lives in the pursuit of compiling worthless accounts of historical facts. 'Stanley and Brucker have set us up with colossi which are just as weird and incomplete as the image of beauty which a Greek composed out of the charms of all the many types of beautiful maidens who were either accidentally or intentionally given to him for his work . . . these of course were masterpieces which would most likely have always been admired and sought by experienced buyers of the arts but they were secretly ridiculed by more sensible people as weird, misshapen growths and chimeras or were sometimes copied for the simple desire of letting the time slip by . . . '[243] The two recorders of temporal experiences, Stanley and Brucker, create colossi which could be thought of as being monstrous wastes of time. They claim to give a definitive and complete exposition of a particular period of time, but they are simply incomplete and cannot be considered to be beautiful if beauty consists in a form of wholeness or integrity. History approaches beauty when a person takes a particular temporal human experience and grasps its integrated meaning in and of itself and then mysteriously relates it to other temporal happenings. But when snatches of temporal happenings are mixed together and called history, one has in a superficially creative sense created a monster. These two men epitomized a kind of enlightened view of history. It was not a view of history which coincided with Voltaire's enlightened view of history, and it certainly differed from Kant's enlightened view of history, just as it should be noted that Hamann's friend, Kant, did not follow strictly Voltaire's enlightened view that history is a completely human experience, because Kant does seek to find a relation in history to godly wisdom.[244]

Man must always seek to grasp that 'the whole historical puzzle of our existence, the impenetrable darkness of its *terminus a quo* and its

---

[243] Nadler, II, p. 78.
[244] Kant, *Idee zu einer allgemeinen Geschichte in weltbürgerlicher Absicht*, in *Werke*, VIII, p. 17 ff. See also Klaus Weyand, 'Kants Geschichtsphilosophie: Ihre Entwicklung und ihr Verhältnis zur Aufklärung', in *Kantstudien*, Hefte 85, Köln, 1964, p. 106.

terminus ad quem, are resolved and explained by the first and primal message of the Word become Flesh.'[245]

The end of history can also appear to be quite eschatological in Hamann's writings because many of them end with a kind of eschatological significance,[246] but it is a special kind of eschatology, usually involving reference to John the Baptist. This could very well indicate that, just as John the Baptist recognized the active communication of God with man in this world in time through Jesus Christ, so eschatology for Hamann is actually the entry of the eternal living God into the temporal now in this world whenever He communicates with a man like John the Baptist who recognizes the communication. Hamann is a man who can never forget that godlessness and depravity on his or any man's part force 'nature, time, and life itself'[247] to work against man as an individual. He derides the fools who do not know that both the law of Holy Scripture and man's reason were given him in order that he might 'know one's sin and ignorance, not to know grace and truth which have to be revealed in history . . . This brief and age-old confession of faith says everything that I personally feel myself in a position to say.'[248] Revelation of man's sin and redemption takes place in history. Faith also is linked to history and is a *fides quaerens intellectum* with the aid of history.

He cannot forget 'how would I continue without this faith!'[249] Faith in Jesus Christ is the heart of his life. His life is part of the great 'Let there be!'[250] which is the creative speech of the Trinity.[251] All creation in time is a word and the word uttered in creation is the Word, the Son of God, who has come into the world. Without this word, man finds that 'all those things that can make a day full of dread and a night full of terror are united in the human life.'[252] Life is not pleasant for the human being when he is overcome by the dread and terror of his own existence.[253] Man in union with the Spirit of God is happier, and Hamann admits that the Spirit of God makes him awake to the world in

---

[245] Nadler, III, p. 192. This view follows Augustine's view of history to a large extent, involving both the Incarnation of Jesus Christ as the central point of history, and our passage through time with the guidance of the resurrected Christ. See Jean Guitton, *The Modernity of Saint Augustine*, translated by A. U. Littledall, Baltimore, 1959.
[246] Ibid., II, p. 107, and III, pp. 77 and 378.
[247] Ibid., I, p. 129. [248] Gildemeister, V, p. 324.
[249] Nadler, I, p. 312. [250] Ibid., III, p. 242.
[251] Ibid., p. 242. [252] Ibid., I, p. 147.
[253] See Søren Kierkegaard, *The Sickness Unto Death* and *Fear and Trembling*, translated with an introduction by Walter Lowrie, Garden City, New York, 1954, as examples of this kind of suffering.

Fascination With Time In This World

a different way. It is a way of being awake which is not filled with terror within the spirit of his own life. 'Man is very close to the recourse of being forced to admit that spirit is to be seen as awake only when it is conscious of God and when it thinks and perceives Him and always sees the presence of God in and around it.'[254]

When God does communicate with the spirit of man, He writes in a form that man can understand. 'How much God the Holy Spirit has humbled Himself in His activity of writing for when He became a history-writer He became one of the most minor and most contemptible, most unimpressive events upon earth.'[255] The Holy Spirit was very condescending in His activity of writing for man about man, but Hamann is always grateful to the Holy Spirit, because man in himself is not capable of any form of communication with God unless God initiates the communication. Hamann is so impressed with man's weakness and the Holy Spirit's mercy that he says 'the Holy Spirit has given to us as His word a book in which He is like a crazy or insane man and a fool, for He actually almost becomes an unholy spirit of our own prideful reason since He used mythical tales, perhaps despicably small events, to relate the story of the Divine.'[256] Man must for ever love Holy Scripture even though it sometimes reads like the writing of an insane man, a fool writing of foolish tales, because these Scriptures, although not through the dead words as written on a page, but as words alive with the Spirit, reveal and communicate God to us.

With the eyes of the Christian, Hamann can see that 'Every aspect of nature was a word, the sign, symbol, and pledge of a new, hidden and inexpressible, yet most profound kind of uniting, interparticipation and mutual giving of divine ideas and energies. Everything that man heard in the beginning, everything that he saw with his eyes and touched with his hands, was a living word—and God was the word. The origin of language in man was as natural and easy and immediate as the games which children play, for the word was in the mouth and heart of man.'[257] God was everywhere for man to see and hear. God today comes in many different ways but man can know that he is always here through the Bible because 'The entire Bible appears to be written with this precise exact purpose: to teach us that God's providence rests in the smallest matters.'[258]

Hamann had sought to encapsulate his creative experiences into one nutshell of experience which is related to history, but, as we have seen,

---

[254] Nadler, I, p. 363.
[255] Ibid., p. 91.
[256] Ibid., II, p. 43.
[257] Nadler, III, p. 32.
[258] Ibid. II, p. 46.

it can be difficult for others to crack that nutshell, and grasping the import of the apparent confusion within can be disconcerting. However, we will make a brief attempt to comprehend what Hamann was doing in time within an historical context, when he was creating in communication with God. He had a temporally subjective and intensely personal bias against 'the public' who always looked for recognizable images of the Enlightenment; he also had a positive bias towards God and an experience of the transcendent in the concreteness of this temporal world. The Creator thus helped to provide images flowing from particular events, whose meanings were sometimes not imaginable to the majority of enlightened readers, but were to Hamann, who helped create the images as a fellow-creator with God. He presented events as occurring in fashions which confused 'the public'. The fellow-creator thus built up various antagonisms in relationship to the public.

As far as 'the public' was concerned, Hamann was condemned to live on the edge of life, on the fringe of respectable society. This creator in many respects did not mind being on the outskirts of enlightened society, for it allowed him to build up relationships only with people who grasped what he was attempting to accomplish; some of these, like Herder, Jacobi, Goethe, and Moser, were not nobodies. The saddest part of this rejection of Hamann as a creator by 'the stupid public' however, was that 'the public' needed precisely what Hamann wanted to give: an insight into the temporal varieties of religiously creative experience. 'The public' lost the very kind of written and spoken experience which it needed. Hamann was relegated to a form of Bohemia, while the enlightened people basked in the glory of the Berlin Circle of elegant thought and writing. But Hamann clung to the right of the writer to express independently of 'the public' what he knew to be creatively valid. He was not dependent upon the state for creating works and in fact he saw that the state helped produce artistic failures whenever it gave too much support to a particular creator. Hamann speaks to the problem of our age on this: to what degree should artists within various disciplines be aided by a federal or state government? Will the money usually have strings attached concerning forms of creativity?

Hamann was seeking to lead people to see that they should view their existence in this world in time in a new manner. Just as the medieval and Renaissance ideas and creative experiences transplanted certain classical and medieval creative experiences, so Hamann wanted to introduce some new experiences into his age which came partially from other ages and other places. He was searching to present a new conception concerning physical–philosophical–theological reality. He was seeking to say that, in combination, they intertwined in a process, a change, a becoming, in which both matter and spirit combined were energy communicating creatively with God. He was dealing with a reality that was relational.[259]

Most of his contemporary opponents were incapable of seeing that the proper content of his works concerned the personally dynamic subjective experience of nature, of mankind, and of God through a succession of instants. The critics tended to see his works as meaningless unsuccessive *non-sequiturs*. He had developed his mind in such a fashion that he could say there is no seeing without hearing, there is no hearing without a form of feeling, touch, there is no thinking without sensationally processional time. As a thought, this notion is hard to think because it lies almost below the level of rational thinking and because it is a ground-thought.[260] Hamann was maddened by the desire to catch hold of what is transient, to discover threads of relatedness in change rather than seek to construct lifeless essentialist patterns of secure reality. He was more interested in creative becoming than in permanent being. He was in a sense amazed at the apparent instability of reality as it transformed itself before his eyes, ears, and touch, and yet he caught hold of a certain security, a certain stability, in this change which created threads of faith flowing from God to man. He decided that the vague and the mysterious were proper means for presenting these divine threads creatively to other persons. The threads helped to form a symbolic wholeness from the apparent sheer change.

He wanted his experiences, which were so firmly based in time, to be represented in such a manner that it took painstaking time to unravel them, to feel, see, and almost hear the threads as they proceeded from God and from his own creativity, in so far as his creativity was a communication of himself with God. He wrote in such a fashion that the objects which he juxtaposed in his writings participated in each other's existences, although most people could not and would not take the time to see how his creative threads held the various objects together so that they could participate in each other's existence. Hamann knew that every written creation was in itself a translation, a form of likeness

---

[259] Although Charles Hartshorne's view of God (or the transcendent) differs quite a bit from Hamann's view, his book, *The Divine Relativity*, does help us to grasp Hamann's views concerning relativity.

[260] Hamann in a sense is wrestling with the difficulties in Heidegger's *Sein und Zeit*. Heidegger was, of course, indirectly influenced by Hamann concerning the question of language and the question of hermeneutics. See Martin Heidegger, *Being and Time*, translated by John Macquarrie and Edward Robinson, New York, 1962.

within itself involving physical activity, philosophical activity, and spiritual activity. The physical, philosophical, and spiritual aspects of Hamann's creations simply cannot be reduced to a rationalistic system. Instinct cannot be reduced to order; drives cannot be totally calculated; temporal experiences cannot be stripped to their essentials and remain true temporal experiences. There may be some subjective displacement of objective experience, but the creator seeks to be faithful to the objective experience while also being faithful to himself, for he grasps that reality for humans is a subjective/objective complex experience.

Hamann gloried in his sense and in his spirit. He could in a sense hear time pass and see the fleshliness of words. He translated the transitoriness of time into new transitory experiences of God, man, and nature. He modelled sensation in such a way as to bring out the half-thought of words without destroying the enfleshed sensation. He knew that time does not stop in reality, but he knew that perceived change depended upon the manner in which man translated his sensual experience of this temporal world into a sensual/spiritual experience that had security in transitoriness. A contradiction in terms? Rather, a 'coincidence of opposites', according to the wisdom of Nicholas of Cusa. He deals with the dissolving and emergent interconnecting movements in his writings. There is a difficulty in making all these connections uniform for to the untrained eye and ear they are basically separate elements. He dealt with accidents in such a way as to make them have a form of aesthetic substance without losing their accidental qualities.

A security in change! The creative expression itself was more important than formal coherence, for the creativity of the expression was what he wanted to be his form. A modern Heraclitus![261] The ignorant enlightened ones might be repelled, but some persons like Herder and Goethe grasped what Hamann was seeking to do and admired the creative wizard of the North. They knew that Hamann created things which were in a sense 'yet unknown', for time is not totally knowable yet, and will never become totally knowable because time is creative change. They knew that there were no proper words in which to confine Hamann's words, for Hamann was a creator of words and that which confines cannot confine itself, especially if it is itself constantly being renewed with new life.

Hamann gave his life to a study of the movement of words as man sought to change them creatively and rearrange them in order to

---

[261] On his views concerning relativity and change, he is certainly more like Heraclitus than Cratylus.

re-express old realities and create new realities. He had an intensity of imagination that many people could not follow, but that is in fact part of his original greatness. He sought to re-express human experience in new modes of writing and overwhelmed many of the dilettante readers of his day. The formal aspects of his writings at times might appear too vague, as his writing verges in the direction of being too temporally individualistic, but it must always be remembered that he could write beautiful Ciceronian passages, French passages, German passages in detail. He also always claimed to have a temporal logic to his writings as he wrote them, so that if they became incomprehensible in parts at a later date he could still say that, at the time of their creation, they had a creative logic controlled by the very temporality in which they were created. Logic changes in time and place.

He wanted to create in the semi-solidity of the written word a fugitive and yet paradoxically secure impression of reality. As a writer in the flesh, he sought to be an amalgamation of the impressions he had received in the world in time. He must seek in one manner or another to communicate everything which had struck his own sensibility in order to be faithful to reality. He hoped that, in being true to his own sensibility in his creations, those who read his creations would be struck by his sensibility also, so that they would truly grasp the experience of what he was seeking to represent. He felt that the heart of written creativity consisted in the right of the writer to consult his own experience of the immediate present. He saw each situation as both contemporary and as transient; he would seek to seize both qualities in his works. In one moment the things he is dealing with will have changed and yet they presented some aspect of God at that particular moment, which gives man a form of *graced security now*. The words, because they are written, have a continuity to them, but their progression re-expresses the fleeting experience which combines many aspects of reality.

Hamann is aware that there are many experiences going on at the same time in the world, and seeks to interrelate these experiences as they flow from Persia or Egypt, from England, France, or Germany. If experiences are not going on at exactly the same time, he knows that various things happened in a particular epoch, the Greek period or the Roman, or the medieval, and he seeks to draw these happenings together more closely so that their time period, their epoch, can be grasped more clearly without losing its mystery. In quantity, Hamann's work was much less than Kant's, but in the revelation of both the particular characteristics of his age and his own singular experience in relation to his understanding of the meaning of language, he is more modern than Kant. He was seeking a new union between fleshly vision and expression in words. He saw in a way that he wanted to imitate what was happening around him, but he also wanted to express his singular, original, individual experience within the imitation of the happenings of the moment. He wanted to include in his imitation of the happenings around him that special quality which exists in each human being as he is moved within and through nature, to experience his God who is also within him. Life is given new lived meaning by being translated into words. Thus Hamann's life was translating experience into words which becomes part of the act of experiencing.

His written works as artistic creations were dependent upon his emotional/reasonable experience. He sought to express through human language the mysterious aspects of temporal experience. He sought to find new representations for new emotions because the emotions of man were not categorized by some schools of enlightened men. He dealt happily with the ambiguous world of the indeterminate.

Where does he get some of his ideas about writing? They erupt from intense feelings. Cold and enlightened caluclations have very little to do with the eruption of this creativity. Works begin within the depths of a man's flesh and blood experience. Hamann in his writings is seeking to awaken in the reader the same type of creative eruptions. He wanted his writings to be quite indistinguishable from his own individual temporal experience and he hoped to lead people to develop their own individual temporal experiences through reading his writings. He wanted each man to see that he has a goal in stating his own beliefs and his own feelings at a particular point in time in communication with God. Each man gives artistically creative expression to his own lived experiences. Thus Hamann, the creator, and his works both revolve around each other, supporting each other, in a contented communication with God.

V

HAMANN'S COMMUNICATION WITH GOD AND WITH HIS FELLOW HUMAN BEINGS

Hamann was fascinated by the reality of incessant temporality. Within the fabric of that incessant temporality flowed the dynamic explosions of creativity, the making of new things. God is a creator and man in communication with God could be a creator. Words are part of that creative flow for they are mutable like other existing realities. It is already known that 'Like numbers, words derive their value from the place which they occupy, and their concepts are mutable in their definitions and relations according to time and place just like coins.'[1] As man creates he writes his thoughts in an intricate pattern of values which are mutable in their meaning precisely because of time and place. Just as coins change from year to year through the creation of new images upon various metals, so words change from year to year through the creative genius of authors because the meaning of language, the meaning of relational symbols, is fleeting in the orders of time and space, which demands a constant renewal here and now of what one was seeking to symbolize in language forms during a previous period of one's life in a particular place.

Hamann acquired his own creative style of writing. It is an original creativity which is however mimetic, in the sense of being influenced by God and other humans. Many people who are not influenced by the gentle inspirations of God can believe that Hamann's style is nonsense, but Hamann always claims 'In my mimetic style there guides a cohesion and a logic glued together more firmly than the concepts found in more lively heads.'[2] All original creations of necessity offer some misinterpretation because 'every sentence, even if it comes from the same mouth and heart, is subject to a vast number of secondary notions which are given to it by those to whom it is addressed.'[3] But some of the misinterpretation of Hamann's by those who read him, flows

---

[1] Nadler, II, p. 71.
[2] Ziesemer-Henkel, I, p. 373. These so-called lively minds are only good at pushing concepts around as they run up and down the staircases of their minds.
[3] Nadler, II, p. 72.

from his immersion in the deepest dependence which man has upon God, which, unfortunately, is no longer explicitly recognized by many of the enlightened persons of his age, for Hamann is dealing first with the ordinary difficulty inherent in communication among human beings and secondly with man's communicative dependence upon God. As has been seen, Wittgenstein recognized the ordinary human problem of fully communicating difficult human experiences truthfully, so that in the *Philosophical Investigations* he was forced to compress his thought into sometimes apparently unconnected paradoxical reflections, just as Hamann sometimes sought to place all his thought into the smallest number of words, into a nutshell, a microscopic forest of symbols which meant something to him and which was expressing a truth, but which possibly meant little to most other people, to most other minds, then and later. Writing is such a delicate task, and one which is also dangerous, because the 'purpose of writing does not consist in an enumeration, weighing, and punctuation of their substitutes [he is referring here to words which are spoken] which amounts totally to a pharisaical tithing of anise, mint, and cummin in relation to the higher, true, and natural purpose which unites speech as well as writing—to some kind of tabernacle, a shekinah, and chariot-throne of our thoughts.'[4] Our thoughts which will be expressed in words reside in a kind of tabernacle, a shekinah; our thoughts are sacred. Somehow, true and natural concepts partake in that very high purpose of establishing the chariot-throne of our thoughts. The spoken word may become a written word; man must not break silence in the sense of the 'silence' in Wittgenstein's *Tractatus Logico-Philosophicus*, but he must also seek to write what he speaks, for the writing, as an extension of the speaking, participates in the conceptual structures which help to create the sacred thoughts residing in the hidden tabernacle of our person. The words are living words of God. Both Emil Brunner and Arno Borst[5] saw in the same vein as Hamann that 'God's word is very much like the human word; in fact it is as human as could be. God's word is given to man, not just an earthly form of speech, but his Word (meaning the Word Incarnate), which comes out of the mouth of God and which man takes with faith. Hamann saw the well-spring of language correctly; the first men heard the living Word of God.'[6] Hamann once said 'Reason and Scripture are one and the same basically: the language of God. My

---

[4] Nadler, II, p. 128.
[5] See Emil Brunner, *The Mediator*, translated by Olive Wyon, Philadelphia, 1947.
[6] Arno Borst, *Der Turmbau von Babel*, Stuttgart, 1957–63, Vol. III, p. 1801.

wish and my *punctum saliens* in my poor little writings is to compress this theme into a nutshell.'[7] This one experience in words, which Kierkegaard said was Hamann's life's ambition to create, this word experience welling forth from and representing the tabernacle, this chariot-throne of thought with its sacred quality, this activity of reason, is an activity of Scripture, for reason is in a sense Scripture. This is not the reason of the enlightened ones whom Hamann despised, but the reason which means the whole person for Hamann; this whole-personed reason is in a sense like Scripture. Somehow, persons are inserted into Scripture through the partial help of reason; somehow the symbols of persons are the symbols of Scripture which is a symbol of God, the language of God—God speaking through the use of language not only as spoken but also as written. God-language is a reality. A creative man like Hamann can express God; expression becomes his sacred chariot-throne of thought, his shekinah.

The poetic genius must explore hidden meanings of language in order to create new linguistic forms from them because he knows that the 'spirit of observation and the spirit of prophecy contain human genius. Everything present belongs to the sphere of the former; everything absent, both past and future, belongs to the sphere of the latter . . . the poetic genius expresses his power in as much as he transforms the visions of the ancient past and the future by means of fictions and represents them in the present.'[8] Hamann's spirit of observation and spirit of prophecy, his poetic genius, must be used to allow him materials of creativity for his message as to who is ultimately God, God-language in human form. God is found in the God-language of the past, the visions of fictions given to other men at other times, and God can be envisaged futurally in the present as man envisages new fictions which are related to but not totally like the fictions used by the geniuses of the past who met God in God-language verging upon human language. God Himself is a genius because He is a creator. There is thus 'un Génie Créateur . . . un Génie Médiateur . . . un Génie Auteur . . . '[9] Goethe explains that as the word was adopted by the Germans it 'was exposed to such misinterpretation that men thought it was necessary to expunge it completely from the German tongue . . . '[10] Hamann puzzles over the question whether 'one has genius

---

[7] Gildemeister, V, p. 246.   [8] Nadler, III, p. 383.
[9] Nadler, II, p. 294. The word Genius came to the Germans from the French and was still somewhat new at that time to the Germans in its meaning.
[10] Goethe, *Dichtung und Wahrheit*, in *Werke*, XXIX, p. 146.

or is a genius,'[11] and opts for a combination of both.[12] He could possibly have become interested in the word from an article in the Königsberg newspaper in 1754.[13]

Hamann always insists that his literary creations flow from his experience of concrete time and space. The creation and giving forth of his letters 'will always depend upon circumstance.'[14] Hamann always remains immersed in the circumstance of his concrete, everyday experiences. Precisely because he remains faithful to his own personal experiences he can even claim on one of his title pages, which are always so important in his authorship, that he will be an original.[15] He is always eager to write original creations as he remarks 'You cannot be so satisfied to be reading as my vexed eye and my finger are in allowing me to write.'[16] Hamann is faithful to his desire of having many senses interrelate in the process of his creative writing. The eye is constantly searching out new sights and his fingers are eager to take up the pen for writing.

Hamann also admires the people who are satisfied to be reading; it will become clear shortly that Hamann knows one must know how to read before one can hope to write. Writing is aided by the reading ability, but writing surpasses reading in its creativity. In Hamann's creations he exclaims 'I express myself in many tongues.'[17] He was so faithful to the concreteness of expressing experience in language that he felt the stuttering of his tongue was related to the myriad experiences of his mind and vice versa.[18] His physical characteristics themselves helped to lend him a form of strangeness in the order of creativity, but the subjects he wished to describe were also dealing with mysterious aspects of reality. He explains 'How can one write about Hierophants (for example) without hierophanting oneself?'[19] How can one indeed write about the strange mysteries of human experience without being strangely mysterious? The enlightened ones felt that Hamann was merely refusing to open his eyes in order to see the clarity which actually exists throughout reality, but the sections on Hamann's style as style, and his arguments with Kant, have demonstrated that Hamann was quite certain that the world was not as rationally clear as the

---

[11] Ziesemer-Henkel, I, p. 275.
[12] Ibid. p. 275, Ziesemer-Henkel, II, p. 80, III, p. 382, and I, pp. 103, 117, 371.
[13] Ibid., I, p. 85.
[14] Nadler, III, p. 138.
[15] Nadler, II, p. 375.
[16] Ibid., III, p. 164.
[17] Ibid., I, p. 396.
[18] Ibid., V, p. 67.
[19] Ibid., III, p. 151.

enlightened ones expected. The world presents itself as a series of mysterious experiences, some of which are hierophantic, so that if a creative person is to write of those experiences his writings must be somewhat mysterious. The writer must also be patient in waiting for the angel of genius to come. The writer must be like the patient waiting in the waters of Bethesda for the angel to come at the appropriate moment to disturb the waters, while imparting insights of genius into his creative activity as a writer.[20]

Before Hamann can write he must experience. Within this experience is the process of reading which helps a man to learn how to write. A man needs a helper, a genius, not only to write creatively but also to read creatively.[21] Hamann read other authors voraciously. He spent all of his spare money on books so that he acquired a huge library during the course of his life. He wrote once later in life that 'the appetite to eat and read is inextinguishable.'[22] He had this inextinguishable appetite for reading during his entire life because he knew that reading would give him new insights for his creating process. Hamann calls his style mimetic in a sense,[23] but, as has already become clear, he is mimetic not in the sense of slavishly copying another person's style, but rather in seeking to re-experience the other person's creative inspirations so that he may create afresh. In this respect one can understand why he always enjoyed saying that he imitates Euripides[24] and Persius.[25] He is seeking to re-experience their creative spark. He reads constantly and always puzzles 'Which is the best author?'[26]

But primarily Hamann is seized by the desire to write.[27] By writing he will partially uncover and reveal to mankind the mysteries of the world.[28] Hamann exults 'I bewitch a book into a person.'[29] He makes his books live. He captures the pulsing life of everyday experience partially within the written word. Just as he had remarked 'Out of children will come people . . . and out of readers authors will come forth',[30] so he is certain that out of the dynamic writings will flow even more desire to experience life, which itself caused the dynamic writings. He has found a circular way of living in which writing is a part. He has what he calls a 'spermatological style'[31] because he is so alive and

---

[20] Roth, II, p. 430.
[21] Ziesemer-Henkel, I, p. 103.
[22] Roth, VII, p. 430.
[23] Ziesemer-Henkel, I, p. 378, and Nadler, III, p. 188.
[24] Nadler, II, p. 178.
[25] Ibid., III, p. 237.
[26] Ibid., p. 183.
[27] Ibid., II, p. 164.
[28] Ziesemer-Henkel, II, p. 54.
[29] Nadler, II, p. 342.
[30] Ibid., p. 341.
[31] Gildemeister, V, p. 48.

dynamic. He wanted himself to be called a spermatologian[32] for the same reason—to show that his writing was utterly dynamic.

He did not want his writings to be receptacles of mesmerized gnosis. 'Since Adam's Fall all gnosis is suspicious like a forbidden fruit.'[33] He wants his readers to know 'Reader! fear you not; I am no ghost.'[34] He presents writings which are enfleshed, and which have the characteristics of pulsing life. He may be 'the voice of a preacher who is a desert to "the public" ',[35] but then he is not much concerned about reaching the 'enlightened Public'; he will reach those who are still alive to the joys of concrete creation. He can say 'I write everything that my Muse dins into me with red running eyes.'[36] He writes it because he is seized by his Muse who dins into him the mysteries of life, mysteries which cannot be slavishly imitated. He can exclaim 'Forgive me the madness of my style of writing.'[37] It is an ironical 'forgive me' and an ironical 'madness', for Hamann is blessed to be seized by the Muse of Creation. He can tell most people 'do not look upon me because I look so black, for the Genius has burnt me.'[38] He is proud to be burnt, to have been blackened in the furnace of creation. He can very happily proclaim 'What I have written, I have written.'[39] His writings are fires of creativity. 'I chose thus my role as an author, with the present postscript [A Flying Letter] about *Golgotha and Scheblimini.*'[40] He states that 'The making clear of those two hieroglyphs will together be the third and last leading question of my entire authorship.'[41] This writing of Hamann's deals with the life, death, and resurrection of the true Son of God.[42]

Hamann exclaims 'As the oldest reader of this rhapsody in Cabbalistic

---

[32] Nadler, II, p. 137.
[33] Roth, VII, p. 253.
[34] Nadler, III, p. 49.
[35] Ibid., II, p. 108. See also Nadler, III, p. 36.
[36] Ibid., II, p. 337.
[37] Ibid., p. 202.
[38] Nadler, II, p. 107.
[39] Ibid., III, p. 153.
[40] Scheblimini means 'Sit at my right side' in reference to Jesus Christ after he has been through the sufferings of Golgotha.
[41] Nadler, III, p. 347.
[42] Some persons insist that Hamann's creativity is religiously related at its heart to the Trinity rather than to the Son of God. There is indeed a hint of a form of true Trinitarianism, which could be analogous to the many-faceted power of creation. Hamann has sometimes written with the desire to demonstrate the many-faceted creative energy of the Trinity. He states 'My authorship had begun with 'To No One' or 'To the Two' and will end in the all perfect Trinity.' Hamann's views of the Trinity may not be totally and explicitly Lutheran, Catholic, or Christian but they do contain that almost Bonaventurian quality of expressing a communicative flow of artistic creation on the part of God. See Nadler *Johann Georg Hamann*, p. 410.

prose I see myself . . . the rhapsodist has read, obeyed, thought, sought, and found pleasing words . . . he has drawn sentence after sentence together, as one aims an arrow on a battle field, and has made his figures, as one measures with a compass or uses a compass to help place tent-pegs . . .—Obelisks and asterisks has he written.'[43] First he experiences reality and then he represents it faithfully in various forms and figures. He has written some obelisk-like lines which may appear bizarre or mysterious and he has written asterisk-like lines with hidden meanings. But in all this apparently strange kind of writing he is only seeking creatively to be faithful to the flow of concrete temporal experience.

Nietzsche could have been writing of Hamann when he writes: 'Those overpowering artists who let a harmony sound forth from every conflict are those who bestow upon things their own power and self-redemption! They express their innermost experience in the symbolism of every work of art they produce—their creativity is gratitude for their existence.'[44] Hamann is seeking to bestow upon things their own power and redemption. He is seeking to show human beings how they can be creatively redeemed and how they can grasp the powers inhering in themselves as creative beings. Hamann creates because he is grateful for his own existence. Ultimately he knows that his existence, including his ability to create, comes from God.

The true creator recognizes his dependence upon God, the greatest creator, and because of grasping this fact 'the author is lucky who can say: if I am weak I am strong',[45] because his real strength will come from the power of God, the Creator. Hamann knows that 'the true genius knows only his dependence and weakness . . . The likeness of his power is a negative dimension.'[46] The genius knows he is dependent upon a kind of muse for his inspiration. In fact, true genius requires so much humility and patience that it can appear at times to be a 'crown of thorns'.[47] The insight keeps the true genius from becoming a public snob.

God is the greatest creator. Hamann has the happy experience that, in a sense, 'All that is godlike is also very human . . . '[48] God seeks to communicate with us 'through creation . . . through poets . . . '[49] God therefore speaks. God is also a painter.[50] The Word of God who is the

---

[43] Nadler, II, p. 217.
[44] Nietzsche, *The Will to Power*, p. 852.
[45] Nadler, II, p. 117.
[46] Nadler, II, p. 117.
[47] Roth, III, p. 174.
[48] Ibid., p. 27.
[49] Ibid., II, p. 213.
[50] Ibid., p. 342.

Son of God is the second creation.[51] Hamann here is not referring to the creation of the Word as Word but to the fact that the Word is the second or new creation leading mankind to a new level of creative activity. When God speaks, His speech is like poetry.[52] Hamann thought poetry was the most perfect form of human speech because it represented most faithfully the creative speech of God. Explication or explanation of reality belongs to and is accomplished by God.[53] God is definitely an author besides being a speaker.[54]

Because God is an author, He loves the creative activity of human writers.[55] Hamann sees God Himself as a creative speaker, writer, and reader. After God's continual personal creation He 'created through nature and writings . . . through the ground of things and figures, through poets and prophets.'[56] The poets and prophets are extensions of the creative activity of God himself.[57] Poetry is the great means of communication, for Christ who is the Poet is not just a copy of the idea of God, nor are the words which are part of His second creation. These words are a communicational bestowing of God Himself.[58] Man helps create words which communicate God. God's word and speech always work.[59] His speech is a continual creative act.[60] Hamann can exclaim 'Each word that comes out of the mouth of God is a creation of thoughts and movements in our souls.'[61] God helps create our thoughts; our thoughts are most creative when they are creatively connected with the words of God. The earth is populated through the words of God's mouth.[62] Man must always be able to grasp that 'the Word is really near you, in your mouth and in your heart.'[63] One should never deceive with the words from one's own mouth because they should proceed from the Word.[64]

God is everywhere in His creation. God speaks about creatures through and in creatures.[65] When one man listens to another man's speech carefully he can hear God's voice.[66] When man reads Scripture he should always praise 'the great maker of these holy books'.[67] Since

---

[51] Ibid., I, p. 282.
[52] Ziesemer-Henkel, I, p. 369.
[53] Nadler, III, p. 132.
[54] Ibid., I, p. 5.
[55] Ibid., II, p. 247.
[56] Ibid., p. 213.
[57] Ziesemer-Henkel, I, p. 367, Nadler, III, pp. 171 and 385.
[58] See F. Blanke, *Die Hamann-Forschung*, Gütersloh, 1956, p. 90, and Erik Peterson, 'Das Problem der Bibelauslegung im Pietismus des 18. Jahrhunderts' in *Zeitschrift für Systematische Theologie*, I, 1923, p. 479.
[59] Nadler, I, p. 85.
[60] Ibid., II, 198.
[61] Ibid., I, p. 64.
[62] Nadler, III, p. 31.
[63] Ibid., I, p. 76.
[64] Ibid., p. 76.
[65] Ibid., III, p. 198.
[66] Ibid., p. 198.
[67] Ibid., I, p. 8.

God is such a great creator Himself, and since much of His creation comes through words, He loves the action of a writer.[68] The writer at times must write in a bizarre fashion in order to represent some of the experiences of God to human beings. Hamann claims that the height of godly wisdom consists in the ability to combine writings which appear to contradict each other, which appear bent upon 'destroying each other',[69] into a new aesthetic creation which will help re-express the myriad mysteries of God. To create something new out of already existing entities is a much greater feat than 'creating something out of nothing'.[70] This passage is obviously an attempt to discredit the scholastic thought that creating out of nothing was a great act and one of the greatest signs of God's creativity. Perhaps that is the case, but in relation to human creativity this 'nothing' was too vacuous to fit Hamann's desire for dealing with concrete things. Man must set out with the dependent power he has from God[71] and create new experiences in this world out of older experiences. He must realize he is weak and that without God he can do very little, but that with God he is strong.[72] Man's speech, which is such a great creative gift, must always be willing and grateful to accept inspiration from above.[73] Man is ultimately a partner with God in the exercise of his freedom and his creative dynamism.[74]

By exercising his freedom in communication with God's freedom man can, through his analogous experience of freedom and in the experience of creating itself, say with Hamann 'This analogy of man to creator gives all creatures their intrinsic value and their character in which trust and faith in all of nature is found.'[75] Man can continue to exclaim that 'Each counteraction of men in nature is a letter and seal of our portion of the godly nature.'[76] Thus man must also desire to be a creator 'to a new, yet presently wasted, land'.[77] He also speaks of taking what appears to be a dead language and breathing new life into it through a new arrangement of words.[78] There are always sections of reality waiting to be recreated afresh, not out of nothing, but out of the aspects now existing which make up these sections of reality, and which are crying to be made new through new arrangements of their being. These lands are waiting to rise from their abodes of present

---

[68] Ibid., II, p. 247.
[69] Ibid., I, p. 264.
[70] Nadler, I, p. 264.
[71] Ibid., II, p. 260.
[72] Ibid., p. 117.
[73] Ibid., III, pp. 27, 37, and 41.
[74] See Bernard Gajek, 'Sprache beim jungen Hamann', Phil. Diss., München, 1959, pp. 74 ff.
[75] Nadler, II, pp. 206 and 207.
[76] Ibid., p. 207.
[77] Ibid., p. 345.
[78] Ibid., p. 183.

listlessness. If man creates well, he can change these wasted lands into lands which he causes 'to be inhabited by beautiful nature'.[79] But man's creative activities must always be dependent upon 'the oracle of Themis'.[80] Man's deepest need and purpose is to create in freedom, so that man must be given the freedom to write.[81]

Through man's creative freedom he can both imitate nature and change nature. 'Man is in nature among all the animals the greatest pantomime.'[82] Rules cannot be set rigidly for these creative pantomimes and imitators because 'Genius cannot set rules.'[83] Creation for human beings always consists somehow in making something new out of already existing entities. Authors may at times appear to be like 'the cuckoo'[84] because they are apparently irrational in their creative activities but the new creation will speak for itself because 'The honorary title of a master of speech and of polyhistories is unnecessary.'[85]

Hamann of course never received great titles, so he could have been defending himself in this statement, but in a more objective sense it is true that great creations speak not only for themselves but also for their authors.[86] He was also objecting to the many people who were receiving worthless 'enlightened' titles. He is, however, on the lookout for the 'aesthetic Moses'.[87] He laments 'The birthday of a genius will, as usual, be accompanied by the martyr's feast of innocent children.'[88] It is inevitable that geniuses must suffer at the hands of those who hate them out of either jealousy or stupidity. The genius must also suffer in the creation of his works, since for a writer the birth of his book takes as much effort as does the birth of her child for a woman.[89] The creator's glory consists in the act of creating itself and also in the created object which speaks for itself and for the creator. The 'unity of the creator mirrors itself in the dialectics of his works'.[90] A true genius has myriad creative abilities. There is a paradoxical unity to his life and works consisting in their very diversity.

Hamann always remembers that his creativity is dependent upon the

---

[79] Ibid., p. 345.
[80] Ibid., p. 345.
[81] Ibid., p. 94.
[82] Ibid., IV, p. 424.
[83] Nadler, IV, p. 424.
[84] Ibid., II, p. 348.
[85] Ibid., p. 123.
[86] One can be reminded of Kierkegaard's feeling that his work, *Fear and Trembling*, would be so great that it alone would be enough to make him an immortal author.
[87] Nadler, II, p. 163.
[88] Ibid., p. 214.
[89] Nadler, II, p. 244.
[90] Ibid., II, p. 204. Hamann certainly does not use the word 'dialectics' in the same way that Hegel will use it at a later time.

Christ who is the Incarnate Word. It is Christ as Incarnate Word who makes human speech and writing healthy.[91] This remaking of both human speech and writing into a new experience of health is in a sense more important than the first creation *ex nihilo* itself.[92] As we have said, the man who will become a creative author is aided by also being a creative reader, because he must know how to read the Word, and the Muse, who stands in a way for the Word, and gives creative ideas, gives them more happily to the good readers.[93] The reader must learn how to use his eyes for reading both books and paintings.[94] The man must begin to exercise his powers of creative imagination.[95] He must learn how to recreate imaginatively what he has observed concerning the flesh and the rest of the world.[96] The man who desires to be an author must always be alive to the experiences of reality. The realities that man sees must be named with great insight.[97] There is a sense in which each man names things for himself in his own creative subjectivity. This will save a person from the danger of a nominalism that merely memorizes. The author must examine all the various aspects of nature with care.[98] Genius comes in a way from luck,[99] but the fruits of genius arise also from industry and from hard work in observing nature.[100]

Hamann is aware that no author, no matter how hard he seeks to be a dazzling genius of creativity hoping to give joy to others, can escape certain recriminations, for 'one simply cannot be an author without censure.'[101] The author as a genius must be martyred by at least part of the 'enlightened public'. He must always be ready to see his work criticized and disliked. Some of the criticisms may even be valid if the criticism flows from a person who is also a creative genius. That is the fate of every decent writer in spite of the fact that 'The author is the best commentator on his works.'[102] The real author speaks 'through blood and fire and smoky mists, in which the speech of the kingdom of heaven consists'.[103] A particular author knows, in a sense more than others, what he wishes to re-express. He it is who speaks through blood and fire and smoky mists. He may be justly censured at times, however, for Hamann sees well that many good creative authors

---

[91] Ibid., II, p. 319.
[92] Ibid., p. 309.
[93] Ibid., II, p. 348.
[94] Ibid., p. 341.
[95] Nadler, II, p. 334.
[96] Ibid., p. 99.
[97] Ibid., p. 189.
[98] Ibid., p. 192.
[99] Ibid., III, p. 190.
[100] Ibid., p. 190.
[101] Ibid., p. 133.
[102] Nadler, II, p. 203.
[103] Ibid., p. 203.

may produce good books in the beginning of their career but then become lazy. In later life, they may write many worthless books but continue to live off their good name. These authors are like hosts who give good wine at the beginning of a party but then go on to give bad wine to their guests after the guests have been mesmerized by a particular taste. In this respect, every good writer should be grateful for criticism which may awaken him from slipshod creativity.[104] How often is it not the case that a man writes one good scholarly work and then becomes a mediocre expert on every aspect of reality! Critics are to be admired if they keep authors honest.[105]

Hamann wants writers to remain ever alert in order to be faithful creators of new experiences. He tells people wanting to be good authors to be steadfast in following all their curiosities and drives; then they will not fall into a single dull style. Every man by nature has a sense of curiosity. A man must exercise his gift of curiosity in questioning about and seeking to know reality. Man must exercise all his drives in order to appreciate the key to human experience—unity in diversity. If man concentrates on one drive to the exclusion of others he will be inherently less human. The quest to be creatively human is diverse and risky but it must be sought out with dynamic tenacity because it is a communication with God.[106] In order for the creative man to be able to re-express these experiences he enjoys through the exercise of all his diverse drives and curiosities he will still need 'Delphic and sibylline speech'.[107] Even when he lives life to the fullest, man still needs the aid of the Muses, and of the all-creating God. Man truly needs the freedom to exercise all his diverse drives and curiosities, for Hamann knows that 'Freedom is the maximum and the minimum of all our creative powers of nature.'[108] Man's ultimate freedom is a paradoxical dependence upon God. The height of man's freedom is to choose freely to be dependent upon God.

Hamann was aware of the fact that man often does not freely admit his dependence upon God for instead he falls in love with himself, just as 'Narcissus loved his image more than his life.'[109] God is ultimately the heart of our lives so that man is fully alive when he is creating through a form of communication with God, but when he only loves himself and his own image man loses his true dynamic ability to live. Hamann knows that man alone without God does not understand

---

[104] Ibid., p. 187.
[106] Nadler, II, p. 172.
[108] Ibid., III, p. 38.
[105] Ibid., p. 334.
[107] Ibid., p. 172.
[109] Nadler, II, p. 209.

himself.[110] The Greeks and Romans were great human beings, but the Moderns should not idolize them totally as the enlightened ones often do.[111] The effort to imitate slavishly the classical style rather than seek new creative objects was a serious problem in Hamann's age.

In its beginning the Renaissance had admired classical beauty but it also used concrete elements of classical beauty to create beautiful new objects that were pulsatingly alive for its own age in Rome, Florence, and other cities. But the Enlightenment often merely admired or imitated past creations and sometimes did so incorrectly. The materials of nature are meant to be refashioned over and over again in order to create fresh beauty. Words making up language are to be refashioned in order to represent realities for contemporary men. Hamann knows that 'Nature and writings are thus the materials of the . . . imitating and creating spirit.'[112] Man must not become enamoured merely with his past creations; he must always seek new ones.

When man excludes God from his creative process he becomes more dependent upon his past creations and must cling to them for security, but if he freely chooses a form of dependence upon God in his creative life he will always be able to make new creations in joy. If 'the public' will not accept its dependence upon God in a radical way for the purpose of true creativity it is because it does not realize that 'Flesh and blood without Spirit is of no use'.[113] These people may think they are alive but they are really dead. They do not begin to grasp the 'magic of words'.[114] For those who are truly alive the secret of life is given: 'Our muse is an infant of the fruitful, many-breasted Mother Nature.'[115] This is one of those many passages in Hamann which can be understood as being totally irreligious, but Mother Nature is for Hamann a metaphor for transcendent dynamism, although it may not necessarily be a Christian transcendent dynamism. The power of God is never far away from the meaning of any of Hamann's words, although it is true that not all his words are strictly Christian in their expression of reality.

Hamann praises the 'priest of the Muses'.[116] The priest of the Muses is he who is able to experience the creative rush of reality and represent it. The common people of any age will benefit greatly 'through the magician of words'.[117] The priest of the Muses experiences that there

---

[110] Ibid., p. 209.
[111] Ibid., p. 209.
[112] Ibid., p. 210.
[113] Nadler, III, p. 237.
[114] Ibid., p. 158.
[115] Ibid., II, p. 96.
[116] Ibid., p. 197.

[117] Nadler, III, p. 159. It must still be admitted however that Hamann did not usually write for the 'Public'.

is 'an aesthetic-electrical magnetism'.[118] Man must speak of this aesthetic-electrical magnetism, and the source of his ability to speak of this wonder is the godly.[119] This godly speech is always mysterious. 'One must be a magician if one wants to read our beautiful spirit.'[120]

Nietzsche, as usual, asks an intriguing question about the reason for creativity on the part of any man. Is the art which a creative man gives to the world a blessing to the world or a curse? Nietzsche asks 'Is art a consequence of dissatisfaction with reality? Or is art an expression of gratitude for happiness enjoyed?'[121] Both aspects in Nietzsche's insight are valid according to one's particular subjective experience of reality.

Since Hamann gratefully admitted his dependence upon the creative dynamism of God in conjunction with a recognition of his own mortality, he created consistently in an effort to express gratitude for happiness enjoyed in time. He can joyfully exclaim 'Mythology here! Poetry is an imitation of beautiful nature. Mythology there!'[122] He sees beauty everywhere in nature. Hamann admires the view of Ceres:

> Hail, many-coloured messenger, that ne'er
> Dost disobey the wife of Jupiter;
> Who, with thy saffron wings, upon my flow'rs
> Diffusest honey drops, refreshing show'rs;
> And with each end of thy blue bow dost crown
> My bosky acres . . .
> Rich scarf to my proud earth—
>
> *The Tempest*, IV.i.76–82.[123]

The messages of the gods are everywhere. Nature is constantly in the process of creating wonder. Hamann rejoices that 'The book of creation reveals an example of all concepts . . . the books of the community reveal an example of secret articles . . . the insight of the writer mirrors itself in the dialect of his works . . . in all a tone of unmeasurable height and depth.'[124] All concepts flow from aspects of creation. The great creative men must always be ready for the 'reception and birth of new ideas and new expressions.'[125] The creative man must always be ready for 'the one syllable blitz':

> Brief as the lightning in the collied night,
> That, in a spleen, unfolds both heaven and earth,
> And ere a man hath power to say, 'Behold!'
> The jaws of darkness do devour it up . . .
>
> *A Midsummer Night's Dream*, I.i.145–8.[126]

---

[118] Ibid., p. 240.　　[119] Ibid., p. 27.　　[120] Ibid., II, p. 342.
[121] Nietzsche, *The Will to Power*, p. 843.
[122] Nadler, II, p. 205.　　[123] Ibid., p. 205.　　[124] Ibid., p. 204.
[125] Ibid., p. 209.　　[126] Ibid., p. 208.

The beauties of creation are temporal and man must be ready to seize them and enjoy them when they appear. This existing creation is a complex creation constantly on the move. Hamann sees this complexity of creation mirrored in the complexity of the reality called language. In a way, one could say that in his writings part of Hamann's specifically paradoxical purpose is to describe the God, God-language, Scripture, Reason, human language, human complexus. All relatively united in a flux of temporal experience although at the same time God remains mysteriously transcendent to the others. Hamann does not desire to be unclear just for the sake of being unclear, but the God, God-language, Scripture, Reason, human language, human complexus may cause him to be unclear at times, so that a man like Salmony with no intention to deride can say of Hamann's writings, 'No other work in the German language is so hard to understand as any one of Hamann's writings. Besides, any comparison with other texts loses the point, even the comparison which is made occasionally with mystic texts.'[127] It may be an overstatement to say that *any one* of his texts is more difficult than all other German texts, but some of them are extremely difficult. Some are also quite clear, however, and many of his letters show that he could be very simple in his writing when he so desired. It remains that when he wished to be complex he could be maddeningly complex. The comparison with mystic texts would most certainly miss the point because Hamann disliked the mystic writings of his times and sought to escape from them as much as possible. Salmony's best point is that comparison with other texts loses the point to a large extent, although one can make many comparisons with Cicero, Horace, Persius,[128] Heraclitus, Plato, and many others. The point is that Hamann is truly an original. He has attempted so succinctly, in his own mysteriously logical manner, to personalize his writings, that most comparisons with other texts are a waste of time and one does not wish to waste time, for time is the heart of the human experience of reality. One could say that at times Hamann borders on being a solipsist because he has created a type of 'private mythical-type language' which is not related to other writings in certain respects, but solipsism on Hamann's part as a total reality is indefensible for all language begins as a communal experience. Thus, in the order of connected processional time, one is always relationally bound up with a community either in the past or in the

---

[127] Alfred Hans Salmony, *Johann Georg Hamanns Metakritische Philosophie*, Zürich, 1958, p. 115.
[128] Although the poetry of Persius is not equal to the poetry of Horace, Hamann was still intrigued by some of its mystery.

future as they influence the present. Hamann must first be read as Hamann and only then, if any man can claim to have grasped his message, may he be related to other writings, even to the writings of Kierkegaard, Herder, Goethe, or Schleiermacher.[129]

Writing is an action of the ever-moving soul, as Demosthenes had observed,[130] and it mirrors the many-faceted appearances of reality. Books are twisting pulsations of reality. Both the author and the reader must be like the 'lover of passion and idiomatic expression'.[131] One must have a love affair with a great book before one can say that he has experienced its many idiomatic levels. Hamann is a great writer; he experiences the fact that he can say to his readers 'You wish much more clarity in my letters, . . . less in oscillating dithyrambs.'[132] But if a book or letter is exceptionally clear one knows that it is not really expressing the myriad mysteries of reality. All great books or letters must be filled with oscillating dithyrambs. Writing should seek to mirror speech which seeks to mirror man's lived experience. Hamann knows that 'one writes what one thinks, one writes what one speaks.'[133]

Hamann was in love with the power of language. He was intrigued by the comments of Pascal[134] on language.[135] He thought Hebraic speech with its concreteness was superb.[136] Hebraic speech is like the 'apocalyptic animal'.[137] Man must always be busy seeking to discover the various meanings of every dialect[138] because dialects are a key to the life of a particular people.

Hamann thought Aristotle was guilty of an excessive categorization of human speech so he makes fun of Aristotle's speech.[139] He wonders how it is that man seeks to be the discoverer of the ultimate source of speech 'while no animal can discover speech and no god dares to discover [the source] of speech.'[140] Hamann's reference to 'god' is perhaps metaphorical. The true God is the source of mysterious speech and if

---

[129] Schleiermacher himself does not seem to give Hamann much credit. Dilthey, however, in his classic life of Schleiermacher, does give Hamann credit for having influenced Schleiermacher. In fact, Hamann's *Socratic Memoirs* is quite similar to Schleiermacher's book, *On Religion: Speeches to the Cultured Despisers.*

[130] Nadler, II, p. 247. [131] Ibid., p. 150.
[132] Ibid., III, p. 141. [133] Ibid., p. 237.
[134] Pascal used his genius in the order of language to be a Christian apologist to the cultured of France. He combined the heart and the mind in a way quite similar to Hamann with the exception of his bent in the direction of mathematics. See Blaise Pascal, *Pensées*, ed. by L. Lafuma, Paris, 1951, and M. L. Hubert, *Pascal's Unfinished Apology: A Study of His Plan*, New Haven, Connecticut, 1952.

[135] Nadler, II, p. 183. [136] Nadler, II, p. 179.
[137] Ibid., II, pp. 181 and 182. [138] Ibid., p. 181.
[139] Ibid., III, p. 37. [140] Ibid., p. 43.

He has mystery at His heart He does not seek to know in a human sense the source of speech. Aristotle was a fool to think he could become a knower of the total meaning of speech. Hamann grasped the myriad problems involved in an epistemological effort to grasp its meaning.

The process of speaking is an essentially dynamic ever-changing phenomenon, for 'the speech appears to have an influence upon the opinions and meanings and the meanings appear to have an influence upon the speech.'[141] There is a constant interweaving of various experiences in speech. Every form of speech has its own peculiar taste.[142] When a person speaks, other people see him to a certain extent according to the way in which he speaks. If he speaks lazily, people will see his physical body in more of a lazy slump, whereas if he speaks energetically his body will appear to be more dynamically structured regardless of whether apparently lazy speech in actuality denotes a lazy body or energetic speech a dynamic body.[143] If a person seeks to speak too correctly he will find that his speech does not convey his experiences correctly.[144] Hamann rejoices in 'all the ambiguities of my word game',[145] because he knows that the degree of ambiguity in speech is a sign of its richness of truthfulness in re-expressing the ambiguity of human concrete, temporal experience. Indeed, the writer Hamann was witty[146] as he sought subtly to reveal the many layers of reality.

Hamann always admired the English poet, Young, and he copies Young in one of his works when Young states 'Speech, thought's canal! Speech, thought's criterion too!'[147] Hamann states 'The base of all human knowledge comes from the exchange of words.'[148] Thus Hamann, or any man who will live life fully, must learn to speak and to write and through God as he is communicating. Reading will also help him to write more effectively. The interchanges between the three will allow him to become a creator. If he is truly creative, other persons will grasp him as a creative person in his books, provided the other persons also have that surge of creativity within them.[149] The basic reason for Hamann's wish to be grasped as creative in his books is that his creativity is a sign of his communication with God and, as has been explained, his experience of God-language is the key to his effort to create for the sake of his readers so that they will experience God through the commingling of God-language and human language. Hamann

---

[145] Ibid., p. 147.
[147] Ibid., II, p. 129.
[149] Ibid., p. 94.
[146] Ibid., III, 253.
[148] Nadler, II, pp. 129 and 125.

will always iterate his basic view of reality by saying 'without abandoning oneself to principles which in part rest upon prejudices of our age, nor scorning the same, because they belong to the elements of our present age and to our connection with it, still the surest and most unshakable ground of all peace is to be satisfied with the pure milk of the Bible in child-like simplicity, to fix upon the light that is given by God, not by man, which shines for us in a dark place until the day breaks in and the Morning Star appears, to cast all our cares upon Him from whom we have the promise that He will care for the destiny of us and ours; to abandon ourselves to the only Mediator and Advocate who speaks better things than that of the first saint and martyr, Abel, and has redeemed us from the idle ways of our fathers. Herein consists the Alpha and Omega of my entire philosophy. More I know not and do not wish to know.'[150] This passage could be considered to be part of Hamann's last will and testament, a general statement of why he lived the way he lived through most of his life and especially in the period of his greatest creative productions. And yet his views of what the Bible was, what Christ was, what God was, what religion was, were not exceptionally orthodox. He was a creative man in his religious experience. The heart of creation is a speaking of God from God, a saying of 'let there be!', and creation is also a note a musical sound of infinite height and depth. Creation is both a musical sound and a speaking forth and both precede a written something, for music and speech make up the acting forces of the written word. This 'let there be!', this note of creation, always has compelling force and is for ever a proof of God's glorious majesty, for His majesty is speaking and sounding the note. In Hamann's eyes all divine activities in creation find as their goal God's honour and glory, for God is the acting force in creating.

The key to the fact that Hamann can create with God, although language and speech were cursed in the Fall and participate in the sin of rebellion against God, is the Incarnation of Jesus Christ and the power of the Holy Spirit in this world. The Son of God, Jesus Christ, truly became flesh and blood in a form of communication and causes human flesh and blood through communication to be able to create outside the curse of the death which came from the Fall. This creative action first proceeds from God. God speaks through His Son in the Spirit to man, day and night.[151] Christ's Incarnation brought us a

---

[150] Walter Lowrie, *Johann Georg Hamann: An Existentialist*, Princeton, New Jersey, 1950, p. 20.
[151] Nadler, I. p. 295.

new life.[152] We rose from the living death we were living in this world through the power of Jesus Christ. Hamann rejoices over 'The Word, that is so near us'.[153]

It is through His presence that man is able to see the mysteries of the world more clearly, yet without their becoming exceptionally unmysterious, so that particular men can represent these mysteries for themselves and also, in a way, experience them in conjunction with their more hidden faith experience, which always precedes and is the ground of their religious symbolic experience.[154] Man can then begin to see that 'He created us after His image.—Because we indeed lost this, He took up our own image—flesh and blood.'[155] This taking up of our image, flesh and blood, does not appear to be the same thing as our creation in the image of God in the first days. The fact that Christ takes on our flesh and blood image implies that His second act of creating is more glorious for us than the first creative act. Christ is one of us! Flesh and blood! 'God came Himself as a man into the world.'[156] Hamann rejoices that He also 'left heaven ... and came into our hearts'[157] through the power of the Holy Spirit. This new revelation in the flesh which is evident especially in the Son in relation to the notion of flesh is the middle point for all human reality. This is the substance of all godly works.[158] God not only created heaven and earth for us, but He came into the world to be with us in flesh and blood.[159] The creativity of this act consists in His self-communication. Hamann exclaims over this creative communication ... You come to me? Oh! God and His son are so gracious that They come to us.'[160]

Through the Incarnation of Christ, man's self rises into a new unity through a new birth.[161] Christ raises man from sin into a new communicative relationship with God.[162] There is no absolute resurrection,[163] for resurrection goes on in this world keeping man alive in a new way, so that he is in this life and yet communicating with God in a new way. Although man is risen in this life from a living death he does remain in various ways 'a sinner'.[164] This is simply a feature of human nature. Perhaps man can never rise to a complete union with God in the

---

[152] Roth, VI, p. 170, and Nadler, I, pp. 128 and 296.
[153] Nadler, I, p. 295. [154] Ibid., p. 266.
[155] Ziesemer-Henkel, I, p. 393. [156] Nadler, I, p. 226.
[157] Ibid., p. 64, III, p. 227, IV, p. 282, and Ziesemer-Henkel, I, p. 385.
[158] Nadler, I, p. 242. [159] Ibid., p. 244.
[160] Ibid., pp. 195, 25, 196, 202, 259, and 255.
[161] Ibid., pp. 132, 150, and 242.
[162] Ibid., II, pp. 11 and 68; III, pp. 149, 304, and 318; Ziesemer-Henkel, II, p. 157.
[163] Gildemeister, V, p. 514. [164] Nadler, IV, p. 282.

sense of being totally free from sin, but he can rise to great heights of communication with God. Hamann is satisfied with a form of resurrection in this life which allows an effective communication with God.

Man is created to speak with God in a new fashion in this world, but 'Man speaks with God only *in* God'.[165] Hamann is attempting to be aware of the fact that the grace of the communication comes from God first. True creativity always comes from God whereas human philosophy, which is part of the glory of the Enlightenment, only appears to be creative. Newton's philosophy of science is mere 'farcical comedy'.[166] Bayle[167] thought he had named everything. People run up and down the staircases of their minds thinking they have conceptualized the heart of reality when in fact they have barely scratched the surface of reality. Hamann says to the people of his age 'our philosophers speak like alchemists . . . the confusion of our speech.'[168] These philosophers may think they are true scientists, but they are merely alchemists. These philosophers act as if they are true thinkers, but they are only rationalists. They think they have rationalized everything into an order, but this order as rationalized only serves to confuse the correct search for truth which is at its heart a partial mystery.

These philosophical 'dogma makers are the biggest stainers of the wonderful works of God.'[169] These people think that they know everything perfectly but they ultimately stain the works of God, one of which is the path towards truth which must accept partial mystery. Because the self is partially mysterious, abstractionist philosophers are actually killing part of their own self-humanity, but they do not begin to know they are self-murderers.[170] The glimmerings of real humanity in them must cry out for dynamic living, but these philosophers always succeed in repressing the life-blood rising up in their own veins through the call of belief. Perhaps others such as Hamann and Herder seek to bring them to the living truth, but people like them are alien to these philosophers, for most critical philosophers understand 'he, she . . . [Only through the] I!'[171] These philosophers become the centre of their own world of truth and neither the personality of God nor another human person can shake them from their own personal, rationalistic viewpoint which is so uncreative.

[165] Nadler, III, p. 224, and I, p. 309.
[166] Ibid., II, p. 367.
[167] Ibid., p. 162. Bayle should not be criticized too harshly on the ground that he sought to qualify various views concerning reality, but he tended to limit those views of reality according to his ability to define them.
[168] Ibid., III, p. 31.   [169] Ibid., I, p. 22.
[170] Nadler, II, p. 97.   [171] Ibid., III, p. 179.

The philosophy of Hamann's time had succeeded in making a 'new Babel'.[172] Enlightened philosophers actually succeed in causing confusion. They use the principle of contradiction in excess[173] because they claim that they wish to be clear, but too constant use of the principle of contradiction ultimately causes confusion about the real truth towards which mankind strives. This incorrect use of mind should be seen as an evil.[174] Without the spirit of God 'the apogee of our genius is a triumph of pagan blasphemy.'[175] Hamann is called pagan at times because he uses figures which contradict theological Christian figures or the religiously disguised figures of secularists like Moses Mendelssohn. But he uses pagan figures precisely in order to escape false theological and religious ones, in the hope that the contradictory figures will arouse new interest in the theological ones and that in a paradoxical way they might lead men towards true religious experience.

The great philosophical religious writers of Hamann's day, such as Starck[176] and Moses Mendelssohn, may have big names, but even though the writer of a popular book may have a great following the book can still be filled with nonsensical philosophical ideas.[177] These ideas may be nonsensical precisely because they claim demonstrative certainty, because they claim to know the process of thinking too well, for as Nietzsche 'a critique [full and entire] of knowledge is senseless: how should a tool be able to criticize itself when it can use only itself for the critique! It cannot even define itself.'[178] Hamann thinks the human mind must communicate with God before it can understand itself too well. Any person who claims to have a good author-system concerning knowledge without the help of God has created a system which is 'like a ballet of limping hypotheses'.[179] This ballet thinks of itself as great, and an enlightened audience may think it the greatest ballet in the world, but for the person who can really see correctly, although in a partially mysterious fashion, it is a disaster, a cruel farce.

Hamann even writes to his friend Kant concerning the *Critique of Pure Reason* that it is not a communication with God but rather an attempt to present a human mind which can communicate *sui generis* with realities in this world. He says to Kant, 'In the end it all appears to me to abound with pedantries, empty word games.'[180] Kant has not really seen that the fate of even the word 'philosophy' itself is in 'times, heads, intercourse, and people'.[181] Ultimately, all philosophical

[172] Ibid., p. 183.
[173] Ibid., p. 296.
[174] Ibid., II, p. 155.
[175] Nadler, II, p. 154.
[176] Starck's influence waned after his death.
[177] Nadler, II, p. 188.
[178] Nietzsche, *The Will to Power*, p. 486.
[179] Nadler, II, p. 189.
[180] Ziesemer-Henkel, IV, p. 285.
[181] Nadler, II, p. 63.

learning must flow from God's speech.[182] All man's creativity must first flow from the amazing dynamism of the God who is with us in His Son and in His Holy Spirit, all three of whom breathe and live with us in everyday temporal experience, making our living deaths into new lives of unbelievably dynamic experience, welling forth into constant new insights and creations for those who have the patience and the energy to create new things out of existing things in and with God.

Hamann is in love with words, their combinations and ever-changing meanings. Words are alive, flowing, creatively acting as they emanate from man. Before they are written they are spoken, and speech is therefore one of man's most creative expressions. Hamann holds that 'in the symbol of speech is the life of the soul revealed.'[183]

M. Knutzen,[184] who taught both Hamann and Kant in their university days, lectured on the fact that speech was an analogy of the creative power of God.[185] The symbol is a revealing process as man reveals his inmost active component which is sometimes called his soul. Hamann's view of what it means to be human is one in which man's soul is always linked with and interpenetrated by his body.[186]

The symbol of speech, which is partially and actively of the body, through the use of the tongue and mouth, reveals man's inner being, and also reveals man's body in a new way for those who can hear and see well. It is for this reason that Hamann's saying, 'Speak that I may see thee!' has such importance in his writings. Various peoples speak so as to manifest themselves in different ways, for each people participates 'in dramatic symbolic images'.[187] If the speaker speaks well, the hearer will perceive the speaker's flesh and soul in an exciting way. Without speech, man's perception of another man's body would differ; it could not reveal itself as well as it can through the act of speaking.

When man speaks, the symbol goes from one mouth to another.[188] The symbol, conceptualized as power and energy, is partially constituted by the mouth for its proper action in the process of speaking. The symbol not only means something in the process of speaking but it is something: it is an active force. E. Burger began to see this point in his book, *J. G. Hamann: Schöpfung and Erlösung im Irrationalismus*,

---

[182] Ziesemer-Henkel, I, 437.   [183] Nadler, I, p. 112.

[184] It is unfortunate that not much is known about M. Knutzen. He must, however, have been an excellent professor since he had a rather formidable effect on both Hamann and Kant.

[185] K. Gründer, *Figur und Geschichte*, Freiberg, 1958, p. 58. See also Roth, II, pp. 156 and 265, III, pp. 62 and 69, and VIII, p. 128.

[186] See Chapters II and III.   [187] Nadler, III, p. 222.

[188] Schmitz-Kallenberg, pp. 14–42.

Communication With God And With His Fellow Human Beings 163

Göttingen, 1929. The symbol of speech, the act of speaking, certainly means something in the rational order, but it is more than it means. Burger grasps how symbolizing exceeds rationality, but he does not grasp the existential character of the symbolizing act as act, just as Whitehead does not grasp the act as creative act when he states that 'The symbols [in reality] do not create their meaning, the meaning is the form of actual effective beings reacting upon us . . . the symbols discover this meaning for us.'[189] The symbols not only discover the meaning, they are actively part of the meaning, which is not a static form for it creates anew.[190]

The symbol is not only more than what can be rationalized about it through and in a series of concepts, in the sense that, if new concepts were found, the symbol could be grasped conceptually. The symbol of speaking is first and foremost a creative force which always partially transcends rationality. This creative force moves from mouth to mouth among human beings and also affects other human senses such as hearing and sight. For those who are blind, a man's speech of a man could be investigated by the touch of the blind man's hand. Even the smell of the speaking man's speech would tell something about him to other people. All these human senses are linked together by various symbolic forces which make up what is termed the body/soul complexus of man.

When man changes his activity from symbolical speech to writing, he has 'symbolical . . . handwriting'.[191] Handwriting, which must express words first spoken, is an extension of the acting force of symbolic speech. In so far as the handwriting is symbolical, it will be forceful, like a two-edged sword, and alive.

Hamann can say that 'Human life appears to consist of a series of symbolical acts by which our souls are able to reveal their invisible natures . . . communicating a perceptible knowledge of their power as existing.'[192] All levels of human life, speaking, writing, eating, drinking, even sleeping, are a series of symbolical acts which reveal man's hidden mysteries to himself and to others. The very heart of man, his apparently invisible soul, communicates a perceptible knowledge to the man himself and to others that he has a deep power of existing, of life, of action. When man grasps that he himself possesses this centre of action, of life, he becomes more consciously aware of his great power, of his

---

[189] A. N. Whitehead, *Symbolism: Its Meaning and Effect*, Cambridge, 1928, pp. 56-7.
[190] Gildemeister, V, p. 612.   [191] Nadler, III, p. 240.
[192] Ibid., II, p. 139.

place in the process of creation. The acts of symbolic life make man's inmost secrets communicatively perceptible.

Hamann knows that most people usually perceive the acts of this world as natural, in the sense of just being there, and as mechanical, in the sense that many persons accepted Cartesianism and its explanations of the determinism of motion according to various laws of nature, which meant that the various mechanical actions were actions consisting in various combinations of material entities. He also knew that, hidden behind these more apparent mechanical, natural, material acts there was a series of symbolical acts which were not merely mechanical, material, or natural in the sense that 'natural' denoted subject to observable laws guided by rational intelligence. Hamann knew that 'Every act, over and above its original and natural, mechanical, and material relation is also capable of many kinds of symbolical, figurative, metaphorical, and typological significations which can be 'investigated and fingered' as little as the intentions and convictions which are behind our acts; however, neither moral nor intellectual impressions can be communicated or transmitted without sensuous expression.'[193] He first mentions that acts can be symbolical. He then continues that they can be figurative, metaphorical, and typological in their significations. As will be seen shortly, Hamann places more stress on the signifying power of symbols than he does on the signifying power of metaphor or typology. He has already spoken of the symbolical acts by which the activity of the inner soul is made visible perceptibly. In this particular quotation, he is limiting the power of the symbol to an act of signifying. This particular view of the power of the symbol is less important than his view that the symbol itself, in its own acting, is a reality over and above its power to signify something. The symbol as acting is the power of human life itself. These various levels of signifying power, however, can be investigated in a reasonable way. They can even be fingered in a sense. In using the word 'fingered' Hamann probably meant both metaphorical fingering of metaphorical signifiers and, in a very vague sense, some form of more physical fingering because, although he says they can be investigated and fingered only superficially, they can be investigated and fingered in so far as intentions and convictions which underly our signifying acts are themselves symbolical acts, because human life at its heart is a series of symbolical acts. In this passage, Hamann is not saying that intentions and convictions cannot be investigated or fingered in an absolute sense; he is stating that they can

[193] Nadler, III, p. 367.

be investigated partially. He knows that reason has its place in investigating and fingering signifiers and intentions and convictions, but the powers of reason are superficial in comparison with the mysteries of the signifiers, intentions, and convictions themselves. He always insists that neither moral nor intellectual impressions can be communicated or transmitted without some kind of sensuous expression and sensuous expressions can be partially investigated and fingered.

God communicates Himself to man through a revealing of Himself which is partially rooted in history, partially rooted in sensuous expressions. Hamann holds that 'He [God] may reveal Himself to the faithful through these signs! . . . all world history is to be thought of as a map . . . '[194] This map not only 'may' reveal God Himself to us in a partial manner, but it *does* as historical fact reveal God Himself to us in a partial manner. We partially grasp God Himself through a form of sensuous expression. God's self may not be sensuous; the heart of his symbolic act may be non-sensuous, but as His symbolic act signifies Himself, He allows it through humble condescension to become partially sensuous. This is the paradoxical expression of God's mysterious condescension which has been seen in the section concerning God's creative historical acting. This is the 'coincidence of opposites'. How can one explain it in a completely rational verifiable manner? This is impossible. But man *experiences* that it happens; he can also know that his experience is not strictly subjective or solipsist because he can verify this communication as a partially sensuous expression. The communication can be partially investigated and fingered. The remainder rests on faith.

There are many who read the map of history and do not perceive the faint contours of God's communication. They may call themselves good map readers and they probably are, but in missing the little hints of God's communication they are not good map readers in the final sense. Hamann lamented that those who do not see the faint contours of God's communication in history and who yet claim to be absolute knowers of reality are the excessively rational enlightened ones. Reason in itself is good, but reasoning in excess becomes partially destructive to man.

Hamann does not link all the active power of a symbol with God. He knows that evil and good exist and that both have power. He can state that the word 'symbol', which symbolizes in itself the act of symbolizing, is, in a way, a pagan word, in the sense that the word

---

[194] Nadler, I, p. 177.

'pagan' is set against that which is Christian.[195] In stating that the word 'symbol' is in a sense pagan he is not clearly saying that it is evil with regard to its partial aspect of being pagan, but it could be viewed as becoming evil in so far as it is pagan from the viewpoint of those who call themselves Christian. As has been seen, Hamann himself has a combination of Christian, Judaic, and so-called pagan tendencies.[196]

In contrast to the possible evil symbol, there is a symbolical circle in history which shows forth God's good works in history. Hamann states that the 'hieroglyphic [hieroglyph or divine symbol] Adam is the history of the whole race in the symbolical circle . . . '[197] The divine symbol, who is Adam, is first and foremost also Jesus Christ for Hamann; this runs through his *Biblical Meditations*. In Hamann's other writings it is not safe to say 'In it, the Bible, Hamann has concentrated his entire creative interpretational power, and has built around it his baroque edifice from polymathy, allegory and symbol—he can hardly write a sentence without citing the Old and New Testaments . . . '[198] The divine symbol also includes the Adam who represents the human race in history. The history of the human race makes up the symbolical circle which has the first Adam as the Alpha and the Second Adam, Christ, as the Omega and rounded end. Christ acts now; in a sense, the end or rounded circle is now whenever and wherever Jesus Christ is acting. Jesus Christ acts in Johann Georg Hamann now. The taking on of flesh by the Son of God was the most special event of world history; it was greater than God's act of creating in the beginning. The Incarnation was however envisaged from the beginning. Hamann can claim that 'Every phenomenon of nature was a word—the sign, symbol, and promise of a new, secret (and at that time) unrepresentable union which was all the more wonderful . . . '[199] Every action of or showing forth of nature was a word, a directed action.[200] The actions of nature were signs, symbols, promises in a way, of the incarnational union between God and man which would take place in Jesus Christ. This union could not be represented in the original concrete order of this world because the

---

[195] Nadler, *Hierophantic Letters*, III, p. 146.
[196] E. C. Salzer insists too much that Hamann's view concerning the manner in which God communicates with man in this world is typical of the 'paganismo nordico' of his age. See E. C. Salzer, 'Il problema dello Hamann dei tempi' in *Rivista di Filosofia Neo-Scholastica*, Milano, 1940, p. 217.
[197] Nadler, II, p. 200.
[198] Richard Benz, *Die Zeit der deutschen Klassik: Kultur des Achtzehnten Jahrhunderts, 1750-1800*, Stuttgart, 1953, p. 197.
[199] Nadler, III, p. 32.
[200] Nature here for Hamann represents his desire to give God (or the transcendent) and the actions of created things their just due.

union had to take place in and of itself as its own active representing of self. The Incarnation, in its very action, was a representing symbol, which presented itself to itself at its heart and only then had the power to show forth, to represent, to express to the rest of reality outside itself its almost inexpressible union. The beginning times signified, symbolized in a weak manner, God's relationship with creation, with mankind, but the Incarnation not only signified and symbolized representationally to the rest of reality God's relationship with creation and with mankind in a powerful fashion—the Incarnation *was* the symbolizing act of union as act.

Hamann's interior life is a representation then of nature, of God, and of itself.[201] Although he usually disagreed with the medieval scholastics, he would probably have agreed with Thomas Aquinas when he says that a symbol can be very much like the thing symbolized.[202] As an image of God, Hamann can imagine God who really is living in him. As a man in communicating with God Hamann can be an image and a ground image, a *Bild* and an *Urbild*, at the same time. Hamann is a symbolizing creature in his every activity. In himself he shows forth the mystery of God's relationship with creation and with mankind, for Hamann's symbolizing action is similar to the symbolizing action of nature, which is similar to the symbolizing action of the Incarnate God, Jesus Christ. His in turn is similar to the symbolizing action of the transcendent/immanent God.

The symbol is power; the symbol is at its heart action. Through their power the symbols of nature have the ability to teach man.[203] Men teach each other through their symbolizing actions. Symbols teach by their power of showing similarities where one might only see contradictions. These are analogical symbols. Analogy will still allow originality for, although things may be 'like' one another, they can still discourage superficial 'imitation' of each other.[204] Symbolizing actions help reveal the 'coincidence of opposites', the similarities between various objects. Symbolizing actions can be mimetic. Hamann can say of one of his works 'the entire work is mimetic'.[205] He does not mean superficially imitative; he means that the symbolizing act can truly imitate various objects and cause them to be represented in a deep way.

[201] Schmitz-Kallenberg, p. 92.
[202] See G. Sievert, *Die Sinne und das Wort*, Düsseldorf, 1956, and *Wort und Bild*, Düsseldorf, 1952, p. 9.
[203] Nadler, I, p. 174.
[204] Ziesemer-Henkel, II, p. 203.
[205] Nadler, II, p. 61. See also Rene Wellek, *A History of Modern Criticism: 1750-1950*, New Haven, Connecticut, 1955, p. 4.

As we saw in our examination of Hamann's style, one object can become almost exactly like another through the mimetic power of the symbolizing act. In contrast, Jesus Christ truly became like a man, although He was also God through the symbolizing power of complete mimesis. He did not become a copy of another man, a mere representation, but He represented within Himself His own representation as a special, singular, individual man. He remained true God but He became also a truly action-orientated man. No man has the power to become totally another man, but God could and does have the power to become totally man in the sense of being, acting, symbolizing with that degree of energy which gives an object the stamp of manhood. Man exhausts most of his energy and symbolic power keeping himself going as an active force. It is still, however, marvellous to see how deeply man can be mimetic. The marvel consists in the great complexities existing within one man, within one self, the many powers within the heart of one human being. Hamann marvels even as to how the *I* can become the symbol for 'Godhead'.[206] Man can fall down and worship his self because it has so much symbolical power. Man can most certainly fall down and worship other men because of their symbolical powers. But if man will be true to his self he will love his self and his power in relation to the power of God. If man will be true to his self he will seek to know his self as did Socrates, the great light in Hamann's life. If man will be true to his self he will grasp the symbolic relationships between his self and the selves of other men. He will imitate active powers of other selves in communication with his own powers, but his imitation will be such that he integrates the powers of the other selves into his own individuality. Thus he himself is not lost as a self or engulfed by the other. A man must be symbolically open to society, to other selves, and open also to himself. Both community and individuality are helpful and good for man. The *I* must not become the Godhead for man, but neither must a particular *I* be swallowed up by the Godhead of the community or the Godhead Himself. The various symbolizing powers must seek to live harmoniously.

Hamann thus exhibits particular views concerning the existence and power of symbols. He is not excessively systematic in his presentation of this central issue of his view of reality; one must always recall that he was intent upon drawing all his views on life from life, in a creative fashion, and just as he considered life in a sense to be like a nutshell at its heart, so he seeks to express his views about life in a

---

[206] Nadler, III, p. 234.

nutshell.[207] It is possible, however, to distinguish in a theological perspective the meaning of symbol for Hamann and its relationship to myth in spite of the fact that he claimed he was no theologian,[208] for, although he may have felt that he was no theologian, he *was* in an objective sense, and therefore, from the viewpoint of others, he was theologizing. In so far as he could never reduce his views of life to life itself, which is just as impossible as reducing life itself to views about life, he was theologizing.

It has been pointed out that symbolizing involves the whole of reality; indeed, it is the heart of reality.[209] Since man is part of reality, man himself is a symbolizing reality.[210] Man represents his more hidden nature to others in a form of symbolic communication. The communication really presents to the perciever a deep representation of the interiority of a particular man. In Hamann's eyes, one of the best ways for particular men to learn how to represent their interiority is through an exhaustive study of Holy Scripture because, from a theological vantage point, the heart of symbolic activity in this world is ultimately Holy Scripture which is an expression of God in this world.[211]

The symbolic act is the heart of representation. Metaphors, figurative language, and myth come forth from the deeper powers of symbolizing reality. Hamann says less about myth, *per se*, than symbol, because myth is dependent upon the power of symbol to give it its own power. Myth is primarily subordinate to symbol because of Hamann's view of time,[212] although Hamann does admire the power of myth as a kind of symbol for the marvel that there are 'a thousand mythological names . . . '[213] In dealing with symbol and myth as related to religion and therefore related to theologizing, Hamann recognizes that there is a 'mythical vein' in religion, but this is located within the vaster power of symbol.[214] He is much more interested in typology as a form of myth than he is in myth itself.[215] He revels in the effort 'to entertain the trade and mystery of typographers'[216] who are related to typology.

Hamann is primarily interested in the symbolic power as that power which allows man at a particular point in time to communicate his interiority. Typology operates in the direction of linking past power

---

[207] Ziesemer-Henkel, II, p. 245 and *Aesthetica in Nuce*.
[209] Ibid., III, p. 242.
[211] Ibid., pp. 171 and 204, and Nadler, I, p. 298.
[213] Nadler, III, p. 224.
[215] Ibid., I, pp. 38 and 123–4.
[208] Nadler, II, p. 115.
[210] Ibid., II, p. 139.
[212] See Chapter IV.
[214] Ibid., pp. 191–2.
[216] Ibid., III, p. 155.

with present power. The myths in a basic sense deal more fully with a 'mythical past' which is still affecting us primarily only because there was a glorious past. The past is always a very important part of time in any myth and the people living in a mythological time must be turned towards the past in their present activity. Hamann is not so interested in the past as past. He is more interested in the present as present and how the past might serve to help the present be more creative. He is very much like the Old Testament in this respect, because the Old Testament use of myth is directed very heavily towards the present.[217] The Hebrew invariably expressed the past only in so far as it would affect the future in a present as present.[218] Hamann had studied Hebrew with great depth and thus of course did not use a solid definition of time. Hebrew does have a notion for a period of time.[219] This period of time quite often expressed something concerning the present, with a today, which is a notion found often in the Old Testament. The Hebrew people were always amazed that God worked in the present in many different ways.[220] Hamann drew heavily from these basically non-mythological but still symbolical views of time with a great sense of gratitude to the Jewish mentality and style of living.[221]

Hamann sees time as symbolically 'present' for God is an activity; 'for God there is no time . . . for everything is present. Yesterday is today and today is today and tomorrow is today.'[222] Time for God becomes the active present, the active heart of the symbolic process, whereas for human beings the active heart of the symbolic process must take time in order for man to become conscious of it himself, and especially for one man to make one of his more hidden symbolic activities visible in a conscious sense to another man or to other men. The representing of the interior symbolic act always takes time. God does it at once because of his great creative power. This 'presentness' of God is in a sense eternity, and God as living active symbolical reality is eternity.

Eternity can be a God who is the simultaneously full and perfect possession of interminable life. Man can only conceive eternity in a time extension, but man can experience eternity, the communication of God in a moment which, although it still has extension, borders on being like eternity itself, and within the process of the 'coincidence

[217] B. S. Childs, *Myth and Reality in the Old Testament*, London, 1968, pp. 76-87.
[218] B. S. Childs, *Myth and Reality in the Old Testament*, p. 77.
[219] Ibid., p. 78.   [220] Ibid., p. 269.
[221] Nadler, III, pp. 309, 306, and 355.   [222] Ibid., I, p. 94.

of opposites' man somehow does really communicate with God, with the eternal, within the symbolic active moment. Hamann seeks consciously, then, to immerse himself in the present, the now, today. The moment, the now, the present, the today become eternity for man in a sense. Hamann can thus exclaim 'As this eternity of days which have been and are yet to be in the world is next to nothing but a today for You [God], so the present day is an eternity for me, my Lord.'[223] On one level of symbolic activity, this today is a representation of eternity for Hamann, but on another level, the eternal communicates directly in symbolic acts with Hamann just as Hamann can experience things in this world through directly experienced symbolic activity and also represent those experiences conceptually, which is less strong than the experience itself. But the symbolic representation is still very exciting and is much better than nothing, a nothing which is the great enemy of symbolic activity. Both God and man can act symbolically now.

Hamann glories in the fact that all reality is a symbol at its heart.[224] By living symbolically now one can, through faith in the Scriptures and nature, enjoy more fully this eternal now or today which is an expression and communication of God Himself. Man will exhaust the limits of the hidden present in the search to discover the meaning of all God's symbols in this world. Hamann, as we saw earlier, exhausts himself in the search for symbolic awareness and creativity because he communicates with God through these processes. He can state as a central notion in this life that 'the spirit of observation and the spirit of prophecy are the holders of the human genius. Everything present belongs to the sphere of the former; everything absent, both past and future, belongs to the sphere of the latter . . . the poetic genius expresses his power inasmuch as he transforms the visions of an ancient past and future by means of imaginings and represents them in the present.'[225]

Man must symbolically seek to bring the past and the future into the present, for it is in the present moment that man attains his eternity, his eternity of communication with God. Writing symbolic language is at the centre of life because 'Next to the riches of God in nature, and arising somehow out of nothing, there is simply no greater creation than that of making concepts and perceptions which are capable of representing heavenly and divine mysteries.'[226] When Hamann speaks of

---

[223] Nadler, I, p. 72.
[224] Ibid., III, p. 242.
[225] Nadler, III, p. 242.
[226] Ibid., I, p. 190.

this form of creativity as somehow arising out of nothing he does not mean *creatio ex nihilo*, because he was not very impressed by that notion. He means that one cannot really trace how and why a particular creative piece is finally created as it comes into existence. Sections of it would appear to come from nowhere. Hamann was always more impressed with the fact that God could transform existing materiality into something new creatively. He was more impressed that God could become man incarnationally than that God could create *ex nihilo*.

Man is seized by the creative Muse, and when the creation is perfected he would almost have to say 'I do not know where all of it came from'. But for man, this creative process is his greatest achievement. God reveals Himself with all of His riches to man in nature. The next most amazing thing in the world is the process of creation. Hamann seeks to make word creations that are 'living, energetic, double-edged, penetrating, narrow, piercing, and critical.'[227] These extraordinary, original, symbolic creations help man at a particular point in time to experience a moment of communication with God.

The best place for Hamann to learn how to be creative with words is the Bible. Scripture is the touchstone for creating religious symbols which are the touchstone for theologizing. He knew that 'without abandoning one's self to notions which in part rest in the prejudices of our age, nor scorning the same, because they belong to the elements of the present age as well as being related to our linking with it, still the best and strongest ground of all peace is to be satisfied with the pure milk of the Bible in childlike simplicity, to fix upon the light given to God, not the light given by man.'[228]

Hamann knew that he might like the Bible because the Lutherans and pietists of his age liked it. He also knew that his perceptions of the Bible were conditioned by the views of the Enlightenment which could appear to be contradictory to those of the Lutheran religion. He was a son both of the Lutheran religion and of the Enlightenment. He was irrevocably linked historically to his own point in time. He grasped that he could not, as a scholar, escape from the conditions of his age into an ivory tower of knowing the languages of other countries and other times, reading books from those ages, totally cut off from and unrelated

---

[227] Nadler, II, p. 263.
[228] Walter Lowrie, *Johann Georg Hamann: An Existentialist*, Princeton, New Jersey, 1950, p. 20.

to the events of his own time. He read the Bible of Christianity as a Lutheran of the eighteenth century. He spoke and wrote as a man of the eighteenth century in Prussia, and the sophisticated people in Paris who taught that language after language could be memorized and that each language must be perfected and freed from concrete historical encumbrances were wrong, for no one can really learn another language as he learns his own mother tongue and no one can write or speak a language correctly unless he speaks that language as it wells up from its past concrete tradition.

Hamann exhausts himself investigating the German language to see God more clearly through creative symbolic acts. Everything points to God symbolically and comes from God symbolically. God is eternal and that which is created can communicate with this eternal event through symbolic creations. The symbolic process allows the world to be world and yet allows the transcendent to communicate with the world and vice versa. The symbolic process for man respects time, for symbolic activity takes time as an activity, but the symbolic process can also cause the 'coincidence of opposites': the eternal can enter into time paradoxically through symbolic creative acts.

Hamann exhausts himself with the Bible, with revelation, because it links him with God and teaches him how he might best be symbolically creative. He speaks of the Scriptures as 'the language of God. My wish and the *punctum saliens* of my poor little writings is to compress this theme into a nutshell.'[229] If people can learn how to begin to read the Scriptures correctly they will begin to participate more fully in a form of creative symbolics. If they then begin to see the stories of the Bible still being lived out in various lives in the present, including their own, they come closer to God through living symbolically in greater depth.

Hamann is seeking to be able to reveal himself symbolically just as God seeks to reveal Himself through symbolic acts in this world. Hamann writes to Lavater 'To tell you about the substructures of my soul . . . a tasting in *signs* that give a fullness that is not empty . . . " the very image of the things", in so far as such can be represented, present, and made visible through a glass darkly.'[230] This is a very difficult passage, but it is a passage that relates beautifully to a passage in Gadamer's *Wahrheit und Methode* which will be cited shortly. In the above passage, Hamann is telling Lavater how he is trying to find various ways of revealing his own interiority. He does not mean by the

---

[229] Gildemeister, V, p. 246.　　　[230] Ziesemer-Henkel, IV, p. 5.

word 'soul' some airy thing, for soul is directly linked with body, though less easily seen without trained eyes.

Hamann wants to reveal the heart of his life. He talks about substructures of his soul in order to show that it has levels of being in act. He will present to people a tasting in signs. The word 'taste' in Hamann's time was very popular in expressing wholehearted experience. 'Signs' in this passage refer to events of a symbolic creative nature. These tasting acts in the order of signs give a true fullness of experience. Hamann means that these signs do not bestow on man abstract knowledge which appears to give a fullness of experience but which actually gives the ivory tower airiness of generalized knowledge. His signs truly give man a taste of life that is concretely alive. Hamann insists that man can create signs that do in a sense make up an image of the thing itself. This is not an absolute likeness of another thing, but it comes close to being so. Hamann can, in so far as it is possible, represent, present, and make visible the interior structures of his soul. Other men as well as he still see through a glass darkly concerning the real state of their own interior life, but men must seek to reveal their interior lives to themselves and each other because it is during this revelation that they also reveal the communicative, creative acts of God, although still through a glass darkly.

Hamann can be related to the great hermeneutist, Gadamer, through the different sections of a quotation and through his insistence that the symbol of a man as a man is the act of a man by which he represents his hidden nature to others in a form of communication. The communication really presents to the perceiver the representing of the interiority of a particular man. Gadamer makes the statement that 'A symbol not only refers, but also presents while it represents. To re-present means to make present what is not there. Thus the symbol represents and also makes immediately present. Precisely because the symbol presents the presence of what it represents, it receives the honour to which that which it symbolizes is entitled.'[231] Gadamer is talking about the difference between representing and re-presenting just as Hamann in his quotation was talking about how a symbol can be represented, and present. A man represents himself through an exterior act of recreation and in the process also makes present to the other his self in its interiority which is usually hidden. Not the entire interiority of his self is made present communicatively in the world exterior to himself, but more of the presentness of his self is communicated than

---

[231] Gadamer, *Wahrheit und Methode*, pp. 264 and 214 ff.

could ever before be communicated. When a genius creates great works of art they receive the honour he, the artist, receives as an individual because they are at least beginning to be a representation of his creative abilities. A recording of Rubenstein receives honour due to Rubenstein in a sense, but if Rubenstein is present then he represents his presence in the playing of the music. He communicates Bach and himself to the people who have the ears to hear. Hamann's famous dictum is always useful: 'Speak that I may see thee'. Just as the Bible makes God present communicatively so Hamann's works will make him present communicatively. His life is a communication.

SELECT BIBLIOGRAPHY

I. HAMANN

1. WORKS

Aus dem Briefwechsel des Magus im Norden, ed. by Schmitz-Kallenberg, Münster, 1917.
Hamanns Schriften, ed. by F. Roth, 7 Bände, Berlin, 1821-5.
Hamann, Johann Georg, *Sämtliche Werke, Historische-Kritische Ausgabe*, ed. by Josef Nadler, Bd. 1-6, Wien, 1949-57.
Johann Georg Hamann, Briefwechsel, ed. by Ziesemer and Henkel, Leipzig, 1949.
Johann Georg Hamann: Lichtstralen aus seinen Schriften und Briefen, Leipzig, 1874.
Mann, Otto, *Hamann: Magus des Nordens, Hauptschriften*, Leipzig, 1937.
Neue Hamanniana, Briefe und andere Dokumente, München, 1905.

2. STUDIES

Blanke, Fritz, *Die Hamann-Forschung*, Gütersloh, 1956.
Blanke, Fritz, *Hamann-Studien*, Zürich, 1956.
Burger, E., *J. G. Hamann: Schöpfung und Erlösung im Irrationalismus*, Göttingen, 1929.
Ernst, P., *Hamann und Bengel*, Königsberg, 1935.
Gajek, B., 'Sprache beim jungen Hamann', Phil. Diss., München, 1959.
Gildemeister, C. H., *Johann Georg Hamann, des Magus im Norden, Leben und Schriften*, 6 Bände, Gotha, 1868.
Gründer, K., *Figur und Geschichte*, Freiburg/München, 1958.
Herde, Heinz, *J. G. Hamann*, Bonn, 1971.
Hoffman, Volker, *Johann Georg Hamanns Philologie: Hamanns Philologie zwischen enzyklopadischer Mikrologie und Hermeneutik*, Stuttgart, 1972.
Knoll, Renate, *Johann Georg Hamann und F. H. Jacobi*, Heidelberg, 1963.
Koepp, Wilhelm, *Der Magie unter Masken*, Göttingen, 1965.
Leese, Kurt, *Krisis und Wende des Christlichen Geistes*, Berlin, 1941.
Leibrecht, W. *God and Man in the Thought of Johann Georg Hamann*, translated by James H. Stam and Martin H. Bertram, Philadelphia, 1966.
Lettau, *Johann Georg Hamann: ein Lehrer und Prophet unseres Volkes*, Gütersloh, 1882.

Lowrie, Walter, *Johann Georg Hamann: An Existentialist*, Princeton, New Jersey, 1950.
Lumpp, Hans-Martin, *Philologia Crucis*, Tübingen, 1970.
Mannack, Eberhardt, *Mystik und Luthertum bei Johann Georg Hamann*, Berlin, 1954.
Metzke, Erwin, *J. G. Hamanns Stellung in der Philosophie des 18 Jahrhunderts*, Halle, 1934.
Nadler, Josef, *Johann Georg Hamann: 1730-1788*, Salzburg, 1949.
Nadler, Josef, *J. G. Hamann: Der Zeuge des Corpus Mysticum*, Salzburg, 1949.
O'Flaherty, J. C., *Unity and Language: A Study in the Philosophy of J. G. Hamann*, Chapel Hill, North Carolina, 1952.
Pöttinger, Margarete, 'Hamanns Humeübersetzung', Phil. Diss., Wien, 1939.
Rothe, Heinrich, 'Hamanns Stellung Zum Judentum', Theo. Diss., Erlangen, 1953.
Salmony, H. A., *Johann Georg Hamanns Metakritische Philosophie*, Zürich, 1958.
Schack, T., *J. G. Hamann*, Copenhagen, 1948.
Simon, Josef, *J. G. Hamann: Schriften zur Sprache*, Frankfurt am Main, 1967.
Smith, R. G., *J. G. Hamann*, London, 1960.
Stahmer, Harold, *Speak That I May See Thee: The Religious Significance of Language*, New York, 1968.
Thoms, Fritz, *Hauptprobleme der Religions-Philosophie bei J. G. Hamann*, Erlangen, 1929.
Unger, R., *Hamanns Sprachtheorie im Zusammenhang seines Denkens*, München, 1905.
Unger, R., *Hamann und die Aufklärung: Studien zur Vorgeschichte des romantischen Geistes im 18 Jahrhundert*, Bd. 1-2, Jena, 1911.
Weber, H., *Hamann und Kant*, Nordlingen, 1903.

II. BOOKS CONSULTED

A Kierkegaard Critique, ed. by Howard Johnson and Niels Thulstrup, New York, 1962.
Adler, Frederick H., 'Herder and Klopstock', Diss., Illinois, 1913.
Alles um Liebe: Goethes Briefe, Ebenhausen bei München, 1948.
Altizer, Thomas, and Beardslee, William, *Truth, Myth and Symbol*, Englewood Cliffs, (New Jersey) 1962.
Altmann, A., *Moses Mendelssohn: Frühschriften*, Tübingen, 1969.
Aristotle, *Metaphysics*, translated by Richard Hope, Ann Arbor, Michigan, 1960.
Armbruster, L., *Objekt und Transyendenz bei Jaspers*, Innsbruck, 1957.
Auberlan, C. A., *Die Theosophie Friedrich Christoph Oetingers nach ihren Grundzügen*, Tübingen, 1847.
Ausgabe von Herders Werke, ed. by B. Suphan, Berlin 1877.

Aus F. H. Jacobis Nachlass: Ungedruckte Briefe von und an Jacobi und Andere, ed. by V. Rudolf Zoeppritz, Leipzig, 1869.

Bamberger, J. P., *Einleitung Paraphrastische Erklärung und Anmerkungen über einige Bücher des Neuen Testaments*, Leipzig, 1761.
Baum, Gunther, *Vernunft und Erkenntnis: Die Philosophie F. H. Jacobis*, Bonn, 1969.
Baumgarten, A. G., *Aesthetica*, Leipzig, 1907.
Bergson, Henri, *The Two Sources of Morality and Religion*, translated by R. A. Audra and H. F. Carter, New York, 1935.
Berkeley, G., *The Works of George Berkeley*, ed. by Fraser, Oxford, 1871.
Beyreuther, Erich, *Zinzendorf und die Christenheit*, Marburg, 1961.
Boehme, Jacob, *The Confessions*, translated by S. Palmer, London, second edition, 1954.
Boehme, Jacob, *The Signature of All Things*, London, 1969.
Boehme, J., *Sämtliche Schriften*, Stuttgart, 1955.
Bohlin, Torsten, *Kierkegaards dogmatische Anschauung in ihrem geschichtlichen Zussamenhang*, Gütersloh, 1927.
Bracken, Ernst von, 'Die Selbstbeobachtung bei Lavater, Beitrag zur Geschichte der Idee der Subjektivitat im 18 Jahrhunderts', Münster, 1932, Diss.
Briefwechsel und Tagebücher der Fürsten Amalie von Gallitzin, Neue Folge, Münster, 1786.
Briefwechsel Zwischen Goethe und F. H. Jacobi, ed. by Alex Jacobi, Leipzig, 1846.
Brown, Raymond, *The Birth of the Messiah*, Garden City, New York, 1977.
Buchdahl, G., *The Image of Newton and Locke in the Age of Reason*, London, 1961.
Budge Wallis, Sir E. A. T., *The Teaching of Amen-Em-Apt: Son of Kenekht*, London, 1924.

Callahan, John G., *Four Views of Time in Ancient Philosophy*, Cambridge, Mass., 1948.
Caponigri, A. R., *Time and Idea: The Theory of History in Giambattista Vico*, London, 1953.
Cassirer, Ernst, *Die Philosophie der Aufklärung*, Tübingen, 1932.
Cassirer, Ernst, *Language and Myth*, translated by Susanne K. Langer, New York, 1946.
Childs, B. S., *Myth and Reality in the Old Testament*, London, 1968.
Collins, J. D., *God in Modern Philosophy*, Chicago, 1959.
Conversations of Goethe with Eckermann and Sorel, translated by John Oxenford, London, 1892.
Cooper, J., *The Life of Socrates*, third edition, London, 1750.
Cues, Nicholas von, *Opera*, Frankfurt am Main, 1962.
Curtius, E. R., 'Das Schematismuskapitel in der Kritik der reinen Vernunft', in *Kant-Studien*; Berlin, 1914.

Danzel, Theodor Wilhelm, *Zur Literatur und Philosophie der Goethezeit*, ed. by Hans Meyer, Stuttgart, 1962.
Derham, William, *Physicotheologie, oder Natur-Leitung zu Gott*, translated by J. A. Fabricius, Hamburg, 1732.
Dilthey, W., *Gesammelte Werke*, Leipzig 1914–36.
Dilthey, W., *Leben Schleiermachers*, ed. by Martin Redeker, Berlin, 1966.
Duncan, G. M., *The Philosophical Works of Leibnitz*, New Haven, Connecticut, 1890.

Ebners, Ferdinand, *Das Wort und die geistigen Realitaten*, Innsbruck, 1921.
Erman, Adolf, *Life in Ancient Egypt*, translated by H. M. Tirad, New York, 1971.
Ernst, Julius, *Der Genie Begriff der Sturmer und Dranger und der Frühromantiker*, Zürich, 1916.

Fabricius, J. A., *Hydrothéologie*, Hamburg, 1734.
Ficino, M., *Théologie Platonicienne de l'Immortalité des Âmes*, ed. by Raymond Marcel, 3 vols., Paris, 1964–70.
Fowler, Thomas, *Shaftesbury and Hutcheson*, London, 1882.
Franger, Wilhelm, *The Milennium of Hieronymus Bosch*, London, 1952.
Franke, Ursula, *Kunst als Erkenntnis: Die Rolle der Sinnlichkeit in der ästhetik des Alexander Gottlieb Baumgarten*, Wiesbaden, 1972.

Gadamer, H. G., *Wahrheit und Methode: Grundzunge einer Philosophischen, Hermeneutik*, Tübingen, 1960.
Gale, Richard, *The Language of Time*, New York, 1968.
Galland, Joseph, *Die Färstin Amalia von Gallitzin und ihre Freunde*, Köln, 1880.
Gervinus, G., *Zur Geschichte der deutschen Dichtung*, Leipzig, 1871.
Gigon, O., *Untersuchungen zu Heraklit*, Leipzig, 1936.
Gilbert, K. E., *A History of Aesthetics*, London, 1939.
Ginsburg, C. D., *The Kabbalah: Its Doctrine, Development and Literature*, London, 1920.
Goethe, J. W., *Poetry and Truth: From my Life*, translated by R. O. Moon, London, 1932.
Goethe, *Dedankausgabe der Werke, Briefe und Gespräche*, ed. by E. Beuten, Zürich, 1949.
Goldmann, Lucien, *Immanuel Kant*, translated by Robert Black, London, 1973.
Goldstein, L., *Moses Mendelssohn und die deutsche Äesthetik*, Königsberg, 1904.
Gueroult, M., *Dynamique et métaphysique leibniziennes*, Paris, 1934.

Hartshorne, Charles, *The Divine Relativity: A Social Conception of God*, New Haven, Connecticut, 1969.

Haym, R., *Herder nach seinem Leben und seinen Werken*, Leipzig, 1936.
Hegels Werke, Berlin, 1835.
Heidegger, Martin, *Being and Time*, translated by John Macquarrie and E. Robinson, New York, 1962.
Herder, J. G., *The Spirit of Hebrew Poetry*, translated by J. Marsch and Edward Smith, Burlington, 1833.
Herman Nees, J. de, *The Development of Kantian Thought: The History of a Doctrine*, translated by A. R. C. Duncan, London, 1962.
Hoffmann, J. G., *Kurtze Fragen von den Natürlichen Dingen, oder Geschöpfen und Werken Gottes*, Halle, 1770.
Hubert, M. L., *Pascal's Unfinished Apology: A Study of His Plan*, New Haven, Connecticut, 1952.
Hume, David, *Treatise on Human Nature*, ed. by L. A. Selby-Bigge, Oxford, 1958.
Hutcheson, Frances, *An Inquiry into the Original of our Ideas of Beauty and Virtue*, London, 1725.

Jacobi, F. H., *Werke*, Leipzig, 1818–25.
James, D. G., *The Augustan Age: The Life of Reason*, London, 1949.
Jaspers, Karl, *Truth and Symbol*, translated by Jean T. Wilde, New York, 1959.
Jung, C. G., *Psychological Types*, New York, 1923.

Kant, Immanuel, *Gesammelte Werke*, ed. by A. Görland and B. Cassirer, Berlin 1913.
Kant, Immanuel, *Religion Within the Limits of Reason Alone*, translated with an introduction by Theodore M. Greene, New York, 1960.
Kant, Immanuel, *Critique of Pure Reason*, translated by Norman Kemp Smith, second edition, London, 1973.
Kemp Smith, Norman, *New Studies in the Philosophy of Descartes*, London, 1952.
Kierkegaard, Søren, *The Sickness unto Death and Fear and Trembling*, translated with an introduction by Walter Lowrie, Garden City, New York, 1954.
Kierkegaard, Søren, *Concluding Unscientific Postscript*, translated by David F. Swenson and Walter Lowrie, London, 1941.
Kirb, G. S., *Heraclitus: The Cosmic Fragments*, Cambridge, 1954.
Koch, J., *Nikolaus von Cues und seine Umwelt*, Heidelberg, 1948.
Kohlschmidt, Werner, *Geschichte der deutschen Literatur von Barock bis zur Klassik*, Stuttgart, 1965.

Lavater, J. C., *Aphorisms of Man*, London, 1788.
Leese, Kurt, *Krisis und Wende des Christlichen Geistes*, Berlin, 1941.
Leibnitz: Selections in the Modern Student's Library, ed. by Philip P. Wiener, New York, 1951.

Selected Bibliography

Lessing, *Gesammelte Werke*, ed. by Paul Rilla, Berlin, 1956.
Lichtenberg, G. A., *A Doctrine of Scattered Occasion*, translated by J. R. Stern, Bloomington, Indiana, 1954.
Locke, J., *Works of John Locke*, London, 1823.
Lotze, Hermann, *Geschichte der Äesthetik in Deutschland*, Leipzig, 1913.
Lowth, Bishop, *Lectures on the Sacred Poetry of the Hebrews*, translated by Joseph Johnson, London, 1793.
Luce, A. A., *Berkeley and Malebranche*, London, 1934.

Mandelstam, Nadezhda, *Hope Against Hope: A Memoir*, translated by Max Hayward, London, 1970.
Marmorstein, A., *The Old Rabbinic Doctrine of God*, Oxford, 1937.
Martensen, H. L., *Jacob Boehme: His Life and Teaching*, translated by T. Rys, London, 1885.
McKeon, R., *The Basic Works of Aristotle*, New York, 1941.
Michaelis, J. D., *Einleitung in die Göttlichen Schriften des Neuen Bundes*, Göttingen, 1750.
Mittheilungen aus dem Tagebuch und Briefwechsel der Fürstin Adelheid Amalia von Gallitzin, Stuttgart, 1868.

Nees, Herman, J. de, *The Development of Kantian Thought: The History of a Doctrine*, translated by A. R. C. Duncan, London, 1962.
Nicolovius, Friedrich, *Mancherley zur Geschichte der metakritischen Invasion*, Königsberg, 1800.
Nietzsche, Friedrich, *Die Philosophie im tragischen Zeitalter der Griechen, Gesammelte Werke*, vol. IV, Munich, 1920–9.
Nietzsche, Friedrich, *The Will To Power*, vol. II, translated by Anthony M. Ludovici, New York, 1924.
Novalis, *Schriften*, ed. by Richard Samuel and Paul Kluchhohn, Leipzig, 1929.
Nufer, W., *Herders Ideen zur Verbindung von Poesie, Musik, und Tanz*, Berlin, 1927.

Oetinger, *Biblisches und Emblematisches Wörterbuch*, Hildesheim, 1969.

Paracelsus, *Selected Writings*, ed. by Jolande Jacobi, New York, 1951.
Pascal, Blaise, *Pensées*, ed. by L. Lafuma, Paris, 1951.
Pfister, O., *Die Frömmigkeit des Grafen Ludwig von Zinzendorf*, Vienna, 1925.
The Philosophy of Ernst Cassirer, ed. by P. A. Schillp, Evansten, Illinois, 1949.
Platner, Ernst, *Neue Anthropologie*, Leipzig, 1790.
Poppe, B., *A. G. Baumgartens, seine Bedeutung und seine Stellung in der Leibniz-Wolffischen Philosophie und seine Beziehung zu Kant*, Münster, 1907.
Price, George, *The Narrow Pass*, London, 1963.

Purdie, Edna, *Studies in German Literature of the Eighteenth Century*, London, 1965.

Rahner, Karl, *The Word: Readings in Theology*, New York, 1964.
Rahner, Karl, *Hearers of The Word*, translated by Michel Richards, New York, 1968.
Randall, J. H., *The Renaissance Philosophy of Man*, Chicago, 1956.
Rasch, Wolfdietrich, *Freundschaftskult und Freundschaftsdichtung im deutschen Schrifttum des 18 Jahrhunderts*, Halle, 1936.
Rosenkranz, Karl, *Geschichte der Kantischen Philosophie*, Leipzig, 1849.
Roth, Leon, *Spinoza, Descartes and Maimonides*, Oxford, 1924.
Russell, Bertrand, *Sceptical Essays*, London, 1927.
Russell, Bertrand, *A Critical Exposition of the Philosophy of Leibnitz*, London, 1937.

Bonaventura, S. *Opera Omnia*, Quaracchi, 1882-1902.
Schick, Edgar B., *Herder's Early Work*, Paris, 1971.
Scholem, G., *On the Kabbalah and its Symbolism*, translated by R. Mannheim, London, 1965.
Shaftesbury, *Characteristics*, ed. by J. M. Robertson, London, 1900.
Simmel, Georg, *Kant*, Leipzig, 1905.
Simonovits, Anna, *Dialektisches Denken in der Philosophy von G. W. Leibnitz*, Berlin, 1968.
Snell, Bruno, *The Discovery of Mind*, translated by T. G. Rosenmeyer, Oxford, 1953.
Søren Kierkegaards Papirer, ed. by P. A. Heiberg, V. Kuhr, and T. Tersting, Copenhagen, 1909-48.
Spinoza, *Opera*, ed. by Carl Gebhardt, Heidelberg, 1924.
Stein, Ludwig, *Hat Kant Hume Widerlegt*, Berlin, 1904.
Strauss, L., *Die Religionskritik Spinoza als Grundlage Seiner Bibelwissenschaft*, Berlin, 1930.
Strawson, P. F., *The Bounds of Sense: An Essay on Kant's 'Critique of Pure Reason'*, London, 1966.

Taylor, Charles, *Hegel*, Cambridge, 1975.
Tertullian, *Concerning the Resurrection of the Flesh*, translated by A. Souter, London, 1922.
The Journals of Kierkegaard, ed. by Alexander Dru, New York, 1959.

The Autobiography of Giambattista Vico, translated by T. G. Bergin and M. H. Fisch, New York, 1944.
Vico, Giambattista, *La Scienza Nuova*, Rome, 1954.

Walzel, Oskar, *German Romanticism*, translated by Alma Elise Lussky, New York, 1932.
Webb, T. E., *The Intellectualism of Locke: An Essay*, Dublin, 1857.
Weiser, Christian F., *Shaftesbury und das deutschen Geistesleben*, Darmstadt, 1969.

Wenley, R., *Kant and his Philosophical Revolution*, Edinburgh, 1910.
Whitehead, A., *Symbolism: Its Meaning and Effect*, Cambridge, 1928.
Wicker, C. V., *Edward Young and the Fear of Death*, Albuquerque, New Mexico, 1952.
Wilkinson, Elizabeth M., *Schiller: Poet or Philosopher?*, Oxford, 1961.
Wittgenstein, Ludwig, *Tractatus-logico-philosophicus*, translated by C. K. Ogden and F. P. Ramsey, London, 1922.
Wolf, Herman, *Versuch einer Geschichte des Geniesbegriffs in der deutschen Äesthetik*, Heidelberg, 1923.
Wolff, Robert P., *Kant's Theory of Mental Activity*, Cambridge, 1963.
Wundt, M., *Die deutsche Schulmetaphysik im Zeitalter der Aufklärung*, Tübingen, 1945.

Young, E., *Original Composition* in *The Complete Works, Poetry and Prose*, London, 1854.

Zilsel, E., *Die Entstehung des Genie-begriffes*, Tübingen, 1926.
Zinn, Ernst, *Wahrheit in Philologie und Dichtung in den Wissenschaften und die Wahrheit*, Tübingen, 1966.

III. ARTICLES

Balthazar, H., 'Hamanns Theologische Äesthetik' in *Philosophisches Jahrbuch der Görresgesellschaft*, Freiburg, Bd. 68, 1960.
Blackall, Eric, 'Hamann's "Fünf Hirten Briefe" 'in *German Life and Letters*, Oxford vol. XVIII, 1964-5.
Bracken, H. M., 'Berkeley on the Immortality of the Soul' in *The Modern Schoolman*, vol. 38, 1960-1.
Grabmann, Martin, 'Aristotles im Zwoelften Jahrhundert', in *Medieval Studies*, Toronto, The Pontifical Institute of Medieval Studies, XII, 1950.
Jørgensen, Sven-Aage, 'Hamann, Bacon, and Tradition', in *Orbis Litterarum*, 16, 1961.
Kendzierski, Lottie K., 'Object and Intention in the Moral Act', *Proceedings of the American Catholic Philosophical Association*, XXIV, 1950.
Klubertanz, George P., 'The Empiricism of Thomistic Ethics', *Proceedings of the American Catholic Philosophical Association*, XXXI, 1957.
Mautner, F. H. and Miller, F., 'Remarks on G. C. Lichtenberg, Humanist-Scientist', in *Isis*, vol. 43, 1952.
Peterson, Erik, 'Das Problem den Bibel auslegung im Pietismus des 18 Jahrhunderts', in *Zeitschrift für Systematische Theologie*, 1923.
Russell, Bertrand, 'The Relations of Sense-data to Physics' in *Scientia*, No. 4, 1914.
Salzer, E. C., 'Il problema dello Hamann nel corso dei tempi', in *Rivista di Filosofia Neo-Scholastica*, Milano, 1940.
Schmitz, F. J., 'The Problem of Individualism and the Crises in the lives of Lessing and Hamann', in *Modern Philology*, vol. XXVII, 1943.

Sharpe, E., 'Psycho-physical Problems Revealed in Language: An Examination of Metaphor', in *International Journal of Psychoanalysis* (21), 1940.

Smith, Morton, 'The Image of God: Notes on the Hellenization of Judaism', *Bulletin of the John Rylands Library*, vol. 40, no. 2, Manchester, March 1958.

Tschackert, H. P., 'Hamanns Universitäts-studien' in *Altpreussische Monatsschrift*, vol. 28, 1891.

Waerden, B. L. Van der, 'Die Arithmetik der Pythagoreer', in *Mathematische Annalin*, vol. 120, 1948.

Verra, Valerio, 'Neue Wege der Hamann-Forschung' in *Philosophische Rundschau*, 7, Jahrgang, 1959, Heft 3/4.

Weber, M., 'Herder als Kritiker', in *Germanistik Studien*, 55, Berlin, 1928.

Weyand, Klaus, 'Kants Geschichtsphilosophie: Ihre Entwicklung und ihr Verhältnis zur Aufklärung', in *Kantstudien*, 84, Köln, 1964.

INDEX

Abel, 111, 158
Abraham, 125
Adam, 37, 127, 146, 166
Agrippa, H. C., 33
Akhamatova, 50
Anselm, 93
Apollo, 44
Aquinas, Thomas, 59, 72, 167
Arimathea, Joseph of, 42
Aristotle, 21, 51, 70, 76, 97, 125, 156
Athanasius, 72
Augustine, 63, 71, 93, 99, 134
Averroes, 71

Balthasar, 42
Baumgarten, 19, 26
Bayle, 44, 160
Beattie, James, 103
Beckett, Samuel, 97
Bensen, George, 27
Benson, Martin, 47
Berens, Catin, 5, 11
Berens, J. C. 2, 4, 32, 48, 88
Berenson, Bernard, 20
Berkeley, 75, 93, 125
Berlin, Isaiah, vii
Blanke, Fritz, 30
Bloomfield, Leonard, 47
Boehme, Jacob, 12, 22, 29, 39, 74
Boerhaave, 73
Bolingbroke, 130
Bonaventure, 20, 72, 146
Borst, 142
Bosch, 29
Brucker, 133
Brunner, Emil, 142
Bruno, Giordano, 33, 42, 54, 73
Bucholtz, 94
Budge, Wallis, 46
Buffon, 1
Burger, E., 162-63

Cassirer, Ernst, 15, 22, 36, 76

Caesar, 10
Cicero, 139, 155
Collins, J. C., vii
Cox, Harvey, 118
Cratylus, 71, 138
Croce, 21
Cusa, Nicholas, 73, 76, 138

Danzel, 100
David, 127
Demosthenes, 7, 17, 156
Derham, William, 45
Descartes, 39, 50, 61, 75, 116, 125, 128
Diderot, 52
Dilthey, 130, 156
Dodds, E. R., 61
Dulles, Avery, VII

Eckhart, Meister, 115
Einstein, 64
Eliade, Mircea, 62
Erasmus, 41
Erman, A. P., 46
Euripides, 145
Ezekiel, 12

Faust, 90
Ferguson, 132
Fuerbach, 105
Ficino, 33, 38
Francke, 66
Frederick the Great, 52

Gadamer, 95, 130, 173-74
Gallitzin, 2, 87
Gildemeister, 89
Goethe, vi, 11, 22, 25, 52, 81, 90, 136, 143, 156

Hamann, Johan Georg,
   birth 2
   career 5, 18, 81
   conversion 5

Index

death 24
marriage 5
and aesthetics 18, 30, 104, 135, 165, 171
and the Bible 5, 85, 148, 169
and Christianity 39, 81, 118, 148
and creativity 30, 39, 46, 95, 107, 123, 131, 137, 169, 179
and enlightenment 12, 64, 153, 172
and God 30, 39, 64, 73, 107, 118, 123, 135, 164, 172
and language 12, 18, 39, 51, 95, 104, 135, 149, 170
and nature 85, 104, 118, 131, 137, 152, 164
and philosophy vi, 12, 30, 95, 107, 131, 164
and style 12, 39, 46, 73, 95, 104, 131, 141, 152, 164, 169
and time 51, 85, 104, 118, 123, 135, 141, 170
Hamlet, 25
Hartshorne, Charles, 73, 137
Hayward, Max, 49
Hegel, Georg Wilhelm, vi, 12, 66, 73
Heidegger, 137
Heinse, 81
Heraclitus, 15, 70, 112, 121, 124, 138, 155
Hercules, 95
Herder, 8, 14, 21, 29, 41, 46, 53, 58, 79, 86, 93, 132, 136, 156
Herodotus, 79
Herostratus, 92
Homer, 70, 97
Horace, 52, 155
Hume, David, 14, 16, 25, 72, 75, 78, 103, 109, 110, 125
Hutcheson, 79

Jacob, 82
Jacobi, 19, 29, 47, 73, 94, 101, 136
Jean Paul, 21, 40
Jeremiah, 114
Jesus, the Christ, vi, 6, 21, 48, 56, 64, 72, 88, 111, 117, 119, 122, 126, 134, 151, 158-59, 166, 168
Job, 86
John, 88
John, the Baptist, 134

Kant, Immanuel, vi, 4, 11, 18, 25, 32, 44, 84, 94, 98, 102, 106, 116, 124, 133, 140, 144, 161
Kaufmann, Walter, 95

Kemp-Smith, 103
Khodasevich, 49
Kierkegaard, Soren, vi, 9, 49, 74, 90, 97, 143, 150, 156
Knutzen, M., 162
Klopstock, 42, 51, 80
Kraft, Peter, 29
Kuhn, Sophie, 25
Kypke, G., 2

Lavater, 39, 42, 80, 173
Lazarus, 90
Leese, Kurt, 61
Leibnitz, 19, 39, 55, 75, 80, 103, 125
Liebrecht, 56
Lessing, 18, 83, 89, 114
Lettau, 13
Levi, R. J. C., 37
Lichtenberg, 39
Lieb, Fritz, 62, 84
Lindner, 1, 6, 16, 27
Locke, 78, 90, 93
Lowth, 24
Lumpp, H. M., 42
Luther, Martin, vii, 2-3, 36, 72, 93

Macquarrie, John, vii
Maimon, Solomon, 14
Maimonédes, 37
Malinowski, 62
Mandelstam, Nadezhda, 48
Mandelstam, Osip, 48
McLaughlin, J.P. vii
Meier, G. F., 20
Mellon, Gertrude, vii
Mendelssohn, Moses, 18, 26, 52, 91, 112. 161
Metzke, E., 36
Michaelis, 24
Michelet, 9
Mocati, P., 51
Moltmann, Jurgen, vii
Montesquieu, 1
Moser, 136
Moses, 19, 150
Mossner, E. C., 110

Nadler, Josef, vii, 42
Newton, 73, 160
Nicolai, Friedrich, 18
Nietzsche, 15, 43, 88, 115, 125, 129, 147, 154, 161
Novalis, 25

Ockham, 72

Oetinger, 39, 77
Ofterdingen, Heinrich, 25
Olsen, Regina, 11

Paracelsus, 22, 73, 81
Pascal, 156
Persius, 145, 155
Philo, 69
Pinget, Roger, 97
Platner, 81
Plato, 16, 44, 71, 125
Plinius Secundus, 26
Pompanazzi, 72, 93
Proclus, 115
Pythagoras, 38, 113

Rahner, Karl, 12
Rambach, 66
Rapin, 16
Ray, John, 45
Reimarus, 89
Rosenbranz, Karl, 84
Roth, vii
Rubenstein, 175
Russell, 77

Salmony, 155
Salzer, E. C., 166
Satan, 33, 58, 66
Scheffner, 95
Schelling, F. W. J., 22
Schiller, 17, 81
Schleiermacher, 84, 130, 156
Schneider, Peter, 53
Schoenach, Otto, 21
Scholem, 36
Schopenhauer, 88

Schultens, Albert, 24
Scotus, Duns, 39, 73
Shaftesbury, 14, 21, 26, 42, 64, 79
Shakespeare, 35, 97
Simon, Josef vii, 95
Smith, Ronald Gregor, 112
Socrates, vi, 10, 15, 26, 34, 43, 78, 115, 121
Spinoza, 19, 39, 74, 93, 116, 125
Stahmer, Harold, 41
Stanley, 133
Starck, 83, 161
Stein, Heinrich, 84
Stillingfleet, 93
Strauss, L., 63
Synesius, 27

Tertullian, 71, 78
Thucydides, 79

Unger

Vico, Giambattista, vii, 21, 30, 51
Voltaire, 133

Wachter, J. G., 36
Walz, 80
Whitehead, 117
Winckelmann, 18, 31, 47
Wittgenstein, 39, 96, 117, 142
Wolff, Christian, 18, 26

Young, Edward, 25, 39, 52, 87, 120, 157

Zizendorf, 78